INTRODUCING

POLICING

CHALLENGES FOR POLICE & AUSTRALIAN COMMUNITIES

INTRODUCING POLICING

CHALLENGES FOR POLICE & AUSTRALIAN COMMUNITIES

Mark Findlay

OXFORD
UNIVERSITY PRESS

OXFORD
UNIVERSITY PRESS

253 Normanby Road, South Melbourne, Victoria 3205, Australia

Oxford University Press is a department of the University of Oxford. It
furthers the University's objective of excellence in research, scholarship, and
education by publishing worldwide in

Oxford New York

Auckland Bangkok Buenos Aires Cape Town Chennai
Dar es Salaam Delhi Hong Kong Istanbul Karachi Kolkata
Kuala Lumpur Madrid Melbourne Mexico City Mumbai Nairobi
São Paulo Shanghai Taipei Tokyo Toronto

OXFORD is a trade mark of Oxford University Press in the UK and in certain
other countries

National Library of Australia
Cataloguing-in-Publication data:

Findlay, Mark.
Introducing policing: challenges for police and Australian communities.

Bibliography.
Includes index.
ISBN 0 19 551621 4.

1. Police – Australia. 2. Community policing – Australia.
I. Title.

363.20994

Typeset by Desktop Concepts Pty Ltd, Melbourne
Printed through Bookpac Production Services, Singapore

Contents

Acknowledgments

This book is the distillation of two decades teaching policing students and of a close association with police and their work throughout Australia and abroad. My students have discussed so many of the essential themes in the text and have been the sounding board for my critical reflections on policing. To all these students, and those in particular who have maintained their generous friendship over the years, I reiterate my gratitude.

Police are a tough audience, but rewarding. Their culture is closed and confused but once cracked it offers rewards to those few outsiders who are given access to the mysteries of the 'job'. In return I have opened up safe and satisfying scholarly environments for police and policing students to interact and grow in their understanding of the place of police within Australian communities. This is a privilege to which this book is offered as a continuing contribution.

I flatter myself that I have had an impact on the emergence of more acute and accountable policing services within the jurisdictions in which I have worked. Yet it is the surprising susceptibility of individual police to the challenge of change which remains in contrast with intransigent police organisations that talk change but disappoint the search for reform. My call for real engagement by police in communities of trust is the message that the book holds out for policing management.

I thank the reviewers and readers of this text for their sharp and intuitive suggestions for revision which I have endeavoured to incorporate. The editorial staff of OUP have been their usual supportive and responsive selves. And to Fran, my A.A., I owe a great debt of gratitude.

The reader is to be warned that this book is nothing more than the title suggests, an introduction. In this moderate compass I draw on the wealth of writing in Australia about policing and I owe a great debt to my colleagues who have turned over more deeply all the issues which this book has no more time than to identify.

A dedication would be too grand for a little project such as this. Therefore I only use it as an opportunity to express my devotion to my children who may read what I write and share my vision for a better world.

Introduction: Policing Australia

Policing is a resilient feature of modern Australian society. European settlement brought with it formalised policing institutions and functions that took root in the earliest days of the Australian colonies.[1] Policing as a state-sponsored function provided an initial social control impetus for government in Australia, and police institutions and organisations essentially promoted an introduced criminal justice inextricably connected to the advancement of white occupancy.

The literature on policing in Australia is significant and well developed.[2] Detailed policing histories feature as part of the academic writing on crime and justice in Australia. As an essential component of *law and order politics* in contemporary Australia[3] current debates about policing focus around:

- policing and governance
- policing and particular social issues such as multiculturalism
- critiques of styles and personalities of policin
- examinations of police ethics, and
- practical issues and operational concerns for policing and its reform.

Notably absent in the scholarly and popular writing on policing Australia is an introduction to essential themes in policing which attempts to position the study and critical examination of the topic within the context of power relations in Australian society which characterise crime control and criminal justice. What follows is an attempt to look at policing within specific modern Australian social situations, while reflecting on the development of civil policing in all its forms. The text builds on a basic understanding of the principles around which criminal justice and crime control are constructed and set to operate, and a preliminary

---

1   See Finnane, M. (1994) 'The "New Police" in Australia' in M. Finnane *Police and Government: Histories of Policing in Australia*, Oxford University Press, Melbourne, chapter 1.

2   The additional readings which conclude this and other chapters confirm this.

3   For a critical analysis of this politics see Hogg, R. & Brown, D. (1998), *Rethinking Law and Order*, Pluto Press, Melbourne.

knowledge concerning the processes of police work.[4] From this the reader is invited to locate their appreciation of the position, practice and potential of policing in Australia within changing economic, political and cultural conditions.

In looking at policing, the book is interested in more than a structural, organisational or operational examination of state police. For the purposes of what follows policing is viewed in the wider sense of regulatory and power relations as demonstrated institutionally, functionally and through the essential relationships of policing. In this respect the discussion of policing themes deals with many forms of social regulation and control which have policing functions. What might be referred to as alternative policing styles[5] feature throughout.

The book is introductory in the sense that it offers the reader a bird's-eye view of the essential features of policing without interrogating any particular issue to such a degree as to distract from a comprehensive and rounded critical understanding of policing as a dynamic process for social change. Further, with social context as the essential style and focus of the text, it offers a grounded, everyday appreciation of the potential and practice of Australian policing.

The manner in which the chapters in this book are presented and their primary topics are dealt with hopefully enables the reader to challenge some commonly assumed notions about the police, while recognising the interests and influence behind recent developments in policing. There is a balance achieved between the essential features of policing such as power, discretion and accountability (often overlooked in operational considerations of police work) and the specific relationships of influence in which the police find themselves as they interact with their various communities. The text presents the opportunity to consult critical writings from a variety of disciplines and perspectives in understanding police work while not alienating some readers by presenting too many competing and complex interpretations.

In Australian society any consideration of policing will identify dichotomies between ideology and practice. In particular, the examination of the evolution of police function as it interacts with other aspects of the criminal justice process highlights the manner in which policing is often a challenge to the achievement of justice. Crucial components of policing such as police culture and independence, remain unrecognised or ineffectively explored. The book addresses this problem. Recent dominant policing strategies such as community-based policing are juxtaposed against wider themes of independence and police governance[6]. The relationship between the police and communities in Australia is explored in a variety of contemporary and problematic situations.

---

4   For this the reader might consult Findlay, M., Odgers, S. & Yeo, S. (1999), *Australian Criminal Justice*, Oxford University Press, Melbourne.

5   See Findlay, M. & Zvekic, U. (1993), *Alternative Policing Styles: Cross-Cultural Perspectives*, Kluwer Law and Taxation Publishers, Deventer.

6   The recurring technique of contrasting essential characteristics of policing with their more controversial contemporary manifestations maintains a critical and applied edge to the book.

The chapters are designed to locate broad policing themes within provocative contexts to stimulate critical debate. In particular, many of the wider issues facing an understanding of policing are given contemporary focus by being placed in particular social, commercial, political, and experiential frames. For example, when examining police culture chapter 8 discusses the fostering of malpractice and the potential for its regulation and change.

Generally the book is conceived in three parts:
- the concepts of policing
- the development and contemporary philosophy of policing, and
- current issues in the institutions and processes of policing.

In particular the text will consider:
- policing ideologies
- histories of policing
- discretion and independence
- the reality of accountability
- representations of policing
- police and the criminal justice process
- police investigation practice
- policing public disorder
- policing social divisions
- police and corruption
- the new investigation agencies
- alternative policing styles, and
- police reform.

While being a straightforward and accessible treatment of policing this text develops a critical thesis. Police and the public are not, as yet, one. Through the examination of power relations that constitute policing, police work within a specific modern Australian social context is observed in terms of actual encounters. While reflecting on the wider development of civil policing in all its forms, the supports and challenges for civil society in Australia, posed by policing, are critically examined. The book commences (in chapter 1) with an examination of concepts of police and policing. All too often the process of policing is viewed as synonymous with state police. This chapter defines policing within criminal justice, exploring a variety of police forms and institutions. What designates and characterises crime control as policing is discussed here.

Chapter 2 ranges across policing history in terms of the way in which historical analysis provides an essential foundation for understanding the relevance and development of particular styles of policing. Australian jurisdictions are the focus for this examination of policing histories and the chapter is concerned with the way history might explain recent developments in policing throughout Australia. The preferred theories of history as they are applied in policing literature are touched upon. The chapter advances an understanding of policing across the widest social context at any particular time in the emergence of modern Australian society, and the institutions of the Australian state, and its commercial terrain.

Chapter 3 talks of police ideologies and focuses on the problematic context of community policing. In so doing the chapter takes ideology as a framework against which contradictory notions such as independence and accountability, original powers and the disciplined service, and police isolation and community policing are analysed and critically reviewed.

Police function in its progression from force to service is the interest of Chapter 4. As both policing agencies and the community consider that investigation is one of the fundamental functions for policing, it is examined as a central feature of police work, with particular reference to trends and specialisation. The chapter analyses the scope and detail of police function looking at expectations of the police in the community, as well as the traditional and transforming parameters of police work via specialisation. Current debate about how policing should control crime problems (such as saturation policing and zero tolerance) is referred to. The recent tensions between consolidating the management of policing services and a community policing presence are viewed in terms of contemporary social control agendas.

Chapter 5 deals with alternative policing. Here we move away from discussing state-sponsored police, while not being restricted to the dichotomy between public and private policing institutions. The chapter examines those forms of policing which are more community-centred rather than necessarily state-sponsored. The scope of policing is revealed through a consideration of private sector police services and policing initiatives that emerge out of community need. The distinction between private and public policing based on police powers, and obligations to policing clients, is teased out. Who pays for policing, who are the clients and what new arrangements are forged between service providers and recipients in a general diversification of policing services is considered here. The chapter explores some of the problems associated with comparative work in the area of researching alternative policing styles.

Police discretion is one of the most significant, but perhaps least well discussed, features of contemporary policing, particularly from the perspective of the police themselves. Chapter 6 relates police discretion to the existence and development of police powers. The *police powers* debate is juxtaposed against the actuality of police discretion in Australia. Recent concerns about the nature and the exercise of police discretion are recognised in the context of the development of police powers in particular, and associated miscarriages of justice. Individual and organisational forms of discretion are identified and related to the aims and practices of policing. The boundaries of the exercise of police discretion within the criminal justice process are developed and particular examples such as Aboriginal deaths in custody are chosen as a focus for discussion.

Police accountability and regulation are the analytical other side of the discussion of police discretion. The historical emergence of police powers essentially based on discretion is a history of conflict with regulation, and its avoidance. Having earlier discussed the structure, form and function of policing, chapter 7 concentrates on the need for accountability in all its many forms. The manner in which police discretion and independence sit with calls for accountability is evaluated against specific attempts to impose stronger accountability regimes, and to defeat these. Boundaries of permission in police work are analysed and methods for requiring accountability explored. Complaints against police and appropriate mechanisms for review are critically examined and alternative forms are speculated upon.

Police culture has been used to explain (and criticise) problems ranging from multicultural policing through to police deviance. Chapter 8 connects cop culture, police malpractice and prospects for change in an attempt to appreciate their interrelations. The chapter explores the association between unique cultures which inhabit police work, and the support which some of these cultures provide for police deviance. Special emphasis is placed on recent investigations into police corruption throughout Australia. An attempt is made in the chapter to suggest the employment of occupational cultures in systems of best practice (rather than malpractice) so as to reveal the connection between culture and the police operational mentality. The role of accountability is returned to, along with notions of police isolation and their challenge to community-centred policing.

A natural theme to follow is Chapter 9's discussion of police and social divisions. In this context social divisions relate to determinants of gender, race, class, age, sexuality, and even employment status. The multicultural and diverse construction of Australian society throws these determinants into stark relief when put against policing relationships and motivations. The topic will examine case studies of selective law enforcement. Of particular interest are issues of police-race relations, the policing of youth, police and gender, and the influence of sexuality on the police organisation. The role played by the police in maintaining social divisions is exposed in the context of such particulars and the manner in which the police confront and negotiate them. Policing ethnicity, culture and custom have specific relevance here relative to their place in contemporary public and media debate.

Chapter 10 explores police professionalism, and the move away from *craft* notions of police work. Police professionalism, the monopoly over specialist knowledge, the nature of the disciplined service, police ethics, education and professional integrity each provide points of reference for analysis. The image of the professional in its broadest sense is compared with police self-image and public expectations. Where do the police sit against other structures of professionalism and what ethics do they claim? Does this reflect the professionalism of criminal justice at large? The essential quest by policing agencies for the respect of the community is reviewed in relation to wider theories of consent and trust.

Police in popular culture is the topic for chapter 11. The ever-increasing significance of policing in the media and modern entertainment is questioned here. Your favourite detective story, movie, video, television program or comic could be under the microscope. This chapter examines the place of the police in popular culture and the ramifications of this for the creation of police imagery. How do representations of the police impact on police and policing in the community? What is the relationship between policing, entertainment and new notions of justice?

The final chapter examines agendas for policing reform. While law reform reverberates through the development of most modern legal systems and more particularly with criminal law and criminal justice in Australia, it has been sporadic and often subject to *law and order* political concerns. Law and order politics is manifest, and exacerbated by the prevalence of discretion in the hands of the police. More recently reform developments in policing have had their origins in concerns about police corruption and malpractice. This chapter will examine the pressures for reform, the processes it takes and the impediments it encounters. The construction of specific agendas for police reform will also be addressed.

The book will provide a resource for further research. Each chapter concludes with a range of additional readings designed to enhance the critical arguments presented under each topic heading.

Selected readings

Brogden, M. et al. (1988), *Introducing Police Work*, Unwin Hyman, London.

Reiner, R. (2000), *The Politics of Policing*, Wheatsheaf, London.

Klockars, C. (1985), *The Idea of Police*, Sage, New York.

Mawby, R. (2002), *Policing Images: Policing, Communication and Legitimacy*, Willan, Devon.

Hall, S. et al. (1978), *Policing the Crisis*, MacMillan, London.

Reiner, R. (ed.) (1996), *Policing*, vols 1 & 2, Dartmouth, Brookfield.

Tonry, M. & Norris, N. (1992) *Modern Policing*, University of Chicago Press, Chicago.

Finnane, M. (1994), *Police and Government: Histories of Policing in Australia*, Oxford University Press, Melbourne.

Finnane, M. (1987), *Policing in Australia: Historical perspectives*, University of New South Wales Press, Sydney.

Chan, J. (1997), *Changing Police Culture: Policing in a Multicultural Society*, Cambridge University Press, Melbourne.

Dixon, D. (1997), *Law in Policing*, Clarendon Press, Oxford.

Dixon, D. (ed.) (1999), *A Culture of Corruption: Changing an Australian Police Service*, Hawkins Press, Sydney.

Neyroud, P. & Beckley, A. (2001), *Policing, Ethics and Human Rights*, Willan, Devon.

Findlay, M. & Zvekic, U. (1993), *Alternative Policing Styles*, Kluwer, Deventer.

Mawby, R. (1990), *Comparative Policing Issues*, Unwin Hyman, London.

Bayley, D. (1994), *Police for the Future*, Oxford University Press, New York.

Cunneen, C. et al. (1989), *The Dynamics of Collective Conflict: Policing the Bathurst Bike Races*, Law Book Company, Sydney.

Newburn, T. & Hayman, S. (2002), *Policing, Surveillance and Social Control: CCTV and Police Monitoring of Suspects*, Willan, Devon.

Coady, T., James, S., Miller, S. & O'Keefe, M. (2000), *Violence and Police Culture*, Melbourne University Press, Melbourne.

Cunneen, C. (2001), *Conflict Politics and Crime, Aboriginal Communities and the Police*, Allen & Unwin, Sydney.

McCulloch, J. (2001), *Blue Army: Paramilitary Policing in Australia*, Melbourne University Press, Melbourne.

White, R. & Alder, C. (1994) *The Police and Young People*, Cambridge University Press, Melbourne.

Collins, J. et al. (2000), *Kebabs, Kids, Cops and Crime*, Pluto Press, Sydney.

Edwards, C. (1999), *Changing Policing Theories for 21st Century Societies*, Federation Press, Sydney.

Chappell, D. & Wilson, P. (1996), *Australian Policing: Contemporary Issues*, Butterworths, Sydney.

Moir, P. & Eijkman, H. (1992), *Policing Australia: Old Issues, New Perspectives*, MacMillan, Sydney.

Lewis, C. (1999), *Complaints Against Police: The Politics of Reform*, Hawkins Press, Sydney.

Enders, M. & Dupont, B. (2001), *Policing the Lucky Country*, Federation Press, Sydney.

Miller, S., Blackler, J. & Alexandra, A. (1997), *Police Ethics*, Allen & Unwin, Sydney.

Evans, D. et al. (1992), *Crime, Policing and Place*, Routledge, London.

Kratcoski, P. et al. (1995), *Issues in Community Policing*, Anderson, Cincinnati.

Klockars, C. et al. (1991), *Thinking About Police: Contemporary Readings*, McGraw Hill, New York.

Greene, J. & Mastrofski, S. (eds.) (1988), *Community Policing: Rhetoric or Reality*, Praeger, New York.

McMannus, M. (1995), *From Fate to Choice: Private Bobbies, Public Beats*, Aldershot, Brookfield.

Reiner, R. & Spencer, S. (1993), *Accountable Policing: Effectiveness, Empowerment and Equity*, Institute for Public Policy Research, London.

Baldwin, R. & Kinsey, R. (1982), *Police Powers and Politics*, Quartet, London.

McConville, M. et al. (1991), *The Case for the Prosecution: Police Suspects and the Construction of Criminality*, Routledge, London.

Barker, T. & Carter, C. (1994), *Police Deviance*, Anderson, Cincinnati.

Leaver, A. (1997), *Investigating Crime*, Law Book Company, Sydney.

Concepts of Police and Policing

Introduction: Policing for Australia

The jurisdictions of policing throughout Australia as a federation are diverse, complex and often interrelated.[1] New South Wales has the largest state police service with over 17,000 personnel. In fact this puts it among the bigger single public policing organisations in the world. Depending on how they are conceived, state, territory and federal police number more than 80,000 throughout Australia.[2] Estimates of private policing in Australia are half again this figure.

Modern Australian policing influences most aspects of social control in Australian society.[3] Governments rely upon the police as a principal agency for enforcing the criminal sanction, for the maintenance of public order and to ensure civil governance through crime prevention and criminal justice. The corporate community now entrusts all levels of its security to private policing arrangements, involving anything from the protection of property through to the gathering of intelligence on competitors.

Community context[4] determines the nature and function of policing. Multicultural Australia has stimulated styles of policing to uniquely reflect, and mould, our social and political priorities. At the same time policing the community divisions which feature across Australia (see chapter 9) challenge the broadest notions of representative and accountable policing.

---

1   In Australia the jurisdiction of the criminal law, while emanating principally from the states and territories, may also be a concern for the Commonwealth. For a more detailed discussion of jurisdiction and policing as a response to this see Findlay, M. (2001), *Problems for the Criminal Law*, Oxford University Press, Melbourne, parts 1 & 2.

2   Including, at the Commonwealth level, customs and state protective services but excluding local government inspectors and security personnel, which would significantly inflate this figure.

3   For an analysis of the performance of police functions within Australian criminal justice see Findlay et al. (fully referenced in n. 4 p. viii) (1999), chapter 3.

4   Throughout this work, community will be used in the broadest sense to cover the collective human context in which policing and its interests are negotiated (i.e. it may mean corporate as well as public communities).

A satisfactory examination of contemporary Australian policing requires detailed recognition of its social context, and of the interests which sponsor police priorities. This recognition should not remain outside the police community, because the police themselves can maintain a dislocated appreciation of their place in Australian society (see chapter 8).

More particularly, a critical analysis of the place of policing in Australia must explain change and diversity in the nature of policing and the community's response to this dynamic. We have come a long way from our colonial policing heritage,[5] and this book will endeavour to explain the transitional situations of policing in Australian community life, and the pathways and stimuli for change.[6]

In his article 'Policing A Post-Modern Society', Reiner[7] talked of the progress of demystifying the 'golden age' of policing through an underlying transformation of social structures and culture. For Australia today this would be represented in multiculturalism as much as any other social process. Reiner proposed a change in the monopolisation structures governing the legitimate use of force as they exist in policing. Despite the continued reliance by police in Australia on the exercise of force, we will argue that respect continues to be more significant for the confirmation of police authority. Respect is conditional on a community's concept of the police and the individual, and shared relationships police to citizen. These can be specifically culturally dependent.

The colonial climate in which policing was established and out of which it developed (social, political and economic) has changed,[8] as has the social structure on which support for police has been based. In an Australian context, policing has tended to maintain a significant role as an agent in this development, particularly in respect of indigenous communities.[9] Policing authority is now more reliant on sometimes unstable and always selective atmospheres of respect, consent and consequent intervention.

Legitimacy of police authority, and the struggle for respect and consent is a significant concern for policing in any form. Reiner identified changes in state police organisation and policy which have unintentionally undermined conventional police legitimacy. Such challenges to public consensus and respect for policing are manifest in contemporary Australian experience and tend to indicate the problematic nature of policing.[10] Reiner particularly pointed to the following features of change, which have resonance for the policing of modern Australia:

---

5   As discussed in Edwards, C. (1999), *Changing Policing Theories for Twenty First Century Societies*, Federation Press, Sydney, Part 1.

6   For a discussion of the political motivations for change in Australian policing see Finnane, M. (2002), *When Police Unionise: The Politics of Law and Order in Australia*, Institute of Criminology, Sydney, chapter 7.

7   [1992] MLR 761.

8   This has not been a gradual or measured progress and reflects the sporadic transition of Australia's migration experience.

9   See Finnane (1994)(fully referenced in n. 1 p. vii), chapter 7.

10 Police–youth relations in certain ethnic communities provide graphic current evidence of this. See Collins, J., Noble, G., Poynting, S. & Tabar, P. (2000), *Kebabs, Kids, Cops and Crime*, Pluto, Melbourne, chapter 6.

1. **Recruitment, training and discipline.** The sophistication of state policing in particular has seen organisational effort to break down the original white, male, macho, middle-class structures of police culture, with limited success. Professionalisation (see chapter 10), specialisation (see chapter 4) and a broadening of the educational base for state police has stimulated developments in police function. However, the predominance of a disciplined service model for state police in Australia has meant that organisation and responsibility issues are hard to break free from a narrow and closed paramilitary tradition.

2. **The rule of law and crisis of police discretion.** While embodying law enforcement as a predominant claim to authority the police in Australia rely on the exercise of police power through discretion. This is not so much a compromise with the rule of law but rather the prevalence of police discretion is invited through the manner in which the law constructs police authority, powers and responsibilities. However, in many Australian communities and for many marginalised groups within them, police discretion and selective enforcement identifies the divisiveness and discrimination inherent within Australian policing (see chapter 9).

3. **Strategies of minimal force and the crisis in police authority.** The more the police attempt to move away from force as the ultimate guarantee of their authority and power, the greater will be their reliance on community consensus. However, in Australia where communities are diverse, respect for police has come under strain and consent is often conditional and requires regular negotiation.[11]

4. **Non-partisanship and the crisis of police isolation.** While community policing has become the catch-phrase for contemporary policing in Australia (see chapter 3) it is difficult to realise. In reality the police and the community are not one. Sectional interests within and without the police tend to endorse an image of communities that support the police, and those that don't. The police community, as a consequence, may feel neither representative of, nor responsive to the young, the foreign or the marginalised in Australian society.

5. **The service role[12] and the crisis of police function.** Police consider 'real' policing as criminal investigation and all that is associated with it. Yet in reality most police time for most police personnel is taken up with the provision of basic services, and information management in particular. Yet along with the police, the public expectation of police is that they are out there protecting property, catching crooks and solving crime. A dilemma for policing, therefore, is to garner the credibility and community consensus which comes from the sympathetic performance of their service function while at the same time not challenging the view that they are crime fighters.

---

11   Again, policing youth is a process which daily evidences such negotiation in situations of selective, discretionary enforcement . See Cunneen, C. & White, R. (2002), *Juvenile Justice: Youth and Crime in Australia*, Oxford University Press, Melbourne, chapter 9.

12   It is worth noting that in order to reclaim a tougher image for police, governments such as New South Wales have dropped any reference to 'service' in official police nomenclature.

6. **Preventive policing and the crisis of police effectiveness.** Crime prevention has asserted itself as a primary direction in community policing. It requires the police to develop community partnerships for prevention, and to adopt proactive rather than reactive approaches to crime. Connected with crime prevention, policing practice has become more reliant on intelligence and crime mapping. These more socially located appreciations of crime risk also invite more sensitive measures of police effectiveness recognising the responsibility of police as being more than criminal investigation, and which take account of community safety expectations.

7. **Police effectiveness and the crisis of self-image.**[13] For too long now, state police, bound to an image of policing principally as criminal investigation, have publicly measured their effectiveness in terms of prosecution success and crime clear-up rates. This has been in accord with their self-image as law enforcers and crime controllers. With the advancement of community policing as the strategic plan for most state police agencies, a crisis in police self-image has arisen, requiring a reinterpretation of what is valued in the policing occupation. This too has invited measures of policing effectiveness associated with the satisfaction of client expectations and the provision of a broad range of community (and not just law enforcement) services.

8. **Accountability and the crisis of responsibility and independence**. Pressures for greater and more diverse police accountability have accompanied the community policing paradigm. Beyond this, and as a consequence of the internationalisation of criminal justice, police accountability measures have broadened out to evaluations of human rights protection.[14] Police have individually and organisationally resisted accountability largely because it is seen as challenging independence and representing external discipline. Police have been slow to realise the positive consequences of openness through accountability to the community, as regards all aspects of policing, even the efficiency of criminal investigation.

For Australia today, Reiner's observation on the potential for policing to challenge democratic government, and governmentality through civil society, are particularly relevant. He centres his argument around class conflict, race conflict, and conflict between the socially marginal and the police establishment. With the disenfranchisement of young people, the unemployed, and the socially marginalised, policing remains essentially directed towards the control of alienated underclasses,[15] rather than the protection of capitalist enterprise and the regulation of the labour force as was a preoccupation for early police forces at the end of the nineteenth century. In this respect policing has not lost its politicality, nor can it be simply assumed that policing is a natural extension of democratic government or free society.

---

13 For a detailed discussion of 'imaging' as it relates to policing, see Mawby, R. (2002), *Policing Images: Policing, Communication and Legitimacy*, Willan, Devon.

14 See Neyroud, P. & Beckley, A. (2001), *Policing, Ethics and Human Rights*, Willan, Devon.

15 See Finnane (1994), section 2.

Definitions of 'the police'

Klockars, in his book *The Idea of Police*[16], suggested that most definitions of the police and policing are norm derivative. They are based on beliefs about what police should do or are supposed to do, along with the purposes for and ends of policing. As such they fail to adequately discuss the actuality of police work.

In addition to normative definitions, it is essential to examine the means employed in policing as well as its outcomes. In so doing, the organisational and institutional presence of the police within modern Australian communities become objects for analysis, beyond viewing police and policing primarily in terms of what they do and don't do.

It is necessary to establish definitions of policing which distinguish police from other groups or individuals using similar means for similar ends. The exercise of legitimate (and sometimes illegitimate) force, for instance, is crucial to notions of the police particularly in their state-sponsored guise. Yet what makes policing different from other functions and institutions of the state-given rights to use force? Coercive force alone may not provide the essential characteristic of policing. It is necessary to inject the issue of authority into a consideration of the exercise of force by the police in order to qualify the role of coercion in contemporary police work.

Police authority is said not only to come from the state but also out of what has been deemed *the original powers of the constable*.[17] The police claim authority as an institution of the state, from the consensus of its citizens, the endorsement of the community, tradition, fear and respect. Were coercive force authorised through state authority to be crucial for police power then there might be little to distinguish the police from the military, and surely there is.

In addition to force and authority, the significance of jurisdiction for the police contributes another crucial feature to the search for the essence of policing. Territoriality such as domain over public space has long been a focus for the exercise of police powers.[18] Police institutions and individuals are given the general right to use coercive force by the state within its domestic territory. The maintenance of civil peace and public order, again traditional concerns for policing, are designated as operational and territorial priorities. However, these functional responsibilities are not exclusive to the police or policing.

The crucial significance of the timing of police interventions, along with their jurisdiction and authority ultimately confirmed through force, rounds off Klockar's attempt at definition. He concludes by reflecting on the statement of Bittner[19]

---

16 (1985), Sage, New York.
17 Historically, and reiterated in the oath of office often taken by police recruits throughout Australia, the Crown rather than the state invests police with authority.
18 Finnane (1994), chapter 5; White, R. & Alder, C. (1994), *The Police and Young People in Australia*, Cambridge University Press, Melbourne, chapter 5.
19 Bittner, E. (1980), *The Functions of Police in Modern Society*, Oelgeschlager, Gunn & Hain, Cambridge, MA.

regarding the right to intervene and the necessity to do so immediately, in order to satisfy community expectations about police responsiveness. Policing, therefore, is a contextual entity, one in which 'something ought not to be happening about which something ought to be done *now*'. For the public (or the corporate client and private police) policing must deal with all those situations in which coercive force may have to be used, authority reasserted, territory reclaimed and order maintained immediately to satisfy the expectations of others. The quality of policing then is measured in terms of responsiveness and resultant client satisfaction.

The police, therefore, can be thought of as a force-based service of first and last resort. Policing, for Klockar, is inevitable for modern, noncommittal civil engagement, and is a particular feature of contemporary urban society.

Policing, it is alleged by those in the business, is not merely for the community but exists and operates on its behalf with one eye on its expectations.[20] The policy aspirations of community policing, however, reveal little about who should play a role in community intervention, why it should be played, or what can be done to shape or control or influence the way any such policing interventions are played out.

Brogden[21] proposed the police occupation as being defined by its specific mandate, powers, and accountabilities. The police task, for him, is primarily about *maintaining consent* which in turn becomes an essential feature of its authority to reproduce social order. In this regard the symbolic (and practical) functions of policing such as the preservation of life, the enforcement of law, and the maintenance of peace are crucial to any definition of police work. Policing is all about the preservation of consent and the structuring of respect in a climate of preconceived expectations.[22]

Different reasons exist for policing by consent based on a variety of expectations and intended outcomes (central to the police or their client base). These are endorsed selectively through encounters between policing agencies and the *community* they service, as well as by the diversification of these encounters through the exercise of discretion.[23] Despite this diversity the central and sometimes strained ideologies of policing remain constant in the face of the shift from *force to service*.[24]

It is impossible to consider a convincing definition of policing, either in a historical sense or contemporary to Australian society today, simply in terms of dom-

---

20   White & Alder (1994), chapter 8.

21   Brogden, M., Jefferson, T & Walklate, S. (1988), *Introducing Police Work*, Unwin Hyman, London, chapter 3.

22   See Brodeur, J. (1983), 'High Policing and Low Policing: Remarks about the Policing of Political Activities', *Social Problems*, vol. 30, no. 5, p. 507.

23   In this I include commercial relationships between corporate clients and private police, community police and their community, as well as the police within their organisation. Encounters can range from the forceful suppression of consent or dismissive domination, through to acquiesence and welfare delivery. Whatever, it is usually the first personal encounter which crucially influences attitudes to police and policing.

24   Finnane, M. (1999), 'From Police Force to Service? Aspects of the Recent History of the NSW Police', in D. Dixon (ed.), *A Culture of Corruption: Changing an Australian Police Service*, Hawkins Press, Sydney;. Avery, J. (1981), *Police – Force or Service*, Butterworths, Sydney.

ination and repression. Having said this there are arguments in favour of such a narrow conceptualisation in the policing of indigenous communities.[25] Ranging expectations for policing, and the variety of community perceptions about what policing should be and what police should represent, tend to challenge the 'domination' model. Even those in the community who fear and distrust the police will sometimes require their intervention. Consent for policing may largely remain conditional and reluctant, but it prevails throughout Australia. The recognition of consent as being at the core of policing authority distinguishes it from essentially repressive exercises of power. This consent may be both tentative and implied, but it is no less real. Consent may be subject to continuing interpretation, reinterpretation and negotiation within Australian communities, but it is not, nor has it been, withdrawn or denied across entire communities despite the fractures which appear between police and the socially marginalised.[26]

Ideology is a powerful component of any policing story. It is particularly so for state-centred or state-based policing organisations and the justification for operational practice. This being said, the individual autonomy of police officers can see them step outside organisational interests and ideology, and will have a significant impact on civil society, producing outcomes often contrary to prevailing policing ideology.[27] One should be cautious not to ignore the importance of individual action when attempting to effectively understand policing.

Policing represents and embodies fundamental contradictions for democratic governments. While policing rests on implied consent, the differential social need for policing is evidence of recurring and perennial challenges to the calculus of community consent. The control of the streets by police relies on broad-based (or at least assumed) respect for its legitimacy, as well as a perception that police operate as an institution with formidable reserves of force. The disenfranchising and de-incorporation of certain citizens from structures of government[28] and the use of the police to require minimum levels of social compliance, demonstrate the extent to which consent-based policing may never leave the realm of ideology. In many respects policing is against the resistance of certain communities in order to retain the respect of other communities.

Bradley would have it that despite changing notions of policing, the mandate and ideologies underpinning their various forms remain remarkably constant.[29]

25 Enders, M. & Dupont, B. (2001), *Policing the Lucky Country*, Hawkins Press, Sydney, Part 2.
26 For an examination of this in relation to police and young alienated males from racial origins, which are the target of moral panics in Australia, see Collins (2000). Concerning the police and motorcyclists see Cunneen, C., Findlay, M., Lynch, R. & Tupper, V. (1989), *Dynamics of Collective Conflict: Riots at the Bathurst Bike Races*, Law Book Company, Sydney.
27 For instance, as discussed in the policing of ethnic minorities, see Chan, J. (1997), *Changing Police Culture: Policing in a Multicultural Society*, Cambridge University Press, Melbourne.
28 See White & Alder (1994).
29 See Bradley, D. & Walker, N. (1986), *Managing the Police, Law, Organisation and Democracy*, Wheatsheaf, Brighton, United Kingdom.

Rapid social and structural change in the latter half of the twentieth century which saw police organisational perspectives move from force to service,[30] have had the tendency to exaggerate the welfare function of state-based police in particular. Aligned with this, the stated significance of community policing and the popular redirection of generalist policing organisational structures away from quasi-military origins has tended to endorse ideologies of police authority in tune with consent rather than force.[31] There can be no doubt that the image of state police as a service rather than an institution of coercion and compulsion has produced more universally agreeable preconceptions about the role of policing in society. Perhaps in contrast with their recent community pose, the state police throughout Australia have shifted towards operational specialisation and claims for professionalism. This has tended not to diminish, in police policy terms, the confirmation of community-based policing as an organisational ethic.

During the late twentieth century throughout Australia there was in policing a constant refining of the managerial reality of police independence (away from accountability), and in some jurisdictions a more direct and consequent recognition of the significant relationship between police and government[32]. The new demographics of Australian policing (see chapter 9) have changed the face of police organisations and significantly influenced the expectations of the state when it comes to the regulation of multicultural communities. Further technologising of police functions has been a consequence of informational innovation and collaboration, not always enthusiastic in nature, with new investigation agencies.[33]

The world of policing today is more complex and conditional than it was when colonial police forces originated in Australia. The search for definitions of policing needs to recognise and reflect the transitional and dynamic relationships that comprise modern policing encounters. Postmodern definitions of policing should reflect on the cultural pluralism and ambivalence of Australian communities when it comes to many of the traditional concerns for policing. There exists in Australia today a multitude of contexts of action and forms of authority which could be conceived of and construed as policing (see chapter 5). We have witnessed here and overseas the decline of the state into fragmented sites of social reproduction. Within such sites exist levels of contest against which policing endeavours are directed. Modern society exists around themes of contingency and the undermining of moral and political absolutes. The social and cultural revolutions, which were a feature at the end of the twentieth century, have required new approaches to policing and new responsibilities for its exercise.

---

30   See Avery (1981).
31   This should not be read as ignoring the continual enhancement of paramilitary capabilities in state policing, through the history of specialist units. See Findlay, M. (1990), *The Tactical Response Group: Some Notes on its History and Organisational Development* (unpublished paper); Cunneen, C. (1991), *The Historical Development of the Special Weapons and Operations Section of the NSW Police Service* (unpublished paper).
32   See Finnane (1994), chapter 9 and conclusion.
33   Also see Findlay et al. (1999), chapter 3.

Reiner identified the following implications of postmodern policing:

1. The *crisis of confidence* in policing leading to a succession of competing agendas for reform
2. *Back to the future* where traditional ideologies of policing remain intact but are undermined in practice
3. A move to the language and style of consumerism where the community is the ultimate consumer and it is made impossible to criticise or contradict *community policing* in principle
4. The development of the police as a *paradigm of the modern* around central and cohesive notions of order
5. The *absence of effective symbols* of unitary order in a pluralistic and fragmented culture
6. State police taking on a *rump role* in maintaining order in public spaces so as to preserve social class through exclusion
7. The *dramaturlogical function* of policing symbolising social order provided by the police rather than their instrumental success in crime control
8. The *internationalisation* of issues for the maintenance of political order and the consequent isolation of conventional approaches of policing, and
9. Policing increasingly reflects *pluralism, disintegration, and fragmentation* in society which are the hallmarks of the postmodern wherein policing bifurcates, specialises and confronts scattered responsibility.

The strategies for achieving a more contemporary and convincing concept of policing, which can survive the pressures of the postmodern, include:

- a replacement of the ideal police character with a more pragmatic conception of responsibility and accountability
- an effort to see the personnel of policing reflecting more diverse and pluralistic demographics in society, and
- the recognition that local policing must be adjusted to the pluralist priorities and cultures of a more diverse social order. I would add to this for policing in Australia a style which is sensitive to disparate and somewhat competing community expectations, and which can surpass the constant law-and-order rhetoric of Australian politics.[34]

Power and policing

In most definitions of policing the involvement of the state, or the interests of large commercial organisations, are taken as given. However, a more all-inclusive way in which policing can be conceived is through the examination of power and

---

34   For a discussion of this rhetoric see Hogg, R. & Brown, D. (1998), *Rethinking Law and Order*, Pluto Press, Sydney; Cowdery, N. (2001), *Getting Justice Wrong: Myths Media and Crime*, Allen & Unwin, Sydney; Collins (2000); Finnane (2002), chapters 1 & 8.

power relationships. Policing is power. Styles of policing are identified through the interaction of interests, power and authority which distinguish the structures and functions of police work.[35] These are in turn constructed around expectations for policing within given cultural and political situational contexts.

A common consideration of the connection between policing and power is the debate about appropriate levels and forms of police powers. This works from the assumption that policing essentially exhibits power and should be invested with specific powers. Claims over police powers and their goals at the very least come from three general sources—the state, community or group interests, and from within policing organisations themselves. These in turn can be analysed at three levels—power relations which designate a particular policing style, power as it is negotiated through policing practice, and power struggles which eventuate as a consequence of policing practice.

Essential to an understanding of police powers is recognition of the place of authority, regulation and decision-making within the style concerned. Any detailed examination of the way in which these features of policing operate will provide particularity when understanding specific policing forms.

Genealogies of power in policing need to be considered specifically. For instance, the power of whom, over whom, and by what means? In the state police scenario, the answer is powers exercised by government, through the police, over the population.

Policing and function

Policing is a process whereby social order and regulation is maintained. Whether this is as a result of repression, by consent, or through collective enterprise, it involves designated and identifiable functions.

Traditionally, central tasks for policing are the maintenance and dissemination of information, the protection of life and property, the maintenance of public order, and ensuring *social happiness*.[36] From the outset, however, police function has required regulation. To this extent, as suggested earlier, it is unwise to separate an examination of what police do from what it is they are expected to do.

A functional focus for policing has long been the maintenance of social and public order. This demonstrates the close connection between policing and governance. It also promotes questions such as whose order and for whom is it maintained?[37] The constitution of what is *social* and *order* opens up an examination of the appropriate environment and priorities for regulation.

---

35 See Findlay & Zvekic (1993), chapters 1 & 2.
36 Pasquino, P. (1991), 'Theatrum Politicum: The Genealogy of Capital', in G. Burchell, C. Gordon, & P. Miller (eds), *Foucault Effect: Studies in Governmentality*, University of Chicago Press, Chicago.
37 For a discussion of this critical perspective see Chambliss, W. & Mankoff, M. (1976), *Whose Law? What Order? A Conflict Approach to Criminology*, Wiley, New York.

Crucial for the development of policing function is the monopolisation of specialist knowledge about crime and justice. Hogg observed that 'the constitution of a model or concept of a "system" (such as criminal justice) is the means by which a knowledge of it is gained'.[38] In particular, one cannot understand the workings of processes such as criminal justice and the knowledge/power which they produce (and on which they rely) if it is assumed that the objects of knowledge (such as crime rates, or policing clear-up rates) are said to exist externally to them. The processes of criminal justice, and policing in particular, produce, contain, reinterpret and market knowledge. Particular fields of knowledge in criminal justice have identifiable boundaries, often determined through the practice of policing. The struggle between specialist and generalised functions is a case in point.

The function of policing in Australia has seen historical transitions from specialist to generalised functions and then back towards more specialist technologies.[39] Despite the existence of more *social* policing functions in Australia today, the specialisation of policing goes on unabated. This parallel development of functions is mirrored in the expansion of public and private policing functions. Boundaries for these functions may depend on levels of specialisation. The state as a principal sponsor of policing in Australia is instrumental in determining and maintaining functional boundaries for police work.

The relationship between policing and government in Australia is a close one. This has always been the case.[40] This relationship endorses functions of policing with identified social and political agendas and presence. In this sense the police can be simultaneously recognised as a welfare and a control agency depending on political imperatives. Recently the state police have been portrayed as a preventive institution essential to government crime control strategies, moving as they are from reactive to proactive commitments.[41] The police are said to endorse and guarantee good government on the one hand and to react to challenges to social disorder on the other. In fact, the repression of dissent by the police is often justified as essential for the maintenance of political and economic order. However, the notion of governance through a separation of powers hard up against the symbiosis of the police and government highlights the complexity of modern democracies.

Policing was one of the earliest executive functions of the colonial state. From the outset, the police, the magistracy and executive government were inextricable. In Australia, control of the police through centralised political power and not localised municipalities has always been a feature of state-based policing. Because of the politicisation of policing, there exists perennial tension between the politicians governing police administration, commissioners of police, and their constables.[42]

---

38 Hogg, R. (1983), 'Perspectives on the Criminal Justice System', in M. Findlay, S. Egger, & J. Sutton (eds), *Issues in Criminal Justice Administration*, Allen & Unwin, Sydney, pp. 3-21.

39 Bolen, J. (1997), *Reform in Policing: Lessons from the Whitrod Era*, Hawkins Press, Sydney, chapters 4 & 5.

40 For a discussion of this relationship see Finnane (1994).

41 See Edwards (1999), chapters 3, 4 & 13.

42 Finnane (1994); Bolen (1997).

Contemporary debate about police function reiterates the need to break the connection between the police and the magistracy, to dismantle centralised police forces, and suppress specialised police agencies with limited remit. In all jurisdictions in Australia there is a shift from reliance on judicial to bureaucratic controls when it comes to the regulation of policing. Even so, the external accountability mechanisms are crucially reliant on internal police investigative discretion.

The significance of policing

Social indicators of the significance of policing in Australia have moved well beyond simple calculations of the number of public and private sector police per head of population. Examining police numbers relative to other essential state and private sector services, and the financial resources invested in policing suggest the current importance of police within Australia and its politics. Particularly at a state and territory level, law-and-order politics in which the police play a central role is continually nominated as an essential election platform. Simple correlations between investment in policing and potentials to control crime are the staple of political rhetoric.[43] The expansion of policing is an increasing investment by the state in a climate where other forms of regulation and control may face reduced public and private-sector budgets.

Since the commencement of white occupancy in Australia, there has been an active connection between the police and settlement. The advancement of Euro-centric interests has accompanied the development of policing in all its forms. Early encounters between police and indigenous resistance is emblematic of the present poor police–Aboriginal relations. The bureaucratic transformation of social relationships between white and black Australians has relied on the ultimate threat of force and dispossession which police powers have endorsed.[44] This atmosphere of selective coercion has spread throughout Australian cities to provide tensions between police and young people, police and the unemployed, police and ethnic communities and any number of other relatively marginalised groups in Australian society.

In Australia, policing was formed and fashioned in socio-political periods of conflict and controversy.[45] The tendency of colonial elites to view lower-order resistance as requiring police intervention has prevailed as a political agenda in Australia. In this respect policing has become a reactionary force within Australian society.

The motivation for the expansion of policing based on specific local issues such as drug-law enforcement, street safety, and traffic regulation provides interesting

---

43   Hogg & Brown (1998), chapters 1 & 2; Finnane (2002), chapters 1, 3 & 6.
44   Finnane (1994), chapter 6.
45   For instance, Finnane (1994), chapter 3; Finnane, M. (1987), *Policing in Australia: Historical Perspectives*, University of NSW Press, Sydney, chapters 4, 6 & 8.

indications of contemporary concerns within Australian political and community life. Many of these concerns generate from a fear of crime and expectations for policing public safety. As with policing itself, these are not uncontentious.

The significance of Australian policing is revealed through struggles over governmentality and police reform. In recent decades governments and politicians have been irreparably damaged by the corruption of police and the failure of reform.[46] The synergy between police and political interests has tended to see shared fortunes along with supportive functions so that policing in Australia is an interdependent rather than independent arm of the state.[47]

Summary: Good and bad policing

In his paper on the topic Braithwaite explores what makes for good and bad policing.[48] He suggested that if we accept that the most appropriate responsibility for policing is the protection of civil dominion (where the freedom for citizens is found within equality, and shared rights and responsibilities) then police performance should be measured against how well they do at that task. In this respect the police, while being committed to the reduction of crime, should focus on crime prevention in collaboration with the community they service. The threat posed to civil society by crime will be reduced when police focus on crucial operational determinants such as the 'subjective certainty of detection'[49], but do so in an atmosphere where the community is comfortable with good police service.

Brathwaite challenges policing in Australia to take community engagement seriously. In doing this, good policing is vitally concerned with human rights through the establishment and maintenance of a safe and free civil society. This book explores ways of meeting such a challenge, as well as the impediments to its realisation. In the chapters that follow, the function, power and significance of policing in many forms will be considered against the diverse communities of Australia. The relationship between police 'communities' and their communities of service is crucial to the reality of *community-centred* policing, explored in chapter 3 and ongoing.

Additional readings

For full reference details refer to the bibliography.
Klockars (1985), chapter 1.

---

46   Dixon (1999), chapters 1 & 6.
47   This is more clearly so through the corporate-client relationship at the heart of private policing.
48   Braithwaite, J. (1992), 'Good and Bad Police Services and How to Pick Them' in P. Moir & H. Eijkman, *Policing Australia: Old issues, New perspectives*, Macmillan, Melbourne, chapter 1.
49   Braithwaite (1992), p. 21ff.

Brogden (1989), chapter 1.

Reiner (1992), chapter 6.

Findlay & Zvekic (1993), chapter 1.

Brogden (1981), 'All Police is Conning Bastards: Policing and the Problems of Consent', in Fine et al.

Reiner, R. (1992), 'Policing a Post Modern Society', *Modern Law Review*, vol. 56, no. 6, pp. 761–781.

Reiner (1997), 'Policing and the Police', in Maguire et al., pp. 997–1049.

Braithwaite, (1992), 'Good and Bad Police Services and How to Pick Them', in Moir & Eijkman, chapter 1.

Leaver (1997), chapter 1.

Dixon (1997), chapter 1.

2

Policing Histories

Introduction

As a bridge to the exploration of policing in contemporary Australia, this chapter very briefly overviews:

1. Concepts of history in policing
2. The early models of policing from which Australian police forces drew structural and operational themes, and
3. The development of policing in Australia.[1]

It is perhaps risky to generalise about the origins of policing as a state function, or about the development of policing in community or commercial contexts. Even so there will be occasion in this chapter to draw out broad themes from the histories of policing which explain the emerging nature of police ideology, operations, and community standing. In this regard the chapter is an argument for the significance of history[2] as a perspective for understanding policing. It does not chart Australian policing histories.

Foundations of Australian policing histories

Particularly in relation to policing Australian communities past and present it is impossible to ignore such issues as police–Aboriginal relations, policing ethnic minorities, policing organised labour, the significant relationship between the police and landed interests, and the close association between the police and the magistracy.[3] In addition, the original social composition of the Australian colonies

---

1   I have decided to make my discussion of policing and history thematic, general and concise. I gain comfort in doing this from the wealth of scholarship on policing histories in Australia contained in more general social histories as well as that which has been purpose-written. For an indication of those working and writing in the field; see Finnane (1987).

2   This chapter is not meant to be a contribution to the history of Australian policing, nor will the reader find multiple references to significant historical events.

3   See Finnane (1994); (2002); Collins et al. (2000).

and the nature of their exiles (introduced and indigenous) declare much about the mandate for policing in its formative stages. The first Australian policing trans- ported and entrenched its originating British interests such as public order mainte- nance, workforce management, safety and health regulation, and the protection of sectoral property interests.

In turn, the make-up of colonial society in Australia largely predetermined the institutional structure and demographics of the first colonial police forces along with their initial priorities. Also, the disparate and far-flung process of colonisa- tion, and the domination of the land by white settlement in particular, was a clear motivation for specialisation in early Australian police units.

For the *'development'* of colonial Australia, relevant policing themes may also be drawn from the histories of policing in other jurisdictional contexts and cultural settings.[4] With these in mind it is possible to reflect on the colonial origins of polic- ing in Australia and their impact on modern Australian policing styles.[5]

Policing histories

Reiner observed that with much of the early historical writing on British policing coming from police officers or those close to the police, the direction of these his- tories was instrumentalist and sometimes apologetic. He divided his discussion of policing histories between what he calls orthodox and 'revisionist' histories.[6] These approaches to British policing histories usefully precede the consideration of polic- ing history in Australia, bearing in mind the claims made for connections between Australian colonial police forces and their English and Irish counterparts.

Regarding the orthodox histories of policing, Reiner characterised a uni-linear approach to analysis where policing grows naturally out of the early Industrial Revolution challenges to public order and the necessities of industrial capitalism. In this context police (particularly state-sponsored police) are a natural structural and functional response to the challenge to *traditional liberties,* posed by social unrest. The early police forces reflected the dominant, but contested, ideologies of justice largely proposed by the propertied classes. They did not allow for the ambiguous challenges to order which social unrest advertised, nor for a recogni- tion of the alternative meanings which such unrest asserted. The police were a symbol that order was apparent and justice clearly self-interested. The only debate

---

4   See D. Hay & F. Sneider (eds) (1989), *Policing and Prosecution in Britain,* Clarendon Press, Oxford.

5   Here in particular one should be careful to consider extraction and augmentation. Visions of policing were not removed from their cultures of origin and frozen in time, but rather from the outset were adapted to the harsh realities of colonial survival and domination.

6   Reiner also described these styles as 'cop-sided' and 'lopsided' approaches to history. See Reiner, R. (2000), *The Politics of the Police,* Wheatsheaf, London, Part I.

in this policing story seems to be about the type and extent of the conflict confronting the police and its origins.

Revisionist histories prefer a 'slice of time' approach to historical analysis. Policing, it is proposed, is examined as any other component part of society at particular periods in its development. This approach to history denies the suggested instrumentalist fit between the police and the requirements of industrialisation. Further, it suggests that the state police arise out of class-based needs for the maintenance of capitalism and private property.

Reiner indicated from this comparison of styles of history that both of these approaches are determinist and tend to distort the origins of policing. It is not factual to rest police histories alone on the notion of the breakdown of earlier forms of social control. Rather, this interpretation suggested that policing emerged in a much wider context of social, economic and political ferment. Change was not simply in the form of control, but rather in the whole environment being controlled, of which the police are a part.

Policing also is not most accurately represented as necessarily the result of the pressures of early capitalism and the regulation of the labour market. The need for policing within and across class groups is also crucial to an understanding of the emergence of specific police styles. Due to a combination of the entrepreneurial activities of reformers in central government (in England) the need for social order was generalised. Supporting this was the perception of the moral panic arising from crime rates and focussed public disorder in rapidly expanding urban contexts. With the development and diffusion of national and local governments throughout Britain during the Industrial Revolution the state required a more sophisticated and intrusive vocational policing service to promote its notion of order and governance. As a part of this the *new police* were required to recognise, at least to some small extent, concerns about local democratic accountabilities. These police became closely linked to the operations and intentions of the state, while assuming a symbolic presence which was sensitive to revolution and domination in other parts of Europe. In addition, policing developed as a crucial component of the repressive dominion of colonialism, and its monopoly of legitimate violence through criminal justice and the penal sanction.

Histories of policing are as much about the historical creation of and contest over police legitimacy as they are a recollection of social facts and themes.[7] Any sensitive and instructive history of policing needs to examine:

- the significance of consent for police authority
- the creation and development of the disciplined service
- the 'rule of law' context for the development of police power

---

7   Robinson, C. (1979), 'Ideology as History: A Look at the Way Some English Police Historians Look at the Police', *Police Studies*, vol. 2, pp. 35–49.

- strategies of minimal force
- the emergence of a service function
- tensions in the relationship between police and the community
- the co-option of the working class into the structures of policing, and
- the prevalence of discretion as a foundation of police power.

Convincing histories of policing confront the manner in which police institutions and operations are inextricably linked with the history of the state.[8] It is important that police histories should examine the foundations of police authority, as well as of its developing jurisdiction. In this respect the positioning of police within public space and the struggle over public order becomes another important theme for policing and political history.

Origins of police authority in Australia

As is the case with much of the recent police reform endeavours in Australia (see chapter 13), policing may be viewed primarily in organisational terms. In this respect police organisational histories feature as an explanation of what police do, how they do it, and why the institutions and individuals of policing exist in the structures of the modern liberal–democratic state.[9]

In order to understand the differences existing in periods of policing and their cultural locations it is necessary to consider the emerging relationship between policing and economic and political transition in Australia.[10] In this respect the differences between original English/Irish police forces[11] and those in Europe, and the unique organisational directions of colonial police forces can be understood.[12] The structures of colonial policing in Australia throughout the early 1800s were largely imported from these Anglo/Irish models, but the exigencies of colonial society forced swift and significant organisational and functional adaptations.[13] More interesting, however, for an appreciation of why policing in Australia is as it is today, are the origins of police authority. These do not so much rest in structural or institutional roots but rather in the functional relationships and political priorities of the early police forces.[14]

---

8   An example of this is Finnane, M. (1994), (previously referred to in n. 1 p. vii).
9   See Reiner, R. (1992), *Chief Constables: Bobbies, Bosses or Bureaucrats?* Oxford University Press, Oxford; Marshall, G. (1965), *Police and Government: The Status and Accountability of the English Constable*, Methuen & Co Ltd, London; Critchley, T.A. (1978), *A History of Police in England & Wales*, Constable, London.
10 See Edwards (1999), chapters 4 & 5.
11 Emsley, C. (1996), *The English Police: A Political and Social History*, Longman, London.
12 See Brethnach, S. (1974), *The Irish Police: From Earliest Times to Present Day*, Anvil Books, Dublin; Carson, W. (1984 &1985), 'Policing the Periphery: The Development of Scottish Policing', parts 1 & 2, *Australian and New Zealand Journal of Criminology*, vol. 17, no. 4, pp. 207–32; vol. 18, no. 1, pp. 3–16.
13 Sturma, M. (1987), 'Policing the Criminal Frontier in Mid Nineteenth Century Australia, Britain and America' in Finnane (1987), chapter 1.
14 Particularly as these relate to indigenous people see Cuneen (2001), chapter 3.

Further, in the search to understand contemporary struggles over police authority, there is the need to explore protest and resistance associated with economic and political change, and the place of police in its regulation, particularly towards the end of the nineteenth century.[15] In the early Australian colonial context, the crime-control agendas which followed on from the regulation of convict life and the repression of indigenous people, for instance, were a history of policing protest and resistance.[16] These sadly have changed little as struggles over the exercise of police authority from its origins in the 1800s and into the new millennium.

Historical development of policing in Australia

The history of policing in the Australian colonies presents a history of contradiction. The central theme around which policing emerged and developed was the need to contain public order in convict society of the early eighteenth century.[17] A bi-product of this was the emergence of an ambiguous attitude to police within the colonies. Policing developed in the context of a popular disrespect for the police and their activities. For instance, the European community to be policed was an anti-authoritarian convict immigrant population out of which poor quality recruits were tempted, or dragooned, into police work. The indigenous populations presented active resistance to policing, particularly as it fostered rural expansion of colonial borders.[18] Expectations for maintenance of public order were not fulfilled in the early days of colonial policing and pressures for reform emerged from political elites which feared a breakdown in public morality, and governability.[19] This in turn was exacerbated by strains among the colonial military and tensions generated by competing interests from within the free community.[20]

The contradictory origins of policing in the colonies featured:

• The fact that the original police force was drawn from an Irish convict population many of whom had been sent to the colonies for acts of resistance against the Irish constabulary. This produced among the police themselves some antipathy towards policing priorities.[21]

---

15   See Barker, D. (2001), 'Barricades and Batons: A Historical Perspective of the Policing of Major Industrial Disorder in Australia', in Enders & Dupont (2001), chapter 15. Mirrors of this struggle in Britain are discussed in Jones, D (1982), *Crime, Protest, Community and Police in Nineteenth Century Britain*, Routledge & Kegan Paul, London.

16   See O'Sullivan, J. (1979), *Mounted Police in NSW*, Rigby, Adelaide. See Connell, R. & Irving, T. (1980), *Class Structure in Australian History: Narrative and Argument*, Longman Cheshire, Melbourne.

17   For a general discussion of the vital relationships of policing and public order see Wright, A. (2002), *Policing: An Introduction to Concepts and Practice*, Willan, Devon, chapter 3.

18   See Cunneen (2001).

19   Sturma, M. (1981), 'Police and Drunkards in Sydney', *Australian Journal of Politics and History*, vol. 27, no. 1. pp. 49–50.

20   Clarke, C.M. (1962), *A History of Australia I: From the Earliest Times to the Age of Macquarie*, Melbourne University Press, Melbourne.

21   Sturma (1987).

- Early recruits represented largely the least employable in the community and those who could otherwise not find a useful government service.
- In the early days of colonial policing there was a high rate of dismissal and resignation among police.
- Corruption was rife.
- Drunkenness and consequent ill-discipline provided a focus for internal regulation in colonial policing. The initial supervision by the magistracy impugned police–judicial independence throughout the development of the colonies.
- The initial decentralisation of police forces led to difficulties with centralised control and regulation.
- The low rates of pay provided to police required the colonial officers to supplement their income in unauthorised ways.
- Certain police units (such as the Gold Police) were not under the particular jurisdiction of policing legislation and the centralised control it envisaged.

Context of settlement and 'state imposition'

Australian policing did not emerge out of community innovation, but rather through state imposition in response to local demands for security, whether these were urban or pastoral.[22] Along with a suspect and antipathetic early policing culture, the wider colonial community represented opposition to the police. The efforts by police to regulate closely the lives and limited recreation of convicts led to regular conflict in the form of challenges to public order. Problems of discipline emerged within the specialised policing units leading to particular flashpoints in authority and power abuse (such as the constant and violent encounters between the Native Police and Border Police with indigenous communities on the fringes of white settlement).[23]

The quality of police work in the colonies, its indulgence, and distance from constitutional legality was itself problematic. For example, the border police were comprised of convicts under sentence or soldiers transported for desertion. This unruly force was regularly in conflict with the free population, while being challenged with maintaining the perimeters and progress of white settlement.

Many of the activities required of early colonial police generated an atmosphere of conflict and isolation from the community. For example, tax collection and revenue-generating activities were the central function for the Gold Police during the gold rushes in New South Wales and Victoria. The Gold Police were essentially a licensing force empowered to ensure state revenue. Associated with this was the ethnic focus of many encounters between the police and gold miners

---

22   Finnane (1994).
23   Sturma (1987).

that exacerbated tensions. The police became the front-line authority for the state under challenge, and concerted rebellion in the mining settlements was directed against the police as the embodiment of the state.

The paramilitary origins of policing in Australia are apparent. For instance, the Mounted Police adopted an organisational presence which was difficult to distinguish from the cavalry. The hierarchy, uniform and operational language were essentially militaristic.

The nature of white settlement in the early colonies and the dispersion of state authority (in particular through the administration of justice) saw a close relationship develop between the police and the rural magistracy. With local magistrates also representing significant landholding interests, the association between the police and justice institutions took on a class-conspiratorial appearance.

All in all through the diversity of policing structures and organisation in the early colonies, the poverty of police populations, and the lack of official superintendence, legislation was required in order to formalise and better regulate state police forces.[24]

Path to centralisation of authority and control

From the origination of New South Wales and Victoria as colonies in particular the administrative functions of policing remained in the principal city. In this sense the power and authority for policing in Australia had always been centralised. The reform initiatives which characterised the mid 1800s and beyond were all about the centralisation of control.[25] The colonial governors were authorised to appoint constables and justices of the peace. In the rural regions the association between the police and the magistracy became strong and powerful. At the local level policing was conducted under the supervision of the magistracy, with magistrates reporting back to the central state.

More apparent centralisation of policing in New South Wales followed the passing of the control of the police over to an executive commissioner, replacing magisterial authority.[26] Yet the impact of such organisational restructuring decreased the further one moved from the capital.

In South Australia there was an early attempt at a greater community-responsible location of police authority. As regards funding at least this extended to an adaptation of the English county police legislation in 1840 requiring contri-

---

24   See for example *Police Regulation Act* (NSW, 1850) which centralised the control of the police and imposed more stringent guidelines for recruiting: *The Police Recruiting Act* (NSW, 1853) which addresses problems associated with recruiting from other jurisdictions. See Finnane, M. (1987), 'The Politics of Police Powers: The Making of Police Offences Acts' in Finnane (1987), p. 88.

25   Finnane (1994).

26   See *Police Act* (NSW) 1860.

bution to the cost of foot patrolling in local districts.[27] This funding approach also acted as a buffer against the retrenchment of colonial expenditure on policing in difficult times. Interestingly Tasmania went against the trend of centralisation where between 1856 and 1898 policing was organised on a municipal basis.

The path to centralised policing in Australia was far from smooth. In the late 1800s struggles between the governors and the judiciary, government and pastoral interests, funding issues, and a new population mix added to problems with the character and performance of the constabulary. Pressures for police reform developed alongside the bureaucratisation of Australian police organisations and remain a feature of the sometimes strained relationships between the police and government, the police and the community.

The legal foundations of contemporary policing in Australia were clearly connected with the emergence of the bureaucratic state as a consequence of the Colonial Acts. A feature of the move to independent government saw the police legislated as state functionaries headed by a Commissioner, or an Inspector General, who administered the police in accordance with the direction of the Colonial Secretary, or the Minister. This purposely excluded the judiciary from controlling police practices.[28]

Policing and public order in Australia: Culture, space and political economy

The ideology of state policing in Australia included the control of crime through prevention and detection, maintaining order through control of dissent and non crime-related municipal concerns for order and stability. In theory this was to be based on the generation and maintenance of community consensus.

Chris Cunneen highlighted what he calls the 'dehistoricised' social consensus of public order.[29] He emphasised in the early days of colonial development in Australia the political and social contest over public space. The police took an important role in the reconstitution of challenges to public order and the control of space. However, in many respects policing became a battle over marginalisation and the discrimination against the disenfranchised. This provided a significant foundation for tension which still remains between alienated groups such as the police and indigenous people. [30]

Consistent with colonial policing experiences in other jurisdictions in Australia the maintenance of public order became the hallmark of colonial police

---

27   Finnane (1994), p. 17.
28   Finnane (1994), chapter 2.
29   See Cunneen (2001).
30   Reynolds, H. (1981), *The Other Side of the Frontier: An Interpretation of the Aboriginal Response to the Invasion and Settlement of Australia*, James Cook University, Townsville.

forces. Several themes emerged from this foundation which have prevailed across policing priorities in Australia today:

1. **The importance of the mob as 'threat'.** The state-based police in Australia have regularly been used for the control of political dissent. More than this police have maintained social boundaries in public recreation, and specific areas of political and social change. The involvement of police in processes of public dissent has seen police individuals and institutions shift to the focus of that dissent as much more than as impartial representatives of public order.[31]

2. **Defining and determining the fear of crime.** As the institution largely responsible for identifying and designating public disorder the police have adopted the role of declaring who makes up the dangerous classes, and against whom they are directed. Policing public order is as much about nominating for the orderly who they should fear as combating the disorderly.

3. **Policing urbanisation and migration.** Australia is one of the most highly urbanised nations in the world. The rapid development of Australian cities in the twentieth century provided a challenge for the organisation and function of policing. This challenge was particularised by the manner in which migrant communities located and interacted in major urban settings. The tensions which emerged from multicultural Australian cities against the narrow background of selective policing priorities, have meant that police/ethnic relations are triggering consequences and challenges in public order.

4. **Inexorable administrative proliferation**. Along with extensive urbanisation and the narrow spatial occupancy of the nation, Australia is also one of the most extensively governed and bureaucratised of countries. The constitutional division of criminal justice in Australia and the state-based obligations for the maintenance of social order have given the police a significant impetus to develop as key features of Australian governance.[32] In addition the intrusion of bureaucratic control across Australian society has progressively come to rely upon the authority of the criminal sanction to endorse many political and social reforms. The police are used to represent these sanctions, and more generally to provide welfare and service functions as part of these reform strategies.

5. **Crisis in early capitalism.** Policing industrial unrest, and the maintenance of a compliant and reliable workforce have depended in many colonial settings on the efforts of state police. Australia has been no different in this regard and even today the police are often called upon to carry out government policy in industrial relations. In addition, state police are now required to defend Australia's position within the global community and to stand against expressions of resistance against globalisation, environmental degradation, and multinational exploitation.

---

31 See Cunneen, Findlay, Lynch & Tupper (1989).
32 Some state police forces are among the largest of comparable organisations in the world.

The police embrace the administrative and operational responsibilities for what Brogden referred to as 'tidying up the disorderly edges of society'.[33] As colonial governments have transferred into more secure states the role of the police in social order control has seen a shift from crude class-based politics to a more liberal, pluralistic, and professional administrative urban reorganisation.

Ethnocentric explanations for police beginnings

With the police being required to perform preventive functions there has been an explicit expectation that the police should represent and protect a particular notion of social order that equates with the priorities of the state. In Australia the development of these priorities can be quite clearly viewed against the demographics of power and authority in early Australian society. These demographics have supported and fostered an ethnocentric style of policing, and have seen the police develop a largely comfortable and reliable administrative compact with the state. In a practical sense the commercial relationship between state-based police and government is obvious in terms of resourcing and institution building. Little wonder therefore that state police will support and endorse the commitments to public order demanded by conservative governments in particular.

Colonial police work was largely the work of the state, or the elite commercial and political interests which supported and maintained governments. This has led to:

- compromises in maintaining the rule of law either in context of consent or of coercion
- the constant delegitimating of indigenous customs or competing community and social orders, and
- the perpetuation of exported inequality which was a bi-product of introduced legal systems and imperial migration structures.

In Australian communities right up until the twentieth century policing was of strangers by strangers. The police provided a major reserve function for government elites and the interests of white settlers in the promotion of colonisation. The professionalisation of policing was directly linked to commercial interests more than community obligation. Towards the end of the 1800s and from then on as Australia diversified its economic and commercial bases (and imported migrant populations to support such diversification) policing became essentially linked to corporate priorities often against the interests of organised labour.[34] In some respects this mirrored their responsibilities to the pastoralist/politicians earlier in

---

33   Brogden, M. (1987), 'The Emergence of the Police: The Colonial Dimension', *British Journal of Criminology*, vol. 27, no. 1, pp. 4–15.
34   See Finnane (1994), chapter 3.

the century in achieving what Finnane identified as their responsibility in 'taking the land' from its indigenous owners as part of the 'government of Aborigines'.[35]

The master–servant role for police in Australia is well founded in the relationship between police and their political 'controllers'.[36] While this has been an uncomfortable alliance against the ideology of operational independence (see chapter 3) the ties between the police and politics in Australia are close and prevailing. They extend from commissioners to ministers,[37] police unions and political parties,[38] as well as police culture and political commitments.[39] The history of the police as servants of political power in Australia and beneficiaries of political patronage is more convincing than any history of the transition of policing from force to service, in a community sense.

Policing the criminal frontier

The relationship between crime and city life in Australia is clear and compelling. Cities (and urbanisation) have become important territories for policing. The socially differential composition of Australian cities has exacerbated discrimination and difference throughout Australian society, and the police have often provided the enforcement of diversity (see chapter 9). Their role in generating fear of crime and disorder has meant that the police have both consciously and unconsciously stimulated social divisions in Australian cities. This tends to equate with the isolated position of many police personnel and organisations from the communities in which they function.

The anxiety of political and commercial elites is often demonstrated through the policing of social disorder. In the re-establishment and maintenance of public order the interests of elites are seen to be synonymous with the interests of good policing.

As the police tend to stereotype challenges to their own authority as equating with challenges to social order more broadly then the public comes to fear the same segments of the community which stand as a challenge to police respect and consensus. For example, policing activity against young males is justified not only in terms of their challenge to policing but also their broader threat to social safety.

In the consideration of policing social order, the disorderly consequences of policing should not be overlooked. In examining histories of social unrest[40] the

35 Finnane (1994), chapter 6.
36 Finnane (1994), chapter 2; Finnane (2002), chapters 3 & 6.
37 See Bolen (1997).
38 Finnane (2002), chapters 5 & 6.
39 Finnane (1987), chapter 8.
40 See S. Humphries (1981), *Hooligans or Rebels: An Oral History of Working Class Childhood and Youth 1889-1939*, Blackwell, Oxford.

potential of the police to exacerbate violent encounters of social resistance is clear. This potential to generate violence through policing has endorsed and supported the tendency for police organisations to become more specialised and reliant on public-order technologies. Police structures have become adapted to the challenge of social disorder and specialised in respect of these challenges. More generally, histories of policing need to consider the relationship between the introduction of policing, shifts in crime both in form and focus, and transition in economic conditions. This can clearly be traced in the rapid social and economic development of Australia following Federation.

Politicisation of Australian policing

The police have grown reliant on governments rather than local communities in Australia for their financial survival. Despite their claims to independence (see chapter 3) Australian police organisations have now emerged as an arm of executive government and public administration.

The politics of police as part of public administration was set in state priorities by the end of the nineteenth century. At this time the largest domains of government employment were education, the railways, and the police which characterised the investment of the developing state with a commitment to centralisation strained by rapidly expanding frontiers.

The emerging relationship between the police and government is revealed through the police–population ratio trends. In the nineteenth century there were relatively high police–population ratios, producing mixed reactions from the community, some comforted by the growing police presence, others resentful of its intrusion.[41] Between the world wars policing numbers fell as a consequence of general manpower shortages, strained government economies, and sporadic crime reporting. Again the police presence went on the increase from the 1940s and in particular after the 1970s due to increased perceptions of public and political unrest, as well as a reorganisation of police work practices. Specialisation and professionalism now combine with the political presence of the police to make police establishments, and in particular the visible presence of policing, a potent political issue in contemporary Australia.

Conclusion: Historical indicators of modern policing

As we have seen, colonial police organisation and functions have developed from:
• pastoralism and the interests of white domination

---

41   Sturma (1987).

- a convict base and the impact of demography policing
- conflictual relationships with indigenous populations and the constant negative encounters between police and social minorities more generally
- the fundamental reliance of governments on policing from the early days of revenue production and protection, through to the endorsement of a wide range of government policy initiatives
- the emergence of workforce management as a policing priority
- the perennial development of master–servant relationships and obligations for policing and politics in Australia
- policing as an essential feature of intensive urbanisation and extensive government across Australia, and
- the perpetuation of policing as an arbiter of Australian multiculturalism

Policing in city and country Australia continues to organise the boundaries of public and private space. Policing has established relationships of accommodation across multicultural Australia and has selectively attempted to support ideologies of democracy in the face of rapid social transition and political change.

Additional readings

For full reference details refer to the bibliography.
Brogden (2000), chapters 4 & 5.
Reiner (2000), Part 1.
Klockars (1985), chapters 3 & 4.
Finnane (1994), chapter 1.
Dixon, (1999), chapter 2.
Finnane (1989), chapters 1, 3 & 9.
Finnane (1987), chapters 1 & 3.
Wood (1997), vol. 1, chapter 3a.
Robinson (1979), 'Ideology as History: A Look at the Way Some English Police Historians Look at the Police', *Police Studies*, vol. 2, no. 2, pp. 35–49.
Neal (1991).
Edwards (1999), chapter 2.
Enders. & Dupont (2001), Part 1.
Cunneen (2001).
McCulloch (2001).

3

Police Ideologies and Community Policing

Introduction

Community-based policing is the prevailing ideology for state police in contemporary Australia.[1] Against a historical development that connects the police to government, and at the same time celebrates the independence and impartiality of their authority, an operational ideology requiring community responsibility seems paradoxical.[2]

It is a paradox not lost on the public or the police. For the police it has produced dilemmas in self-image[3] and accountability; for the community, confusion and frustrated expectations. Even so, there is great promise in community policing and its ramifications for community-centred criminal-justice delivery. This chapter looks at the translation of community ideologies into police work, and foreshadows the more detailed consideration of accountability in chapter 7.

The history of policing in Australia has indicated different responses to political direction.[4] It has been said that the police are guided by largely unarticulated political, moral and policy considerations that determine their response to political directions. Where specific directions and/or the mechanics of their attempted enforcement do not offend these general and particular interests (or may actually strengthen them), the police are willing to comply. Where this is not the case the police will seek ways of resisting the policy. This can be seen in the recent trajectory of community-based policing from ideology to operational manifesto.

---

1   Glare, K. (1991), 'Community Policing in a Multicultural Australia', in McKillop & Vernon.
2   Lurigio, A. & Rosenbaum, D. (1970), 'Community Policing: Major Issues and Unanswered Questions', in M. Dantzkler (ed.), *Contemporary Policing: Personnel Issues and Trends*, Butterworth Heinemann, New York, pp. 195–216.
3   For a discussion of officer reaction to community policing see MacIntyre, S. & Prenzler, T. (1997), 'Officer Perspectives on Community Policing', *Current Issues in Criminal Justice*, vol. 9, no. 1, pp. 34–55.
4   For example, see Bolen (1997).

In this respect the exercise of police discretion is crucial for the realisation of policing ideologies. Discretion, both individually and organisationally, may indeed be independent (even self-interested) and at times at odds with other executive policy.[5]

Common law principle holds the police are accountable to the law, and where controversy over their independence arises it tends to focus on their relations with government. The essential and general independence of the police as an institution of the democratic state has largely remained above question in considerations of Australian government, both for the police themselves and for the state. As regards private policing, notions of independence are conditional on the commercial environment in which services are designated and for which they are contracted.[6]

To talk about police power and responsibility as being only accountable under the law is far too limited an explanation for their exercise in practice. In many cases the law institutes huge discretion in terms of the structure and exercise of police power, and associated accountability. Rarely is it that the law specifically imposes responsibilities or corrects errors in the exercise of police powers, in any definitive way.[7] As chapter 7 suggests, police accountability in Australia is more an administrative province than a legislative requirement. Community-based policing, however, requires accountability to the public as the client of policing.

The reality of community policing

A useful dimension for testing the reality of community policing is the historical origin of state-based police services. In Australia, early policing initiatives were clearly connected to the interests of land-owners and the white colonial state.[8] The police themselves in their Victorian (nineteenth-century) form were directed against the leisure and public behaviour of the working classes and the unemployed. The police have always been connected with the regulation of labour forces and the development of interests in capital. In this respect history does not support notions of broad and inclusive community policing.

One might ask what is the difference between the visible forms of community-based policing in Australia and their actual impact? An answer to this should go beyond the rhetoric of police ideologies and look closely at the realisation of

---

5   An example of this, where police resistance took on its own political dimension, can be seen in Eggar, S. & Findlay, M. (1988), 'The Politics of Police Discretion', in M. Findlay & R. Hogg (eds), *Understanding Crime and Criminal Justice*, Law Book Company, Sydney, pp 209–23.

6   A historical discussion of this is found in Bowden, T. (1978), *Beyond the Limits of the Law*, Penguin, Harmondsworth, chapters 4 & 5.

7   To some extent an exception to this legislation such as the *Police Powers and Responsibilities Act* (Qld); *Law Enforcement (Powers and Responsibilities) Act* (NSW).

8   See Finnane (1987), chapters 1, 2 & 3.

community expectations for policing. As policing moves from preventive to proactive modes we need to critically analyse the widest social effect on community policing. Essential to this, the complexity of communities in Australia needs to be recognised. Flowing from this is the examination of whether community-based policing can be achieved through communities themselves or imposed from outside.

Certainly, from the point of view of conventional criminal investigation, it might be that the most positive dimension of community-based policing is the freer flow of information and communications. This, however, needs to go beyond a one-way process. While the police have a legitimate right to expect the provision of useful information for the purposes of crime prevention and control emerging from the community, the community itself has a right to know what the police do with this information and how it impacts on citizens' rights and responsibilities.

Ultimately community policing is about consensus. The ideology of community policing is a campaign for consensus. For it to have reality as a generator of further consensus across diverse communities, community-based policing needs to move well beyond the realm of ideology. The same could be said for the exercise of criminal justice outside policing. The police are a community within the wider process of justice. Agency cooperation within criminal justice is essential in contributing to the achievement of community policing goals.

Finally, new management strategies for policing which endorse a community focus must permeate through all levels of the police community in order that they should take root. If community policing is to move beyond a statement of ideals and have impact for those who endorse it, the nature of the relationship between police and the community, local and managerial, must have potency on a daily basis.

Ideology of independence?

Conventionally, and as confirmed through case law, the office of the police constable claims independence of control by government or by the state. The constable has in common law tradition, an independent discretionary responsibility to enforce the law and cannot be directed in relation to such enforcement.[9] It follows that in principle police authority in the structure of the disciplined service does not determine the original law enforcement actions of subordinates as declared in the oath of office. In reality this is both unrealistic and not reflected in policing practice.[10]

---

9 See *Enever v. R* (1906) 3 CLR 969; *AG for NSW v Perpetual Trustee Co* (1952) 85 CLR 237. For a discussion of the case law see Milte, K. & Webber, T. (1977), *Police in Australia: Development, Function and Procedures*, Butterworths, Sydney, chapter 11.

10 Police commissioners can and will order their offices to intervene or refrain from acting in order to maintain order. See *R v. Chief Constable of Devon and Cornwall, Ex parte Central Electricity Generating Board* [1982] Q.B. 458. In this case Lord Denning took the view that it was of the first importance that the police could decide on their own responsibility what action should be taken to preserve the peace.

Despite the apparent paradox the ideology of policing rests on the notion of independence. In this respect independence is designated from:

1. Executive direction
2. Statutory intervention
3. Direction of government, and
4. Interference with the independence of the individual constable.

However, like the generality (and ambiguity) surrounding the notion of original powers, the actuality of police independence requires questioning. This is confounded by the managerial and supervision necessities of a quasi-military authority structure. For instance, in some Australian jurisdictions police legislation requires senior police to be subject to the direction of the Commissioner of Police by the Minister.[11] Police commissioners have the power of superintendence over their staff, and that power obviously relies on traditional management principles within the structure of the disciplined service. Mr Justice Lusher[12] attempted to draw a distinction on the basis of independence between the functions of government in the administration of justice and law enforcement, and almost all other administrative functions. He viewed the former as only government by the law and not being governed through the powers of the executive. Why Lusher chose to make this distinction based on law enforcement is not clear, beyond the fact that he wished to defer a legal authority holding the police to be independent while at the same time recognising the essentially close relationship between the police and government at an administrative level.[13] In addition, this distinction seems to cut across traditional notions of ministerial responsibility. It might be explained to some extent by the notion of the separation of powers, however, the special status of the police within that separation doctrine does not seem clear. Neither does the place of the police within the executive/government state.

Lusher read down the statutory 'direction' provisions in police regulation legislation, in order to complement the ideology of independence. His position was that a constable when acting as a peace officer is not exercising delegated authority and the law of agency has no application. Yet how does this explain the master and servant relationship between the police officer, the commissioner and the state? In addition, in what way does this ideology accept the compliance of the police with the democratic authority of the state? If independent, how do the police stand obliged to the community? Does the doctrine of original powers arise from attempts at avoiding employer's liability rather than establishing levels of executive accountability? The case law seems to evidence the former.

If independence-based, policing ideology relies on broad but challenged notions of this central concept. It takes the form of an unsustainable immunity from executive control while accepting supervision by superior officers. It depends

---

11   For example, *Police Regulation Act* (NSW) 1899.
12   As a commissioner of inquiry into NSW Police Administration, Parliament of NSW, 29 April 1981.
13   For a discussion of this argument, see Hogg, R. & Hawker, B. (1983), 'The Politics of Police Independence', *Legal Services Bulletin*, vol. 8, pp. 160–5 & 221–3.

on artificial administrative distinctions such as efficiency and effectiveness versus law enforcement.

The political utility of issues of independence becomes apparent when the close relationship between the state and the police is exposed. The police are pre- • sented as having autonomous political power within their own organisation. Behind this façade of political independence exists a complex inter-relationship between government, the state, and the police. The tensions inherent in such an ideological and functional paradox are resolved through the exercise of police discretion (see chapter 6).

Why is the independence notion so attractive to police organisations and their officers? One might anticipate that ascription to independence leaves the individual police officer largely on his or her own when it comes to responsibility for the exercise of police powers, or as regards the master–servant relationship.[14] An answer is perhaps that the police see independence as a shield against accountability. Because independence is viewed as likely to obscure or avoid clear hierarchies of accountability individual police officers are led to believe that this is to their advantage. Unfortunately, any such confidence demonstrates a general misunderstanding about both the exercise of discretion and resultant accountability, in the context of a disciplined service. In practice, police officers are placed in an invidious position when it comes to internal, organisational responsibility, and the protections of vicarious liability. Unless paths of delegation are clear, or the powers which are exercised by individual police, are specific, it is all too easy for the state, the organisation of policing, and senior officers to pass responsibility down the line.

Secrecy and occupational solidarity, features of the disciplined service, also pressurise the position of the individual officer away from being able to claim the protection of a clear line of authority. An example of this and one which will be discussed later (see chapter 4) is the situation with the use of police informants. Any denial of operational or organisational imperatives that motivates or constrains the actual use of police discretion in favour of endorsing this notion of independence, further complicates the position of police officers. Questions then arise for whom do they exercise their discretion and from whom can they claim immunity? Immunity and independence are of little value to individual operatives if they remain at the level of ideology.

Therefore, by simply looking at the example of the ideology of independence we are on notice that police ideologies are complex, contradictory and very often ambiguous.[15] Obvious dichotomies open up between police ideology and operational practice. For instance, policing may operate in a variety of compulsory or discriminatory contexts quite contrary to the central ideologies of responsible and representative government. The vagaries and inconsistency of policing ideology

---

14   See *Griffiths v. Haines* [1983] ALJR 108.
15   For a discussion of this and related matters see Wright, A. (2002), *Policing: An Introduction to Concepts and Practice*, Willan, Devon, chapter 2.

are compounded by imprecise and sometimes compromised notions of justice which it is said to serve.

Ideological aims of policing

When looking at state-based police in particular their broad aims include:
- crime control
- the protection of citizens and their property
- the upholding of justice
- the denunciation of criminality, and
- the maintenance of order and democracy.

It is useful to distinguish these broad ideological aims from operational goals for policing. Operational goals are influenced by:
1. Community expectations
2. Individual and organisational police perceptions of their function
3. Characteristics of the community being policed
4. Internal bureaucratic constraints
5. Individual and collective interpretations of the law
6. Professional standards
7. Pressure from other agencies of justice in particular, and
8. Occupational solidarity.

At the operational level conflict between general aims and particular goals can be identified as between:
- law versus policing priorities (where the exercise of police power is either internally regulated or its boundaries of permission can sometimes represent deviation from legality)
- operational processes of policing and ideologies which govern other aspects of the criminal-justice system
- the significance of discretion for policing and the operation of individualised justice, and
- isolation from meaningful contact with policing clients and the aspiration of community policing.

Prevailing corporate ideologies in state-based policing

In Australia since the 1980s, the stated mission of most state-sponsored police services has been one of community-based policing.[16] This mission implicates the

---

16   See Wright (2002), chapter 6, particularly as it challenges symbolic representations of community policing by recognising community diversity and the police role within it.

community in crime prevention and locates the police and policing within a community context. It is intended to complement notions of 'the community' and its expectations for public safety and social order. The focus is on the professionalisation of police services for the community as clients.

In so saying, the values of policing remain largely individualised and profoundly selective. The core ideology (as represented in the oath of office taken by most police) talks about upholding the rule of law, protecting the rights and freedoms of the citizen and is directed towards 'client satisfaction and efficiency' in a particularist form. Clients are the law abiding, the 'silent majority', those who share the police notion of public order. They are not the young, the marginalised, the ethnically and racially diverse, or the 'troublemakers'.

Most police services designate leadership principles reflecting service and community accountability, but fail to detail the methods for its achievement, along with diversification of community consensus and confidence. Even where it has become more attractive in law-and-order politics to prefer force to service in describing the functions of state police, the direction of both is said to be legitimised by community concerns and their satisfaction.

While community policing aspirations have taken hold of policing management ideology, questions have been asked about the translation of these principles through the ranks, to individual operational police. In reality, many of these individuals suspect that their alienation from the community means community policing strategies may have limited relevance for the communities in which they are required to work.

What is community-based policing?

David Bailey defined community policing in function and output terms.[17] He emphasised:

- community-based crime prevention
- patrol deployment for non-emergency interaction with the public
- active solicitation of requests for service not involving criminal matters, and
- creation of mechanisms for grassroots feedback from the community.

Reflecting her interest in diverse communities, and perhaps aware of the dangers inherent for operational policing in the 'community' conceived as monolithic, monocultural and homogenous, Chan preferred a definition which highlighted the accountability of policing to its many communities.[18] Such accountability to *local communities* is supposed to exert influence upon occupational culture by provid-

---

17 Bayley, D. (1986), *Community Policing in Australia — An Appraisal: Working Paper Report Series*, Australian Centre for Police Research, Paynehan.
18 Chan (1997), pp. 58–61.

ing an 'alternative reference group away from the immediate work-group influ-ence of police peers'.[19]

Cunneen identified the concept of community as essential when coming to terms with 'community-based policing as an operational entity as well as an ideo-logical commitment'.[20] Recognising that some communities have a history of poor relations with the police will help to explain the less-than-uniform application and acceptance of community policing as a strategy. It also highlights the unreality of expecting the police and every community to be 'one'.

It is this sense of unreality which also explains the uneven translation of com-munity-based policing from a bureaucratic mission to an individual officer's ethic. Police on the beat are the first to realise whether they have a community into which they can become positively involved. They know that the community is a problematic, dynamic and diverse entity where respect is not constant and consen-sus is not to be assumed.

Community policing as a concept in policy statements and guidelines is diffi-cult to translate into practice. This makes it no less worthy of the endeavour. Indeed some of the reasons for its resistance are just the issues on which police and communities must reflect if aspirations for the community ownership and embed-edness of policing are to be realised in a society such as Australia where communi-ties are diverse and policing pervasive.

Conventional policing: Where does the community fit?

Returning to the notion of independence, conventional policing ideology cele-brates individual responsibility and discretion in contrast with the police as civil servants, officers in a disciplined service, and as community representatives. Real-istically this independence is qualified by the accepted obligations of police to their communities. Once these responsibilities are nominated and understood, the ques-tion remains, responsible to whom? Is it to the community, the government, the police organisation, or the culture of policing occupations? The answer to this question may lie in the location of police authority. If we accept that this authority, based as it is on the notion of original powers and delegation, now relies on com-munity consensus, then accountability to the community cannot be overlooked by the state police. It is crucial to the effective structuring of any community policing response.

---

19   Brogden, M. & Shearing, C. (1993), *Policing for a New South Africa*, Routledge, London, p 104.
20   Cunneen, C. (1991), 'Problems in the Implementation of Community Policing Strategies', in S. McKillop & J. Vernon, *The Police and the Community in the 1990s*, Australian Institute of Criminology, Canberra.

Independence and isolation: Where does policing fit?

The ideology of community stands apart from those notions of policing which advance individuality and independence. In saying this, however, the concept of community is itself problematic.[21] In respect of policing, what form does the community take? Whose community is it, and whose notion of community-based policing does it expect?

In Australia, the policy of multiculturalism works from the notion that communities are heterogeneous and have a right to be so. As regards policing in this context, the communities within which it operates have widely different expectations and a range of different views when it comes to the reception of police initiatives. Respect for police, community to community, as well as within Australian communities, varies. Also, the attitude of the police to different communities will be influenced by the predispositions of police to the cultures and contexts of these communities.[22]

The relationship between consensus, respect and police authority is, as I have mentioned previously, essential to an understanding of police power. In the context of community-based policing, consensus needs to be examined against the community in which particular policing activities occur. When thinking of consensus one needs to determine whether the community is a democratic concept, and whether the appearance of consensus (like the community liaison structures) actually rests on selective communications between community representatives and the police. In addition, are there mechanisms through which most of the community can be implicated in policing, and thereby real consensus in a common endeavour maintained?

For individual police operatives, and for policing management, the language of community has particular significance; however, this may not be a uniformly held view. It is not coincidental that when state-based police organisations moved to change their identity from force to service they highlighted their location in the community. However, as mentioned earlier in this chapter, the operational objectives of policing and the isolation of police within their communities further removes the police from a valued and effective community connection. The police community, which itself is largely homogeneous, seeks shared value structures for its comfort and connection with the community it polices. In many situations however, the respect and loyalty which police seek is absent among communities due to historical tensions between the police and certain ethnic or indigenous groups, and the manner in which policing fractures and continues to divide the community on the basis of gender, age, sexuality, race, and class.

---

21 For a discussion of the problematic symbol of community as it relates to criminal justice see Cohen, S. (1985), *Visions of Social Control*, Polity Press, Oxford, chapter 4.

22 For a discussion of police attitudes to ethnic variance in Australia see Collins (2000); Chan (1997).

Another problem when considering police isolation within their communities is confusion over the concept of the client/customer relationship. For state-based police it is problematic who are their customers, and how they relate to both specific and more general community interests.

Certain operational characteristics of policing may have the capacity to isolate further the police from community acceptance and recognition. Selective law enforcement, for example, is expected by the criminal-justice process and enabled through the discretionary character and operation of police power. Selective enforcement is a feature of the way in which police manage encounters with the public.[23] As such it may be essentially divisive.

The tendency for the police to be isolated from communities and important groups within communities creates a tension within community policing ideology. This tension is not addressed through the representation of the police as independent, and the community as morally or politically homogeneous. Multiculturalism is a challenge for policing rather than an impediment to the achievement of community policing.

Police in the community or the community monitoring the police?

Earlier we posed the question *whom do the police represent?* In the chapter which examines cop culture (chapter 8), it will become clearer that police organisational and operational imperatives tend to suggest synthesis with certain types of communities and certain expectations for policing. Notions such as the community are not synonymous with, nor are they necessarily represented by, the democratic state. The communities in which the police are comfortable are further limited, and the police cannot uniformly be one with the community, despite ideological pronouncements to the contrary.

Further, one needs to ask what is the community interest in policing? For some communities in Australia, such as those comprising Aboriginal people, or young ethnic males, the interest if any is in avoiding contact with the police or minimising the need for police encounters. A fundamental issue around which community policing tends to focus, in its more conventional form, is the maintenance of public order. Again, this is a situation where one needs to question whose order is being policed and what form it takes. Contests over public space have been at the heart of state-based policing since its earliest origins. In Australia this emphasis has continued and focussed recently on indigenous people and youth.[24]

---

23 See Travis, G. (1983), 'Police Discretions in Law Enforcement: A Study of Section 5 of the NSW Offences in Public Places Act 1979', in Findlay, Egger, & Sutton, chapter 14.

24 For the history of the struggle of police–Aboriginal relations and its location in public space see Cunneen, C. (2001) *Conflicts, Politics and Crime: Aboriginal Communities and the Police*, Allen & Unwin, Sydney.

The determination of public order has rested largely with the police and police discretion. The police on the other hand see themselves as acting on behalf of the common good in the maintenance of peace and good order for that community which largely endorses and respects the police, and is the constituency of the tabloid press and talk-back radio.

While there has been a recent recognition of community-based policing as an important ideology for the police, at the same time state policing agencies have developed their tactical response capacities recognising a more hard-edged approach to social control. These modes and mechanics of policing feature today in Australian urban communities where consent is in contest and community policing may have broken down.

Crime prevention as an important operational commitment for the police is sometimes seen as a link with communities and their implication in policing. Again, however, is it accurate to audit police as crime prevention and control agents through community victimisation surveys and the satisfaction they suggest?[25] The real test for community-based policing is to evaluate critically the relationship between the police and the *dispossessed within communities*. In this regard policing diverse communities itself has the potential to create division and be divisive when these communities contain the young, the under-employed and the different.[26] Recent trends towards the co-opting of communities or community representatives through endeavours such as Neighbourhood Watch are an attempt to do more than claim community support. Some might say that when the police choose to talk to the middle-class community representative they in fact deny the voice of the dispossessed. This may indicate why recently Neighbourhood Watch has been devalued both by police and the communities in which it operates.

Through an acceptance of community policing the state-based police have colonised community control initiatives. This has sometimes reduced the effectiveness of these initiatives and certainly tends to distance the community from its own responsibilities for control. As such this is a criticism of police management over family-group conferencing.[27]

In certain situations, however, policing by the community becomes the only alternative where the state withdraws its sponsored policing services or divests itself from policing concerns of the community. Further, where policing becomes something for purchase, the nature of policing and its quality will vary from community to community, based on socio-economic measures. In Australia already, in

25   See Hogg, R. et al. (1994), 'Counting Crime: Are Victim Surveys the Answer' (unpublished conference paper); Travis, G. et al. (1995), 'The International Crime Surveys: Some Methodological Concerns', *Current Issues in Criminal Justice*, vol. 6, no. 3, pp. 346–61.

26   Crowther, C. (2000), 'Thinking About the Underclass: Towards a Political Economy of Policing', *Theoretical Criminology*, vol. 4, no. 2, pp. 149–67.

27   See Blagg, H. (1977), 'A Just Measure of Shame: Aboriginal Youth Conferencing in Australia', *British Journal of Criminology*, vol. 37, no. 4, p. 481.

urban settings, wealthier suburbs are choosing to employ private sector policing facilities to protect suburban public disorder from private property.[28] It has been suggested that a consequence of this in other cultures has been the downgrading of state-based policing services for similar areas of need.[29] Our discussion of private policing later in the book (chapter 5), will explore more fully the selective provision of policing services based on differential community wealth. Suffice to say here that such a characteristic of policing obviously tends to challenge uniform expectations at the heart of community-based policing ideology.

Community policing is perhaps most under challenge in areas where state authority and presence is rejected.[30]

Conclusion

Community policing suggests that if the community is the client then the efficiency and effectiveness of police practice should be measured against the satisfaction of the community with its policing. However, accepting as we do the problematic nature of the relationship between the police and the community, is it realistic to measure the values of all aspects of policing against community satisfaction? And in any case with heterogeneous communities how is that satisfaction to be universalised?

Additional readings

For full reference details refer to the bibliography.

Hogg & Hawker (1983), 'The Politics of Police Independence', *Legal Services Bulletin*, vol. 8, pp. 160–5, pp. 221–3.

Mawby (2002), chapters 3 & 8.

Brown & Sutton (1997), 'Problem Oriented Policing and Organisational Form: Lessons from a Victorian experiment', *Current Issues in Criminal Justice*, vol. 9, no. 1, pp. 21–33.

Macintyre & Prenzler (1997), 'Officer Perspectives on Community Policing', *Current Issues in Criminal Justice*, vol. 9, no. 1, pp. 34–55.

James & Sutton (1998), 'Policing Drugs in the Third Millennium: The Dilemmas of Community Based Philosophies', *Current Issues in Criminal Justice*, vol. 9, no. 3, pp. 217–27.

---

28   See Martin, C. (2000), 'Crime and Control in Australian Urban Space', *Current Issues in Criminal Justice*, vol. 12, no. 1, pp. 79–92.

29   See 'The Problem with Policing: Black Settlements in South Africa' in Brogden, M. & Shearing, C. (1993) (fully referenced in n. 18 p. 35).

30   See Findlay & Zvekic (1993), Part 2, chapters 5, 6, 7, 8 & 9.

de Lint (2000), 'Autonomy, Regulation and the Police Beat', *Social and Legal Studies*, vol. 9, no. 1, pp. 55–84.

Jesilow & Parsons (2000), 'Community Policing as Peacemaking', *Policing & Society*, vol. 10, no. 2, pp. 163–82.

Skogan & Harnett (1997).

Freckleton & Selby (1988), chapter 4.

Griffiths v. Haines [1983] ALJR 108.

Marshall (1965), chapters 1,2 & 3.

Baldwin & Kinsey (1982), chapter 1.

White (1994), 'Street Life, Police Practises and Youth Behaviour', in White & Alder, chapter 5.

Cunneen (1991), 'Problems in the Implementation of Community Policing Strategies', in McKillop & Vernon.

Silverman (1995), 'Community Policing: The Implementation Gap', in Kratcoski et al., chapter 3.

Brogden (1988), chapter 8.

Bayley (1989), 'Community Policing in Australia: An Appraisal', in Chappell & Wilson, chapter 4.

Bayley (1988), 'Community Policing: A Report from the Devil's Advocate', in Greene & Mastrofski.

4

Police Function: Criminal Investigation and Specialisation

Introduction

This chapter will examine broad foundations for policing function and locate these within the context of particular expectations for policing practice. Those who work within policing, who represent what policing is in society, and the community that receives police services, share expectations. Essentially these relate to criminal investigation, and portray policing as a process of conventional detective work. In reality when focussing on what policing agencies do, the criminal investigation component is not the most significant area of function whatever the form of policing. This would suggest that the professional and public appreciation of policing function may have little to do with actual practice. The symbolic significance of criminal investigation, therefore, and the justification it provides for specialised policing practices and technologies is important when evaluating policing function where image contests with reality for the creation of representations and expectations. What follows is an endeavour to relate the scope of police function to the particular imperatives of criminal investigation and the specialisation that functional priority promotes. The investigation and specialisation focus accords with popular representations of policing rather than the more routine and mundane actuality of police function. The critical examination of representations will call up consideration of more regular police functions. This is to understand what police do as against what they and we expect them to do.

Factors influencing police function

It would be incorrect to assume that policing function is determined from a single source. State interests, community expectation, and organisational and individual policing priorities will directly influence the creation and prioritising of particular policing functions. In detail these influences include:

1. **Traditions and conventions of policing.** As mentioned previously (chapter 2), state-based policing grew out of a concern for public-order maintenance. Private-sector policing has always had an interest in the securing of capital and the regulation of labour. Community-centred policing initiatives develop to reflect those functions that are not covered effectively either by state-based police or private police services.

2. **Political expedience.** With state-based police in particular, governments have become more reliant on their role as a general public service. In fact the police are one of the few remaining twenty-four-hour services throughout Australia. The police have become incorporated in a range of welfare, licensing, information, and security service deliveries which previously may have been the responsibility of other sectors of government, or of community agencies. It is a feature of most legislation in Australia nowadays that obligations created by statute will require policy enforcement. Further, in a variety of different public and private enterprises, private and state police are now more regularly integrated in the provision of policing services.[1]

3. **Police perception.** The police as an organisation and as individuals are as likely to be influenced by perceptions about policing as the rest of the community. Popular representations of policing, therefore, will have an important impact on the way in which police view themselves and translate this into the performance of function. The impact that police have on the operation of their function is particularly significant bearing in mind the scope and degree of police discretion.

4. **Community expectations.** As is the case with the police, communities' expectations of police function may be moulded by popular culture in addition to the changing concerns within communities regarding safety, security, and service delivery. Communities across Australia are not homogeneous and therefore expectations for police function within communities will vary and take particular forms. Sometimes these may in fact compete with one another and challenge the performance of police function.

5. **Media representation.** Popular wisdom about policing is in part created as a consequence of media reporting, and the manner in which policing is seen as entertainment within various media forms. The relationship between the media and the police (see chapter 12) is symbiotic and in certain situations uncritical. For instance, much of the reporting of crime and social order in the tabloid press throughout Australia takes the form of reproducing police accounts. These official accounts will endorse particular functions and heighten expectations for their delivery.

6. **The nature of the community being policed.** Australian policing services are delivered to a wide variety of communities and differentially to various components within those communities. In fact, in certain situations policing services may be

---

1   For example, reflect on the policing of the Sydney Olympics.

withdrawn or excluded from those elements within communities that do not provide the police with respect or consensus in the operation of their function. In large
Australian urban settings notions like 'the community' and 'consensus' may not be
readily identifiable and therefore the police may find the appropriate delivery of
their functions difficult and ambiguous in a community policing context.

7. **Internal bureaucratic constraints.** Police function is, for the state-based
police, the product of management priorities. Police executives are sensitive to
political discourse on crime control and often try to model their functional direction to reflect that discourse. As a public service organisation, state policing
requires government resourcing and in that respect is sensitive to government policy. Private-sector police have a clearer commercial connection to the requirements of their clients when it comes to function.

8. **Organisational policy.** Particularly in a disciplined service function, individual
police officers will depend on rank, experience, and specialist designation. The traditional division between plain clothes and uniform police is a symbolic reflection
of the different functions performed by these operatives.

9. **Discretion and structures of responsibility.** The exercise of police function
is discretionary in so far as the powers which enable various functions arise from
discretionary authority. Structures of responsibility are the consequence of wide
police discretion and more recently in Australia have predetermined the way in
which certain police functions are performed.

10. **Individual and collective determinations of the law**. As law enforcement
agents the police are charged with transferring legal regulations into street practice. Again, discretion plays an important part here. Selective law enforcement is a
feature of police function and it could be argued is an essential process in the maintenance of limited criminal-justice resources.[2]

11. **Professional standards and job satisfaction.** In later chapters we will discuss contemporary claims by police for professional status (chapters 10 & 13).
Along with professionalism comes some independent control over the formulation
and exercise of function. In addition, 'best practice' policing has important ramifications for the manner in which police functions are performed.

12. **Pressures from other agencies.** Police have been identified as 'gate keepers'
of the criminal-justice process.[3] The functional priorities of the police may either
complement or run contrary to those of other agencies within the criminal-justice
process. While criminal justice is the product of a variety of different operations,
institutions and functions, the police perform the initial important role in designating the form that justice will take through the process.

13. **Occupational solidarity.** Our later discussion of policing culture (chapter 12)
will identify the significance of occupational solidarity when it comes to the actual

2   For a wider discussion of this see Findlay, Odgers & Yeo (1999), chapter 3.
3   For a discussion of the manner in which the police fuel the criminal justice process see Ashworth, A.
    (1998), *The Criminal Process: An Evaluative Study*, Oxford University Press, Oxford.

performance of police function. There are occasions where the performance of police function will be deviant or may miscarry rather than ensure a justice outcome. Occupational solidarity is often essential to corrupt or deviant policing functions and the barriers which are presented to accountability.

Individual and organisational functions

There is a dichotomy between what police organisations represent as their important functions and what individual police will prioritise or prefer for police work. The differences which exist between individual and institutional functions become most apparent at street level when organisational functions are translated into practice. The nature and scope of police discretion facilitates this translation and allows for differences.

It is important to remember that a distinction can also be drawn between those functions having a symbolic significance and those which are considered relevant in the context of actual policing work. For example, state police have recently argued for the significance of having a tactical-response function against terrorist activities and serious incidents of public disorder.[4] In fact, in Australia such situations are rare and the tactical-response police units retain largely symbolic purpose. At a functional level these units have been used more and more for general policing duties and this has tended to cause some confusion among police and negative outcomes in relation to public safety.[5]

The distinction between police force and service has brought about a shift in the emphasis on police function. While coercive force and its manifestations in policing remain essential to the job, in its wider public manifestations the police choose to identify service as their main concern. In this respect they talk of the community as their client and endeavour to emphasise those functions with a service dimension. Individual police themselves, however, are less comfortable with this type of service and prefer to rely on the underpinning of force when it comes to their own interpretation of their work.

Recent emphasis in crime control on prevention has had a demonstrable impact on the priorities in police functions. Both state-based and private sector policing are engaged in preventive strategies many of which involve community endorsement or input. It is not necessarily the case that these preventive functions should challenge the more traditional reactive policing functions such as criminal investigations. Nor

---

4   This produced a significant investment in this capacity, along with an expansion of intelligence-gathering and sophisticated surveillance capacities in anticipation of Olympic security threats in Sydney during 2000.

5   Cunneen, C. (1990), 'Aboriginal-Police Relations in Redfern: With Special Reference to the "Police Raid" of 8 February 1990', *Report Commissioned by the National Inquiry into Racist Violence*, Human Rights and Equal Opportunities Commission, Sydney.

should recent attempts at proactive policing beyond the realm of crime prevention be viewed necessarily as in contest with preventive functions. In a climate of limited resourcing, however, proactive or reactive policing will draw some emphasis away from crime prevention as an essential motivator of policing function.

There is little doubt that police functions are essentially implemented and maintained as a factor of the territory or domain in which policing activity is carried out. For instance, crime prevention for policing is a community-based initiative. Proactive and reactive policing may have more particular and specific directions and be used against challenges to police claims over territory such as public space.

Further, territory or domain for policing determines and delimits the persons who will become the subjects of police attention. On a one-to-one basis the exercise of police discretion in the performance of any particular function is heavily dependent on the circumstances in which the police encounter particular individuals and the manner in which they may stereotype these encounters. [6] In endeavouring to understand the way in which police functions will appear as part of police work, it is important to recall the relationship between the aims for policing, their historical origins, and function, which is determined by bureaucratic structure, political expectations and constraints.

In so doing, one must not minimise the significance of discretion over the formulation of functional imperatives, the exercise of police function, and the structures governing that exercise.

Another clue to any apparent dilemma between individual and organisational functions is to appreciate the relationship between the structure of different forms of policing and their function. For instance, the New Police in metropolitan London, as created by Sir Robert Peel, were originally uniformed and unarmed, relying heavily on the development of citizen respect for their authority which in turn would make it possible for them to do their work.[7] The structure of this early police force determined the manner in which they would perform their functions as *moral missionaries* among the *dangerous classes*. The maintenance of respect was essential to this structure and function of policing.

Respect and its maintenance, along with the generation of community consent, is an essential feature of most policing structures. The maintenance of respect becomes a primary function for policing in this context.[8] Its operational importance is transferred through consensus-based policing and its political significance is demonstrated by the acceptance of community-based policing as the principal policing style.

6   See Travis (1983).
7   For an examination of this see Reiner, R. (2000), chapters 1 & 2.
8   Findlay, M. (1992), 'Police Authority, Respect and Shaming', *Current Issues in Criminal Justice*, vol. 5, no. 1, pp. 29–41.

The importance of 'threat' in determining police functions

Silver foreshadowed in his examination of the relationship between early policing and class disorder,[9] the connection between urbanisation, crime control and collective resistance. In doing this he identified the development of policing functions. Silver saw the intervention of police in the contest for public order as a dynamic process where the mechanisms of crime control, such as policing, played a key role in formulating the nature of resistance. He went on to suggest the creation of police forces was dependent on the ideological representation of 'threat'. This threat is both to the police as individuals and organisations, as well as to the notion of state order they are charged to protect. Along with this is the tendency of policing discourse and operational priorities to imbue community conceptions of fear about crime with compatible perceptions of threat[10].

For Silver, the historical function of police in response to threat takes its form because of:

- inadequate government controls
- poor avocational policing
- ambiguous and low-level public morality
- mixing of racial groups
- public disorder
- idleness of the unemployed
- plurality in the classes being policed
- a self-indulgent and socially contingent wealthy class, and
- the growth of cities without social roots.

A function of the police in this context was to identify those against whom they directed their functions as *dangerous*. The stereotyping of the 'dangerous classes' was an early policing technique in the struggle for public order.[11] In so doing the police were able to focus the 'crime' threat in society on certain class behaviours and class origins. These behaviours and origins were seen by the police as inextricably connected with challenges to public order which the police function was designed to meet. Disorder was seen as generated by:

- socio-economic inequality
- a close association in a physical sense between the rich and the poor
- traditions of collective violence as a legitimate expression of dissent

---

9 Silver, A. (1967), 'The Demands of Order in a Civil Society: A Review of Some Themes in the History of Urban Crime, Police and Riot in Britain' in D. Bordua (ed.), *The Police: Six Sociological Essays*, New York. Wiley & Sons, pp. 1–24.

10 Recently, the significance of perceptions about crime and justice and the place of fear within both, has been recognised as a crucial formulator of law-and-order politics. See Hogg & Brown (1998).

11 The commitment to stereotyping in the pursuit of social threat of the disorderly has prevailed as an essential feature of policing.

- an absence of strong social buffers to cordon off dissent
- a language of confrontation developing between the socially marginalised and the police (as well as the interests they protected)
- a clear distinction in terms of class and race in communities
- an anticipation and publication of the threat these factors posed to the police
- urban environments under strain
- the criminalisation of urban classes as a consequence of socio-economic development, and
- class alienation.

Alternatively, however, disorder was identified as resistance to the police determination of good order.

Socio-political foundations of the police function

Klockars has identified that no police system or process can be understood apart from the social and political system within which it works.[12] In this respect the threats posed to police that require functional responses emerge from wider social and political contexts. It was this perception of a more diversified and widespread threat throughout society that led the police away from the avocational forms and into vocational, state-sponsored civil police forces. Whether these changes were function driven, or were as a consequence of the needs of the developing state, is difficult to determine. However, the structures of policing, particularly in their militaristic and uniformed appearance where the use of force is an underlying option, could be seen as determined by the conceptualisation of any threat through opposition, and any competing representations of social order. For example, police patrols in public spaces have taken on the appearance of colonisation, and a formalistic endeavour to secure or regain police territory. The police (with a quick response force to public disorder) designate their interests in controlling both time and space, when pitched against collective and community threat (disorder). In this respect the functions of policing have developed as a consequence of contests over territories as well as recreation. These contests delimit and determine the people who will become the focus of police attention and on which a pyramid structure of police responsibility is constructed.

The development and marketing of police functions

As we have already mentioned, the shift away from avocational policing has created a whole new public-service and private-sector policing design for and on

---

12   Klockars, C. *et al* (1991), *Thinking About Police: Contemporary Readings*, New York, McGraw Hill.

behalf of the state and commercial interests. Through a concentration on control and prevention of crime in public space the early vocational police forces identified the determination and maintenance of public order as a primary function. Essential to this was the need to mark out and protect territories within which legitimate policing could predominate and in which the police could confront and control those whom they deemed as threats to such claims. Once police accepted their role as one of order maintenance it was a reluctant graduation from policing public to private domains such as domestic violence.[13] A good example of this is the police responsibility for licensing a whole range of commercial activities and relationships. In their earliest forms these functions were directed towards industrial safety and the effective and efficient operation of employer–employee relationships. The police function in licensing was one which determined the nature of relationships and identified situations in which the police might intervene in order to sustain the conditions over these relationships. Again, the licensing function was an essential implementation of police concerns for territory.[14]

The activation of police functions is effected by what is known as the police *working personality*. This personality accepts a particular social balance as being crucial to the performance of police functions within a very particular world view. Therefore, policing becomes a set of specific functions that work within and maintain that social balance and world view commensurate as it is with the police working personality as any other legitimate influence. Such a balance requires an appreciation by the police of appropriate social distance from challenges to their independence or compromises to their discretion. However, this social distance is selectively applied within the considerations of their working personality.[15]

The actual exercise of police functions is as much influenced by *control waves* as by *crime waves*. Recently throughout Australian jurisdictions, law-and-order politics has taken control over the development of police functions.[16] Bearing in mind their essential role in determining measures of crime within the community, and as a consequence generating fear of crime and its consequences throughout the community, the police are far from impotent in the orchestration of control waves, which in turn may influence the development of policing functions.

To some extent the role of the police is now community dependent. This means that beyond the political rhetoric for police preference, community expectation and the media's representation of it, community policing has an important and formative

---

13 In certain contexts in contemporary Australian society this shift has not been comfortable for police. With their involvement in domestic violence, for instance, the police have been forced to rethink their attitudes to private relationships, and the 'real' functions of policing in the maintenance of domestic order and safety. See School of Social Science and Policy (1997), *Report on Police Attitudes to Domestic Violence*, University of NSW, Sydney.

14 Carson, W. (1970), 'White Collar Crime and the Enforcement of Factory Legislation', *British Journal of Criminology*, vol. 10, no. 4, pp. 383–98.

15 Such considerations develop into and arise out of what is known as 'cop culture'. See chapter 8.

16 See Hogg & Brown (1988).

influence over the development of policing functions. This is well illustrated in the tensions which have recently emerged when several Australian police bureaucracies advocated more centralist and specialist organisation and allocation of resources. The public has questioned such developments against the understandings of community policing as fundamental for the delivery of police services in Australia. The community has become the benchmark for change.

The nature of police function

Policing may be divided very generally into repressive, preventive, political, service, conflict resolution, and punishment priorities. Within these broad headings a variety of different activities may appear to overlap. This is an obvious consequence of the complexity of policing functions.

The classical repressive functions of policing include:

- patrol
- the protection of private property
- public order maintenance
- criminal investigation, and
- reporting and information-gathering.

The last of these, police information functions, have expanded enormously in recent years. The state police, in particular, provide a repository of information for activities which range from particular criminal investigation requirements through licensing and accreditation and across many different sources of public-sector intelligence. If one were to spend a short time observing the operation of any average police station or policing environment in Australia, the importance of the information-gathering, collection, retention and dissemination function would be apparent.

Crime-prevention functions also focus on patrol because of the need to locate the police visibly within as many community contexts as possible. General deterrence, said to flow from this visibility, has important preventive functions claimed for it. The police adopt educative and developmental roles in their attempt to prevent specific forms of criminal behaviour among particular classes in the community (e.g. traffic offences and improved driving courses). In addition, the crime-prevention functions of policing are where there is greatest interaction between the police and community groups.[17]

As representatives of the state and protectors of its institutions, the state police provide an inherently political function. In addition, it might be argued that by the particular notions of public order the police maintain, the exercise of their discretion in the performance of their functions is political, both in a selective and

---

17   For a wider discussion of this within specific political contexts see Hogg, R. & Brown, D. (1990), 'Criminal Justice Policy in Australia', in I. Taylor (ed.), *The Social Effects of Free Market Policies*, Harvester, London.

a broad sense. In the effecting of government crime control policy, police selectively promote some dominant political ideologies while resisting others they do not see as complementing their concept of social order. Through their support of the conservative state, the police legitimise its monopoly over crime control and accept from the state legitimacy in their authority.

Since the transition from force to service, most state policing agencies throughout Australia have recognised the significance of their welfare and protective intervention functions. For example, with respect to domestic violence, police now both individually and organisationally understand the necessity to intervene in private domestic domains whereas in the past they were reluctant to do so.[18] This has not simply come as a consequence of accepting political realities or the pressure of interest groups in the community, but rather from the realisation by police that domestic violence contains elements of what they consider to be 'real policing'.[19]

On the notion of real policing, in order that the police as individuals will accept a particular function as reflecting their expectations for their work, a close connection with crime and crime prevention seems to be essential. Police as a state agency have always maintained some functions which have punishment as their consequence. The exercise of limited corporal punishment by the police, both legitimate and otherwise, has until recently been an accepted element of the police occupational personality.

To replace some of the more apparent punishment functions in policing, police agencies have developed an interest in conflict resolution. The expansion of juvenile cautioning by police is a good example of this trend. Juvenile and family group conferencing is another area in which the police in Australia have taken pivotal roles.[20]

In respect of their adjudication functions, the police provide many instances where they make determinations on custody, bail, detention, arrest, charge and prosecution. Each of these decisions will have a vital impact on the further processes of criminal justice at later stages.

Criminal investigation: The archetypal function[21]

Both in terms of the impression police have of themselves, and of the expectations from the wider community, criminal investigation and a crime-control focus for policing is naturally recognised as a primary function. Seemingly irrelevant to this

---

18   For instance see NSW Police Service (2000) *Domestic Violence Policy and Standing Operating Procedures* Sydney; NSW Ombudsman (1999) *Policing Domestic Violence in NSW*, Office of the Ombudsman, Sydney; Stanko, E. (1985), *Intimate Intrusions: Women's Experience of Male Violence*, Routledge & Kegan Paul, London.

19   Stanko (1985).

20   For a discussion of this see Strang, H. & Braithwaite, J. (2000) (eds), *Restorative Justice: Philosophy to Practice*, Ashgate, London.

21   For a useful critical examination of the crime-investigation function, the origins of the investigative culture, investigation as gatekeeping, and 'the myth of crime fighting' see Wright (2002), chapter 4.

is the reality that the majority of policing operatives and perhaps the greater proportion of policing time and energies are not directed towards criminal investigation in any essential form. This takes us then to consider the symbolic significance of criminal investigation as a policing function.

Part of the reason for the importance of criminal investigation in the police perception of their own function is the way in which they have utilised the success of investigations as a measure of their performance. Detection rates, clear-up rates, successful prosecutions, and conviction rates are all employed by police management and individual police themselves to determine if further policing functions are worthwhile. This is endorsed by popular culture expectations of what the police should be doing.

Often criticism is raised of police (in contexts where their functions may be considered misdirected) that they should be out there catching criminals and cleaning up crime rather than performing a more common but less exotic function such as traffic control. Police commissioners have often said that the bureaucracy of accountability holds them back from their primary function of detecting crime and bringing criminals to justice. The symbolic impact of this rhetoric is difficult to challenge. It then all comes back to the reinforcement of misconceived perceptions about police function or its apparent disproportion.

Methods of investigation are also the subject of divergence between expectation and reality. For instance, the standard way in which a homicide is cleared up by the police comes as a consequence of the offender confessing very soon after the homicide has been committed. Popular culture representations of policing homicide would have the police involved in extensive and sophisticated searches for, and analysis of, material evidence in an attempt to piece together scenarios which led sometimes tortuously to a class of suspects and then to the right offender. Yet in practice a more regular and important technique for modern police investigation of crimes is a reliance on the admissions and confessions of the accused.[22] Once these have been obtained the police are sometimes reluctant to proceed to any corroborative analysis of material evidence. This has resulted in a range of criticisms of policing practice when it comes to the obtaining of admissions and confessions.

More recently the police have come to relay on a variety of sophisticated information technologies in an attempt to investigate modern crime such as fraud and corruption. DNA testing is now championed by the police, in part as evidence of the scientific forensic basis for their investigation techniques. Even so, while modern technologies are available to the police and they are investing in these, old-style techniques still play an important role in the production of police evidence. For instance, the use of criminal informers (prison informants in particular) has generated interesting debates in Australian jurisdictions about the appropriateness or otherwise of police investigations.[23]

---

22   For a discussion of DNA testing throughout Australia see Institute of Criminology (2001), *Use of DNA in the Criminal Justice System*, Institute of Criminology, Sydney.

23   See Brown, D. (1993), 'Notes on the Culture of Prison Informing', *Current Issues in Criminal Justice*, vol. 5, no. 1, pp. 54–71.

With what has come to be known as victimless crimes (such as drug abuse and many crimes involving morality) new surveillance, intelligence-gathering, and information access techniques, are being used by police. In particular, modern communication technologies have provided the opportunity for police to intercept communications which were not available to them in times gone by. This has also necessitated the development of new legislation constructing police powers. An example of this is with the regulation of forensic procedures. Initially, at a federal level, the Model Criminal Code Officers' Committee recommended uniform legislation covering forensic procedures. The Model Bill was largely translated into the Commonwealth legislation but in its *Crimes (Forensic Procedures) Act* the New South Wales government broadened the thresholds for testing and recognised more liberally the exercise of police discretion in determining when and whether to require forensic samples.[24]

The generation and expansion of new investigation bodies has had its impact on conventional police-investigation practice. Whether the more conventional state-sponsored police have been incorporated into the activities of these new investigation bodies or whether they have simply adopted their techniques and claims for power, what has been produced is a sophistication of investigation practice in modern policing.[25]

In Australian jurisdictions there is an increasingly clear influence of law and legal regulation over police work. For example, legislation governing appropriate procedures for the detention, questioning, and obtaining evidence from suspects has produced various adaptations in an investigation practice[26]. In addition, both legislative and administrative guidelines have reformulated investigation practice. For instance, the audio and sometimes visual recording by police of a suspect's record of interview is now a matter of widespread common practice. It is interesting that in many states in Australia the principal source of guidelines for investigation techniques emerges from the police themselves (in the form of commissioner's instructions). In some states such as Queensland[27] these investigation requirements have been codified and stipulated in detail in legislation. However, this source of regulation is not the rule.

Much of the police criminal-investigation practice rests still on the exercise of police discretion, and the demarcations existing in police working personalities. For example, it has not been until recently that the police have conceded to the uniformed divisions of their services clear responsibilities for criminal investigation. This was once only the domain of detectives and those who gained specialist experience in criminal investigation.

---

24 In 2002–3 the author was the principal investigator in a review of the *Crimes (Forensic Procedures) Act* for the NSW Attorney General. For a discussion of the review see Findlay, M. & Grix, J. (2003), 'Challenging DNA in Court', *Current Issues in Criminal Justice*, vol. 14, no. 3, pp. 269–82.
25 For a wider discussion of these agencies, see Findlay et al. (1999), chapter 3.
26 See Findlay et al. (1999), chapter 3.
27 See *Police Powers and Responsibilities Act* (Qld).

For the private sector, again the popular representation of policing is the detective or the specialist investigator working for clients to supplement state police investigation and detection practices (or deficiencies). Consistent with state police and the observations made so far this is really only a minor part of what private-sector police do when compared with their responsibilities in security maintenance and the preservation of private property.

Criminal investigation and specialisation

In the popular representations of policing there has always been a specialist overtone to the delivery of criminal investigation. The symbol of the detective responsible for the exercise of investigation functions is essential to this notion.

Another feature of the relationship between policing and specialisation has been the generation of opportunities it has created for corruption and malpractice. Recent royal commissions and commissions of inquiry in Australia have clearly identified the potential of specialist squads within public-sector policing to generate cultures of their own around which malpractice is a feature. Also, within these specialist cultures, the prosecution and conviction outcomes of investigations become so significant and so pressing that police practice is adapted (sometimes *extra legally*) to assist and ensure these outcomes.

Some areas of police specialisation, drug-law enforcement in particular, represent environments of opportunity where specialists face considerable temptation to indulge in illegal practice. In certain situations, suspect or compromising investigation techniques, at least implicitly condoned by police managers, place added strain on street police particularly in their association with offenders. For instance, undercover policing in drug-law enforcement where police operatives are required to embrace the drug culture and sometimes to foster drug transactions in order to lead to *control outcomes* are particularly problematic.[28]

In an attempt to address the association between specialisation and malpractice, many police services throughout Australia have shifted their organisational emphasis away from specialisation. For example, in New South Wales following the commissionership of John Avery, policing was regionalised and the specialist squads (largely contained in the Central Investigation Bureau) were disbanded because they had fostered factionalism and corruption. Where specialisation was necessary it was positioned out in the regions within a taskforce model. However, the reality of criminal investigation is that certain specialist knowledge and experience will facilitate better investigation practice. Therefore, it has not taken long in New South Wales for a return to specialisation in the name of criminal investigation. Now in this state, a central management agency for specialist investigation

---

28   See Manning, P. & Redlinger, L. (1977), 'Invitational Edges of Corruption: Some Consequences of Narcotics Law Enforcement', in P. Rock (ed.), *Drugs and Politics*, Transaction Books, London.

skills and personnel is thriving. At the same time, to appease the preferences of politicians who use the special squads as a model for targeted and elite policing, units like the armed hold-up squad are reborn.

Specialisation in modern policing is not limited to the more sophisticated levels of criminal investigation. Since the popular acceptance of *zero tolerance* policing in the US and now in some Australian jurisdictions,[29] street police and uniformed police officers are required to employ criminal investigation skills such as *stereotyping*, profiling, crime mapping, and the generation of police intelligence. In fact, the main source of police intelligence around which many major criminal investigations revolve is the information obtained from low-level plain-clothes police officers on the street.

Contemporary specialisation: A challenge to regulation

There is no doubt that specialisation within policing generates different and more close-knit police cultures. These subcultures within the broader policing culture are likely to be resistant to reform and difficult to make accountable.[30] In order to overcome this dilemma, a range of issues needs to be recognised in reforming police organisational strategies when specialisation is involved:

- The need for efficient policing in controlling crime and the associated need to generate measures of efficiencies, which are not realistically connected to the outcomes of criminal investigations, such as successful prosecutions
- The creation of new measures of efficiency which are unconnected with policing organisational outcomes and more directly associated with best-practice policing
- The recognition that the major sources of detection information about crime are victims, witnesses or the perpetrator. In this respect there needs to be a redirection of understanding about police intelligence and the dissemination of policing information. Further, the more efficient flow of information, from the public to the police, needs to be broadcast as a crucial consequence of a vibrant and inclusive community policing strategy.[31]
- A determination of specialist functions relative to particular aims for policing. The functions of policing are largely determined by organisational structures, modes of deployment, forms of supervision, internal rules and instructions, training, customary practices, etc. In this respect the diversity of policing and police function needs to be appreciated.

---

29   Darcy, D. (1999), 'Zero Tolerance—Not Quite the Influence on NSW Policing Some Would Have You Believe', *Current Issues in Criminal Justice*, vol. 10, no. 3, pp. 290–8.

30   Brown, D. (1998), 'The Royal Commission into the NSW Police Service: Process Corruption and the Limits of Judicial Reflexivity', *Current Issues in Criminal Justice*, vol. 9, no. 3, pp. 228–40.

31   See Wright (2002), chapter 6 for a discussion of policing community justice.

- Recognition that the functions of policing are heterogeneous and highly differentiated, including the investigation of crime and the information management on which it essentially relies.
- Understanding the use of the criminal law and procedure by police during investigation as governing the normative conditions under which they are exercising their powers. This is more so in the contemporary era of codification.
- An appreciation of the problem in seeing crime as an undifferentiated entity opposed to the state and to police. There needs to be a reinterpretation of crime to reflect upon the relationship between police, the community and their information sources when it comes to investigation and detection practices. To facilitate this, crime should be understood as relationships and all that entails, rather than in focusing on personalities, behaviours and situations.
- A recognition of the difficulty within policing when attempting to control police through centralised mechanisms of management. The idea of police being accountable to the democratic state is undermined by clandestine police relationships and cultures at the heart of police specialisation.
- Specialisation needs to coexist with the most general commitment throughout police practice to a problem-oriented approach. This will require organisational change not only a reordering of policing priorities towards specialist units and services. As Brown and Sutton observed of the Victoria Police[32]:

> ...Australian conceptions of the problem-oriented model are that it is a technology of policing that can be added to police organisations as they pursue the continuing goal of modernisation...isolating one section of a large organisation (such as the police) is a strategy with a high likelihood of failure...it is not till such a section is challenged to step outside the bounds of conventional thinking and practice that the very real limitations within which it works will be revealed.[33]

Conclusion

The function of policing is neither singular nor necessarily inherent within any particular policing style. Traditionally police have adopted broad crime-control and order-maintenance functions. But associated with these are a wide range of information maintenance, welfare service and security obligations to various sectors of the community. An emphasis on any particular function will obviously be somewhat dependent upon political and community priorities at the time, as well as the 'best practice' preferences of the policing organisation.

32 Brown, M. & Sutton, A. (1997), 'Problem Oriented Policing and Organisational Form: Lessons from a Victorian Experiment', *Current Issues in Criminal Justice*, vol. 9, no.1, pp. 21–31.
33 Brown & Sutton (1997), pp.30 & 31.

Additional readings

For full reference details refer to the bibliography.

Findlay & Zvekic (1993), chapter 3.

Brodeur (1983), 'High Policing and Low Policing: Remarks about Policing of Political Activities', *Social Problems*, vol. 30, no. 5, pp. 507–20.

Silver (1967), 'The Demand for Order in a Civil Society', in Bordua, pp. 1–24.

Hogg (1987), 'The Politics of Criminal Investigation', in Wickham, pp. 120–40.

Briody (2002), 'The Effects of DNA Evidence on Sexual Assault Cases in Court', *Current Issues in Criminal Justice*, vol. 14, no. 2, pp. 159–81.

Innes (2002), 'The Process Structures of Police Homicide Investigations', *British Journal of Criminology*, vol. 42, no. 4, pp. 668–88.

Dixon & Maher (2001), 'The Cost of Crackdowns: Policing Cabramatta's Heroin Market', *Current Issues in Criminal Justice*, vol. 13, no. 1, pp. 5–22.

Ericson (1981)

Waddington (1999), 'Swatting Police Paramilitarisation', *Policing and Society*, vol. 9, no. 2, pp. 125–40.

Leaver (1997), chapters 2–6.

McConville (1991), chapters 2, 3, 4, 5, & 6.

Baldwin & Kinsey (1982), chapters 2, 3 & 5.

Brogden (1988), chapter 3.

Wood (1997), chapter 7.

Klockars (1985), chapters 2, 3, & 4.

Grabosky (1989), 'Efficiency and Effectiveness in Australian Policing: A Citizens Guide to Police Services' in Chappell & Wilson, chapter 10.

Kelling & Coles (1996).

5

Alternative Policing

Introduction: What is alternative?

In considering alternative policing styles it is not sufficient to present simple dichotomies such as:

1. Public/private police
2. Formal/informal police, and
3. Community/professional policing.

As with policing in general, alternative policing styles arise out of the series of choices regarding how to police particular problems. These choices are influenced by, and will influence the goals, structures and practices of, the policing style selected. The need to choose a particular policing style will be met within complex forms, functions and influences of social control in general. [1]

In its broader form policing may be viewed as particular interactions of interests, power and authority which distinguish the structures and functions of a particular policing style. Forms of policing are constructed around the expectations for their function. Within a given cultural, political and situational context, styles of policing will emerge and operate specifically to address the demands of these contexts. These styles in many respects are structural adaptations of already existing power relationships within society.

Analysing styles of policing

Styles of policing are best conceived as different ways of doing police work. They are not simply the manifestations of form, function or expectation, but incorporate

---

1 Findlay, M. & Zvekic, U. (1988), *Informal Mechanisms of Crime Control*, UNISDRI, Rome.

all of these. In the creation of a style of policing there is a negotiation of under-standings about police work, and aspirations for its impact on society. A style of policing is deemed so by whatever source of interest recognises its place and prac-tices within a community. In this respect policing styles are usually culturally spe-cific and often dynamic in their development.

In order to analyse the differences between policing styles, it is useful to enquire into their responses to particular social interests. Structural variables style-to-style are apparent and essential in any comparison of policing, in particular con-texts. Revealing differences between policing styles will rely on recognising the dif-ferences in the context within which they operate.

A style of policing may be described in terms of its sources of authority, its reg-ulatory frameworks, and its decision-making processes which affect the power relations between a police style, the state, and the community. These may also be powerfully dependant on the *imaging* or representation of a style of policing which proponents (and opponents) advance.[2]

The analysis of styles of policing may be more functional. In this respect aims, outcomes, perceptions, and discourses on policing give substance to the interactive social reality of police power and authority.

Various models exist for explaining police styles.

1. **Interaction**. Policing is the personification and institutionalisation of power relations within specific social contexts. More than this, police work is transitional and dynamic within these contexts. Police styles are a combination of structure and action, and specifically represent layers of interaction which can explain char-acteristics of policing such as isolation, discretionary enforcement, resistance to accountability, cop culture, police deviance, etc. The challenge to analysts of polic-ing is to discover the origin and the development of hierarchies of police interac-tion when considering the relative power relationships comprising policing.

2. **Opportunity and market structures.** A market model for police services is inextricably connected both to the interests authorising policing, and client need. These in turn may be inextricable. The closer the connection the more likely it is that a style of policing can claim inclusion in community justice strategies.[3]

The regulatory role of police over the market is essential for the creation of a variety of different opportunities both legitimate and illegitimate.[4] This notion of opportunity will include the objectives for policing as well as situations where fur-ther policing responses may be required. Discretionary decision-making, a feature

---

2   For a discussion of imaging policing and the crucial role it plays in claims for legitimacy, see Mawby (2002), especially chapters 3, 7 & 8.

3   See Wright (2002), chapter 6.

4   Findlay, M. (1994), 'Breaking the Crime-Control Nexus: Market Models of Corruption and Opportunity' in D. Chappell & P. Wilson (eds), *The Australian Criminal Justice System: The Mid 1990s*, Butterworths, Syd-ney, pp. 270–82.

of all modern bureaucratic policing styles, is essential for the creation of opportunity within these market structures.

3. **Integrative conflict.** The dialectics of ideology and function in policing gain their meaning from the contextual setting of any policing style. Policing promotes conflict as much as it has the potential for its resolution.[5] 'Triggering events' bring about an immediate need for a police response and this response is receptive to the needs and interests of those sponsoring police organisations. Structural differentiation in relation to policing occurs in response to conflict and challenges over the authority it exerts. The importance of consensus and respect on which police authority so often rests is emphasised in a model which examines policing in the context of conflict and differential challenge. They are also essential to those styles of policing claiming professionalism as a component status.[6]

4. **Power relations.** As suggested earlier, policing may be defined in terms of its representations of power and authority. These power relations designate particular policing styles. Forms of power may be negotiated through policing practice. The power struggles which will eventuate through, and as a consequence of, policing practice, can have a crucial impact on the development of policing styles and their essential legitimation.[7] Cyclical relationships exist between policing, structures of authority, and sources and representations of power.

Analysing structures and functions of policing

It is common to examine forms of policing in structural terms. While this has a tendency to construct differences around institutions and organisations, rather than practice and outcomes, it still provides a helpful framework for comparing different styles of policing. Standard indicators of various policing styles will include:

- forms of participation in the policing exercise
- volunteerism
- professionalism and vocation
- bureaucratic organisation
- client focus
- visibility (particularly in the exercise of discretion)
- jurisdiction, and
- the place of force and compulsion in police authority.

Structural analysis is also useful when grouping different styles of policing together. Such grouping is a natural consequence of examining the contextual

---

5   Wright (2002), chapter 2.
6   Mawby (2002), chapter 2.
7   Mawby (2002), chapter 3.

significance of different policing styles within their social and community origins. Structural groupings may be drawn together around:

- covert policing (where a policing style may be pitted against the state-sponsored or conventional forms of policing)
- subcontract policing (where community or commercial interests employ individuals and institutions to carry out policing functions even in confrontation with other conventional policing styles, or in order to supplement these styles)
- entrepreneurial and privatised policing
- consensual or 'blind-eye' policing (where formal or conventional policing condones informal policing activities which they themselves may feel constrained to exercise)
- co-optive policing (where particular social and community interests are drawn into the policing style itself)
- compulsory or obligatory policing (in which civilians are formally required to engage in representative policing functions), and
- confrontational policing (where rather than negotiating or accommodating the incursion of state-centred policing the confrontational community posture resists the action of formal police).[8]

Very often a structural analysis of policing styles will be incorporated into considerations of function. Policing function will also provide a framework for discrimination against the expectations and aspirations of police work arising from a particular style. As observed earlier, policing functions (see chapter 4) are difficult to distinguish as separate enterprises and this is a problem associated with functional analyses of policing, along with the fact that statements concerning police function are so often normative.[9] In any case, principal themes regarding police function as it relates to alternative styles include:

- classical repressive functions (patrolling, security protection of property, order maintenance, crime reporting and investigation)
- crime-prevention functions (patrolling, community warning, promotion of social development and institutions of positive socialisation)
- policing political imperatives and governmental interests (political and moral policing, promotion of any dominant political ideology, reserves of paramilitary force[10])
- welfare assistance and social service (intervention for victims, family protection, assistance to other service agencies)

---

8 For a more detailed examination of the structural analysis of policing styles see Findlay & Zvekic (1993), chapter 2.
9 For a view about police function which proposes a rational analysis see Wright (2002), chapter 2.
10 In the Australian context see McCulloch, J. (2001), *Blue Army: Paramilitary Policing in Australia*, Melbourne University Press, Melbourne.

- conflict resolution, shaming and punishment (cautions, conferencing, adjudication, corporal punishment, detention)
- licensing and permissive functions
- public order and peacekeeping, and
- information management.

Issues of authority, regulation and decision-making

Issues of authority, regulation and decision-making draw their significance from two analytical perspectives: policing as a process of interaction within particular environments of interest and power configuration, and policing as a durable repetitive pattern of social interaction. Alternative styles rest on unique sources of authority (e.g. confrontational, consensus, state-sponsored legitimacy, and commercial/contractual interests which they serve). These sources of authority may be diverse, ambiguous and often are the product of power struggles. Regulation of this authority may operate internally, externally and a combination of both (see chapters 6 & 7).[11] Discretion and accountability patterns are what designate the decision-making process of a policing style.

Contextual parameters of policing

The contextual parameters of a policing style as well as the community in which it operates provide a sense of reality to the analysis of policing as power relations. The use of jurisdiction adds a normative perspective to the segregation and expanse of police work. In this there is the potential to reflect on the dynamics of policing alone while recognising, but not being restricted by, the normative aspirations for any particular policing style. In so doing, policing styles can be considered in terms of:

- spatial distribution (where does the protection of life and property occur, or not, and for whom, and how?)
- political transfiguration (what is the political course, predominance and acceptance of policing?)[12]
- context (of conflict and support, of isolation and integration, of manifest and latent functions, in transition), and
- alternative styles of justice possible through different approaches to policing.

---

11 For a detailed discussion of accountability as a regulator of police authority and the discretion it fosters see Edwards (1999), Part 3.

12 This was the context for the transformation of policing in the new South Africa. See Brogden, M. & Shearing, C. (1993), *Policing for a New South Africa*, Routledge, London.

Policing styles in transition

It is essential now to take the discussion of alternative policing from the level of abstract modelling back to practice. Much of what we have discussed about policing so far in this text has been in the style of state-sponsored police services. This style of policing is essentially partisan, and despite ideologies of independence and community, such policing does not speak well within and for the communities it serves. The politicality of state policing complicates expectations for objectivity and representativeness, impartiality and commitment, while confounding the legitimacy it might claim through association with these themes. Therefore, what is it that state-sponsored police work should claim when seeking its definition as well as its authority?

Its role in the guaranteeing of a particular type of order is well documented.[13] The role of the police in defining and demarcating orderly behaviour sets them against and apart from certain groups within the community. Public-order policing necessarily advances the interests of some against others. Through this function policing culture becomes determined largely by what it represents and what it rejects in the struggle over its definition of good order.

However, like all policing styles, state policing is dynamic.[14] There is a program for change in state police cultures recognising that:

- problems exist with the ownership of change
- problems exist with the actuality of change
- communities may not be drawn into the process of change without real consultation and communication which is often impeded by the nature and legitimacy of this form of police work
- change may only occur at certain levels of the disciplined service, and
- until openness is the context in which accountability is achieved a transition to community-based policing will not be achieved.

Public/private dichotomy?

The distinction between private and public police styles is not a simple dichotomy.[15] It goes to the substance of the definition of policing in exposing the controversial issue of client focus. Rather than being divided, both public and private designations may work together for policing in resolving and complementing

---

13 See Wright (2002), chapter 3 for a discussion of public order policing as peacekeeping.
14 In Japan, for instance, it has been required to adapt to local community needs in a very particular fashion in order to enhance its legitimacy and relevance. See Bayley, D. (1986), *Patterns of Policing: A Comparative International Analysis*, Rutgers University Press, New Brunswick, N.J.
15 This is widely discussed in the essays in Matthews, R. (ed.) (1989), *Privatising Criminal Justice*, Sage, London.

sometimes strained relationships between the public and private spheres of social control and justice maintenance.

Public and private police work within and on behalf of different communities.[16] Both recognise the artificial division of labour in policing. Developments in state-centred policing have occurred irrespective of the explosion in private policing services. This is not to deny the connection between the two styles. The rise of commercially contracted policing has recently been stimulated by a conscious withdrawal of the public police from areas of previous responsibility and from certain traditional public functions. For instance, the public police rely on private-sector insurance agencies to report on and compensate for a wide range of property crime. More recently state police managements have suggested divesting, licensing, and traffic functions to private policing. They have already removed these responsibilities in large measure to local government security arms which may then be contracted out.

Historically, the public police institutions did not emerge to entirely substitute for private-sector policing, particularly in the areas of private security and space.[17] In Australia the police were initially a franchise of the military and in that respect, while it could be said that they were public, they were not the executive institution we know them as today.

Public police organisations introduced a new ideological overlay into policing–that being the ideology of independence, foreign to private policing arrangements. In addition, public policing shifted the client focus away from the commercial employer to the state (as the representative of the law and of the community) and more recently to aspects of the community itself. This corresponded with the gradual exclusion of individual victims and petitioners in favour of state prosecutions in the name of the community at large and its interests.

Now with the integration of private policing within multinational corporate models, private policing has moved well outside the interests of states and communities. Accountability is to the corporation, jurisdiction is global and obligations are entirely commercialised. This presents significant challenges for conventional notions of democratic governmentality when the state chooses (for ideological and commercial reasons) to divest its policing functions to these multinational interests or to engage in public/private partnerships for the securing of criminal-justice services. The new focus on crime control as risk management tends to foster this confusion in regulatory responsibilities.[18]

Recent arguments concerning the professionalisation of public policing have placed the relative standing of private police, their training, and accountability into stark relief. The fact that the state police in Australia license the private police

---

16   The commercial dimension of private policing is discussed in South, N. (1988), *Policing for Profit: The Private Security Sector*, Sage, London.

17   See Johnston, L. (1992), *The Rebirth of Private Policing*, Routledge, London, Part 1.

18   See Wright (2002), chapter 5; Edwards (1999), chapter 13.

raises an atmosphere of competition and subservience which further divides the two styles.

In relation to jurisdiction, particularly with the monitoring and controlling of public space, the private and public police styles in Australia increasingly have shared complementary functions. For instance, the security of large shopping malls is the domain of the private police backed up by state police when crimes are committed. The *enemy* is uncontested in policing terms and the appreciation of threat is common. The technologies for policing (such as closed-circuit television) may be in private ownership, with the problems this poses for accountability and ancillary challenges to privacy and personal integrity.

The authority given to public or private policing styles will be inextricably dependant on:
• client focus (who is the policing for?)
• commercial connection (who pays for the policing?)
• contractual connection (what is policing obliged to do?), and
• reliance on force (what backs-up police power, and answers resistance to authority?).

Private policing styles

It has been suggested so far that policing is a product of social context. Policing is a process where professionalised vocational organisations have taken over the community responsibility for policing and have responded to the dynamic challenges to public order, private property, political predominance, and commercial and community interest.

It makes sense, therefore, that along with the expansion of the public and private sectors of the Australian economy and the pervasive influence of multinational as well as state bureaucracies, that private commerciality will represent a significant context for policing, concurrent with the development of the state police. The diversification of social justice in Australian communities, along with notions of citizenship and social responsibility in Australia's corporate and commercial worlds, has meant that private police have developed as functional and organisational contrasts to state police. In this respect the public/private divide may depend on the interests which each style represents.

At the commencement of this century in Australia there were around 120,000 private-sector police operatives working in a variety of different policing styles. This is half again the state police service numbers in Australia. Private policing is a booming industry with an estimated billion-dollar turnover. Operationally, private police have assumed something like 20% of the areas conventionally policed by state agencies, including crowd control, building and precinct security, transport protection, and the movement of prisoners. This percentage increases significantly if we consider those operational areas where the state and private police actively cooperate, sharing resources and jurisdiction.

Private policing has developed rapidly in Australia for the following reasons:

1. The fiscal, resource and legitimacy crises in public-sector policing, which may be viewed as part of wider strains on funding public-sector bureaucracies
2. Challenges for public-sector policing to divert resources to areas of specialisation and higher technology, in order to meet the influence of the new investigation and prosecution agencies. This leads to a shift in state policing priorities away from conventional security, protection and public-order functions.
3. Confrontational industrial regulation and the need to police the consequences of industry restructuring and structural unemployment
4. The development of corporatised police partnerships (particularly in loss protection, and client protection)
5. Marketing of private policing services by multinational owners
6. The diversified structural properties of globalised enterprise. There is now a push by multinational and major financial corporations to contain security and control issues within their corporate structures and away from public criminal justice. This sits with a desire to avoid state-sponsored accountability.
7. Compatible corporatisation (and globalisation) of private policing services and structures
8. Growth in more autonomous forms of civil action in social control. Communities now contract policing services in response to a fear of crime, rather than await the initiative of state police, beyond their control. This is also evidenced through the empowerment (and sometimes the isolation) of victims.
9. The emergence (stimulated through popular representations of policing) of expectations for 'instant' justice
10. The emerging relationships between state police and private sponsorship
11. The association between state-police and volunteerism
12. Criminal-justice institutions now being approached as institutions of last resort. This involves trends such as an increased use of mediation, and a greater reliance on commercial surveillance of civil life.
13. The development of discipline and public order through surveillance. Such mechanical surveillance, particularly in urban public space which might otherwise have been patrolled personally by state-police, is now mechanically watched, not individualised, nor essentially punitive, nor is it necessarily correctional.

Perhaps the most significant problem with the growth of private policing rests in its qualified accountability. While private police may exercise similar powers to the state police they are only accountable through their specific contractual relationships, and general licensing obligations. Wider accountability to the state police through the licensing process is marginal. In addition, the nature of private policing contracts, their limited visibility, and the manner in which they may be negotiated, exacerbates questions of accountability to the public good.

With private policing being initially a commercial relationship requiring a 'user-pays' motivation, the notion emerges that some fundamental and basic policing work may move beyond the reach of some within the community, while the state police draw back from these functions in the wake of private sector policing incursions. This may lead to a recasting of the role of public policing away from, and no longer on behalf of, the whole of the community and those regularly victimised in particular.

The concern about standards of policing in the private sector and their compatibility with those claimed for public police is also important. Private police, similar to state police, need to be viewed as a service with unique powers and outreach. There is a public-interest dimension to private policing which cannot be denied simply by its commercial and contractual context.

The benefits on the other hand of private-sector policing include:
• It is chiefly proactive as opposed to primarily reactive state police.
• It is seen by many as alleviating the state police from some of the more mundane and routine tasks, thereby allowing them to 'get on with real police work'.
• It provides immediate security and protection to private homes and businesses which the state police simply cannot or will not offer. These services may of necessity require the financial commitment from those who receive them.
• Complementary public and commercial interests are served through the use of surveillance and patrol security in other areas of the public domain by private police. For instance, public surveillance cameras which are introduced and situated for specific security or traffic-flow functions may also provide a wealth of information in other criminal-investigation contexts.

With the proliferation of new forms of public surveillance, largely motivated by private and corporate interests, the potential for the invasion of privacy is significant. So too is the consequent, and often undetected but pervasive, expansion of policing function across community life.

Concerns for other liberties have also emerged from the experience of private policing in other jurisdictions. For example, in the USA surveys have shown that over 20% of private-sector police personnel have witnessed or taken part in actions which exceed their authority.[19]

New boundaries for private-policing styles

The following provides just a brief list of contexts in which private or community initiated policing has developed a recent presence in Australia:

---

19   See O'Toole, G. (1978), *The Private Sector—Private Spies, Renta Cops and the Police Industrial Complex*, Norton & Company, New York.

1. Private security patrols—where armed or unarmed guards patrol a range of public and private jurisdictions to provide personal and property protection.
2. Internal security patrols—where armed or unarmed guards are employed by organisations to provide security (hospitals, railways, universities, shopping malls, casinos, nightclubs, libraries, museums, etc.). Many of these patrols are uniformed and use vehicles with similar markings to those of the state police.
3. Loss-prevention officers—internal security officers employed by private-sector organisations such as department stores whose main aim is to prevent or minimise the loss of stock through shoplifting.
4. Private investigators—organisations which offer investigative and surveillance services hired for a range of purposes such as missing persons, divorce cases, insurance fraud, workers compensation fraud, etc. The relationships between this policing style and the state police have been traditionally uneasy.
5. Police volunteers—in certain jurisdictions volunteers have been recruited to act as information providers and intermediaries between the state-sponsored police and the community. These operatives usually work out of a shop front physically separated from the local police station. They do not possess sworn powers of any kind but refer matters to the police if required. By the mid 1990s over 100 volunteer police were operating in New South Wales in 23 patrols.
6. Neighbourhood Watch/Marine Watch/Safety House Program—these are community policing initiatives in which the public acts as informant to the state police regarding criminal occurrences in their community. Principally these volunteers act as deterrents and provide support for police and the community in the event that a crime is committed, and for the victim in situations where it is appropriate.
7. Risk assessors—in a wide range of commercial and corporate environments there is developing an obsession with risk assessment and minimisation. Along with this is a broad interest in the policing potential of compliance strategies. Private analysts, investigators and assessors are taking up roles to meet these market needs by transferring from areas such as risk insurance into risk prevention.
8. Public-sector inspectors—in the areas of motor transport, environmental protection, work cover, the provision of health services, and local government there have developed a network of inspectors and rangers with many of the public-order functions of the state police. These inspectors may be specifically empowered under statute to carry out a range of regulatory functions which then are endorsed by the state police in situations where the regulations may be breached.

Therefore, it is clear in Australia that even with the provision of what we might consider core state functions it would be incorrect to assume that the style of state-sponsored police predominates. In the diversification of policing styles throughout Australia some of the issues for state police that we will confront in the remainder of this text, are both more relevant and urgent for analysis in respect of less visible, accountable and more pervasive policing styles. On the other hand state and private-sector police could have much to learn from more participatory, representative, community-centred policing initiatives.

Conclusion

Alternative policing is a comparative concept. The more common forms of policing, such as state-centred police organisations, become the referent against which comparisons are drawn. This inevitably leads to certain themes about policing predominating largely due to their representation and reflection in the most common policing forms. For example, state-centred policing confirms important social and political imperatives for the state such as the organisation of labour and the power relations essential to contemporary commerce. State-centred police, through their close connection with state imperatives, determine the context and coverage of their claims over criminal justice and its legitimacy. With criminal justice in modern bureaucratic states having become the monopoly of the state, the close connection between the government and the police is both obvious and inevitable. On the other hand, the problems associated with this relationship have, in many communities, stimulated a rethinking of policing expectations and responsibilities.[20]

Additional readings

For full reference details refer to the bibliography.

Findlay & Zvekic (1993).

Findlay & Zvekic (1992), 'Analysing Alternative Policing Styles' (unpublished conference paper).

Xiaoming (2002), 'Community and Policing Strategies: A Chinese Approach to Crime Control', *Policing and Society*, vol. 12, no. 1, pp. 1–14.

Gans (2000), 'Privately Paid Public Policing: Law and Practice', *Policing & Society*, vol. 10, no. 2, pp. 183–208.

Gill & Hoot (1998), 'Exploring Investigative Policing: A Study of Private Detectives in Britain', *British Journal of Criminology*, vol. 37, no. 4, pp. 549–67.

Davids & Hanack (1988), 'Policing, Accountability and Citizenship in a Market State', *Australian and New Zealand Journal of Criminology*, vol. 31, no. 1, pp. 38–68.

Mawby (1990), chapters 1, 11 & 12.

---

20   Mathews, R. (1988), *Informal Justice?* Sage, London.

Johnston (1991), 'Privatising and Police Function: 'New Police' to New Policing', in Reiner & Cross, chapter 1.

Johnston (1993), 'Privatisation and Protection: Spatial and Sectoral Ideologies in British Policing and Crime Prevention', *Modern Law Review*, vol. 56, no. 6, pp. 771–92.

Reynolds & Wilson (1996), 'Private Policing: Creating New Options', in Chappell & Wilson, chapter 14.

Spitzer & Scull (1977), 'Privatisation and Capitalist Development: The Case of Private Police', *Social Problems*, vol. 25, no. 1, pp. 18–29.

Noaks (2000), 'Private Cops on the Block: A Review of the Role of Private Security in Residential Communities', *Policing & Society*, vol. 10, no. 2, pp. 143–62.

Findlay (1993), 'Police Authority, Respect and Shaming', *Current Issues in Criminal Justice*, vol. 5, no. 1, pp. 29–41.

Johnston(1992), part II South (1988), chapters 1 & 9.

6

Police Discretion and Police Powers

Introduction

In this chapter we will examine not only the existence and workings of police discretion but also the manner in which it underpins the nature of police powers. In Australia, discretion is part of policing in terms of conventional and accepted organisational practice. Only in some circumstances it is legitimated through legislation[1]. Discretion is the mechanism through which both law enforcement and non-law enforcement activities can be distinguished and administered by police, for the wider purposes of criminal justice as they see them. In addition, discretion sometimes allows the police to extend or step outside the boundaries of the law in order to achieve any of their particular functions. In this sense discretion can be viewed as the context in which both legitimate and illegitimate policing occurs.

What is discretion?

Discretion when applied to criminal justice is any and all of the following:
- Individual decisions
- Decision-making, and
- The process through which decisions are made.

Police discretion may be individually or collectively exercised, as well as being an essential feature of the institutions and operations of policing. Police power rests on discretion. Within a disciplined service, discretion obviously works within set boundaries that are determined by the organisation of police work. This is not

---

1   See *Police Powers and Responsibilities Act* (Qld.); *Law Enforcement (Powers and Responsibilities) Act* (NSW).

to diminish the individual influences that operate on discretion where police have significant control over their decision-making and daily encounters with individual members of the community.

Discretion is crucial to the operation of the criminal-justice process at large.[2] Klockars[3] alleged discretion is the basis of the operation of criminal justice and without it criminal justice as the process we know would not function. In so doing he identified discretion as:

• the process of individual or collective decision-making
• as a continuum across which a variety of decisions are made
• being predetermined by rules
• influenced by the reality of independence as to agencies within the system
• emphasising the importance of delegation
• counterbalanced by accountability
• both stipulated and assumed by the context in which it is exercised, and
• both individual and organisational in its form.

Discretion exists 'whenever effective limits on his, her, or its power leave the officer free to make choices among possible courses of action or inaction'.[4]

Davis saw discretion for policing 'as a tool indispensable for the individualisation of justice'. He talked of discretion allowing for 'governments of law and of men, where rules alone cannot cope with the complexity of modern government'.[5] Discretion provides the principal source of creativeness within the administration of law and is essential to selective law enforcement from a police perspective. It could be said that where the law ends discretion begins and the exercise of discretion may mean beneficence or tyranny, justice or injustice, reasonableness or arbitrariness.

Bottomley argued that the meaning of law and law enforcement is essentially transferred through the exercise of discretion.[6] In this process discretion is crucially influenced by the characteristics of the parties to the process: 'Not only are the individual needs of the client taken into account but the decisions themselves are very likely to be influenced by the individual characteristics and values of the decision-makers'.[7]

Discretion operates within a framework of laws, rules and definitions. Issues such as the elements of the offence, the demeanour of the offender, the visibility of discretions exercised, and regulation, public expectations and accountability may determine the outcomes of any discretionary decision-making. At an operational

---

2 See Ashworth, (1994), chapter 1; Findlay, Odgers & Yeo, (1999), chapter 4.
3 (1985) p. 93.
4 Klockars (1985), p. 91.
5 Davis, K. (1969), *Discretionary Justice*, University of Illinois Press, Urbana; Davis, K. (1975), *Police Discretion*, West Publishing, St Paul.
6 Bottomley, K. (1973), *Decisions in the Penal Process*, Martin Robertson, Oxford.
7 Bottomley (1973), p. 119.

level, discretion in criminal justice and policing discretion in particular, may be regulated by:

- perceptions of how justice agencies will function, whether these come from within the system or are represented from community and media interests
- internal bureaucratic constraints such as the structures of a disciplined service such as the police
- interpretations of the law where its substance and application depend on the decisions of individuals
- professional standards and job satisfaction
- pressures from other agencies, whether direct, (such as the Office of the Director of Public Prosecutions on the police) or indirect, where the operation of one component of the system impacts on the potential of another (for example, sentencing practice and prison overcrowding), and
- occupational solidarity which is an isolating and consolidating factor of all criminal-justice agencies.

Discretion allows compromise and expediency to act as considerations in the criminal-justice process. For example, some observers of policing[8] suggest that conflict between the law governing police powers and police operations in practice is resolved through the individual and collective exercise of discretion. In settling any such conflict the police may even usurp the roles performed by other agencies of the determiners of guilt or the executers of penalties.

Police discretion

Bearing in mind these preceding comments on the place of discretion within criminal justice and its significance for policing, it is important to determine specifically the context in which discretion and its exercise can determine a particular policing style. In this, the ideology of independence should play a central role in the logic of discretion as an individualistic mechanism for police powers.

For police officers, discretion and its prevalence are dependent on:

- legal limits such as the definition of an offence
- the visibility of its exercise, and the context in which discretionary encounters occur
- accountability for its exercise, both formal and informal
- the demeanour of those encountered by police and the respect or otherwise that they demonstrate, and
- general public expectations of the exercise of police powers.[9]

---

8 Skolnick, J. (1966), *Justice Without Trial: Law Enforcement in a Democratic Society*, Wiley, New York.
9 For discussion of the issues which impinge on the individual exercise of police discretion see Travis (1983), pp. 212–19.

Preconditions for the exercise of police discretion, at both individual and organisational levels, are influenced by the appreciation by the police of their function. These perceptions in turn depend on the way in which police perceive challenges and resistance to their function, or situations in which the law and the legal process stand in the way of what they consider to be a just outcome.

Skolnick alleged that policing is all about balancing the tension between legal regulation and crime-control imperatives. In this he argued that the police use discretion to bring about what they and many in the community believe to be just outcomes which would otherwise be interfered with by due process.[10] McBarnet, however, would have it that the manner in which the law creates police powers tends to institutionalise the opportunity for the police to use discretion to interpret justice as they see fit. For her, the dichotomies suggested by Skolnick are false, as they are a function of the class nature of society and of its laws. Her arguments undermine the notion that the fairness and efficiency of criminal justice rests on the exercise of discretion and would be challenged through a strict adherence to existing law. McBarnet concludes the law itself does not conform to the ideology of legality. She argues rather that in its substantive and procedural content the law positively contradicts the precepts of due process, and that consequently there is no fundamental conflict between the formal system of law and the informal practices of agencies such as the police and the courts. Police discretion, the potential for selectivity, discrimination, and other practices usually labelled as abuses or informal accommodations to conflicting demands are shown to be positively confirmed by, and affirmed in the law.[11]

Whether we prefer to see the exercise of discretion as Skolnick does (a way of resolving conflicting challenges of justice), or as McBarnet suggests (evidence of a deviation from legality institutionalised in the law itself), it is beyond argument that policing is about the exercise of discretion enabling the police to set the direction for future criminal-justice decision-making.

Exercise of discretion

As mentioned earlier, discretion is both an individual and an organisational feature of policing. Individually it is directed towards:
- the generation of respect
- crime solving and successful prosecutions
- immunity protection
- self-advancement and job satisfaction for individual police, and

---

10   See Skolnick (1966).
11   McBarnet, D. (1978), 'False Dichotomies in Criminal Justice Research', in J. Baldwin & K. Bottomley (eds), *Criminal Justice*, Martin Robertson, Oxford; see also McBarnet, D. (1979), 'Arrest: The Legal Context of Policing', in S. Holdaway (ed.) *The British Police*, Edward Arnold, London. See also Hogg (1983), p. 7.

- endorsing individual concepts of appropriate police work.

   On the organisational level, discretion is used for:

- the maintenance of authority
- crime detection, prevention and security
- the satisfaction of community perceptions
- organisational cohesion, and
- public tranquillity.

   Travis's study[12] identified four principal factors affecting the exercise of police discretion. These are the behaviour of the offender, the behaviour of the police agent, the locale and time of the encounter, and operational targeting. For behaviour, the offender's characteristics and status are significant. So the status and characteristics of the police officer are determined (as these may be for the citizen or suspect as well) by gender, sexuality, race, class, and social placement. Regarding locale and time issues such as drug ingestion, the physical or ideological threat posed by the encounter and its social context are relevant. Operational targeting, media campaigns, responsive police organisation and strategies, and the resultant public image of police will impact on the exercise of discretion.

   A significant difficulty in analysing or evaluating police discretion arises from the fact that police operatives themselves diminish or misunderstand its place in their work. This is made more problematic by the essential need to recognise police discretion when evaluating police work and policing styles. Important reasons for recognition include:

1.   The necessary ambiguity involved in the language of rules and laws governing policing means that the law can only give general guidance to the exercise of police powers. In this respect, interpretation of rules and laws by police requires individual judgment, along with administrative guidance from within the police organisation.[13]

2.   Discretion is a necessary outcome of limited resources both in terms of criminal justice as a whole and policing in particular.

3.   Consequences of the conceptualisation of justice and 'good policing'.

   When talking about the exercise of police function we referred to the political and organisational basis of police discretion.[14] This is often concealed by the ideology of police independence and impartiality. Political, organisational and industrial determinants of discretion generally are not recognised, articulated or regulated in the operation of police powers. The isolation of policing within the community and the individuality of its exercise exacerbates the problems of recognition and control as they relate to discretion.

---

12   See Travis (1983).

13   Such guidance often takes the form of instructions or guidelines issued by police commissioners over the exercise of police powers in the area of investigation, detention, and court appearance.

14   See Eggar & Findlay (1988).

The regularity of discretionary decision-making in the face of a lack of its recognition can be explained by often unarticulated policing policies (such as those relating to the maintenance of respect and discretionary reactions to suspects), the occupational culture of policing, and the institutional values of the organisation which may compete with laws and rules (such as loyalty over legality).

Policing domestic violence: A case-study in discretion

Police are unique among most bureaucratic agencies in that the degree of discretion which they exercise increases as one moves down the line of managerial responsibility. Also the extent of discretion as a feature of police work is inversely proportional to the visibility of a police–citizen encounter. These features have a particular impact on the policing of domestic violence.

As with all law, legislation governing the control of domestic violence in Australian jurisdictions does not anticipate full enforcement and gives police some latitude in deciding whether or not to intervene. Recently, as a consequence of criticisms about the police failing to enforce breaches of apprehended violence orders in particular, certain jurisdictions now require that the police designate reasons for deciding not to act. Another regulation of police discretion not to enforce domestic violence laws has been the introduction of legislative requirements forcing police to enter and search premises when a domestic dispute is the reason for them being called out and they believe firearms are on the premises.

Why is it that police are reluctant to intervene in domestic violence? It is common for police to declare a distinction in their jurisdiction between public and private domains. Police are reluctant to get involved in domestic disputes particularly when they do not view them as *real crime*. This view has been combated by the statistics demonstrating the significant connection between female homicide victims and their histories of domestic abuse.

The ambiguity in the interpretation of domestic violence within police culture tends to complicate effective domestic-violence policing. This has recently been recognised in most Australian police organisations and as a result specialist education and training programs have been instituted to sensitise male police officers in particular to the reality of domestic violence and the danger it poses to women and children within all communities.

Stanko's work on rank-and-file cop culture[15] as an explanation for inaction in the policing of domestic violence reveals representations by male police that the violence is the victim's fault, and as a contest between male rights and female blame. If the police confront domestic violence by scrutinising what they see as the

---

15   Stanko, E. (1989), 'Policing Battering: Missing the Mark', in J. Hanmer et al. (eds), *Women, Policing and Male Violence*, Routledge, London, chapter 7.

complicity of the victim's behaviour then protective intervention will be less likely, particularly if male police empathise with the male perpetrator of the violence. It has been suggested that one reason for an unbalanced empathy such as this is the personal association male police may have with domestic violence in their own personal relationships or when they were children.

Another reason suggested by police for non-intervention, especially in repeat offence situations, is the reluctant victim. Police are negatively disposed to women they see as weak for not being able to remove themselves from violent relationships. This poor disposition by police to victims is exacerbated by the not irregular occurrence of victims wishing to withdraw complaints when matters get to court, or becoming reluctant witnesses in these settings.[16] Stanko is correct in arguing that a feminist critique of domestic power relations needs to be employed here to divert inappropriate blame from victims that justifies unbalanced policing practice.[17]

It would be wrong to suggest that all policing of domestic violence is of such a nature. In fact, sensitive and committed management strategies in policing organisations, fuelled by spiralling domestic-violence figures have brought about significant changes in biased occupational cultures resistant to protective policing practices. Even so, the conventional focus of police function on street crime above domestic violence reflects a conception of law and order which is suggestive of discrimination and downgrading the criminalisation of male violence in domestic settings.[18] If occupational cultures of policing contribute to this then no doubt they will influence the exercise of discretion and the emphasis and outcomes of selective enforcement.

Policing domestic violence throws into sharp focus the relationship between conditional legality, occupational culture, and selective law enforcement. In discharging (or avoiding) this function, individual police can translate their own understandings of appropriate domestic behaviour into discriminatory policing outcomes, the consequences of which can endanger the safety of a significant and vulnerable community. The allocation of policing resources towards domestic violence and a more literal application of police powers in the area on the other hand can ensure a more limited discretion in favour of victims and away from masculine violence.

Selective enforcement

Police do not enforce all the laws all of the time. The tensions within the exercise of police discretion as a technique for utilising police powers, are constantly

---

16 Mugford, J. et al. (1993), *Australian Capital Territory Domestic Violence Research: Report to the Australian Capital Territory Community Law Reform Committee*, Australian Institute of Criminology, Canberra.

17 Stanko, E. (1995), 'Policing Domestic Violence: Dilemmas and Contradictions', *Australian and New Zealand Journal of Criminology* (special issue), pp. 31–44.

18 Messerschmidt, J. (1993), *Masculinities and Crime: Critique and Reconceptualisaton of Theory*, Rowman & Littlefield, Maryland.

between action and inaction. In fact the significance of police discretion in no small part rests on its fundamental connection with the selective activation of significant police powers and the individual interpretation of when to enforce the law.

Through selective law enforcement the police become *gatekeepers* of the criminal-justice process. The majority of all minor criminal events which come to police attention in Australia do not progress beyond police decisions. Therefore, the role of the police as agents of diversion from the rest of the criminal justice process is important.

Selective law enforcement as practiced by police tends to be challenged at least in theory by the universality of the rule of law, the separation of powers that Davis refers to as *government of laws*. However beyond these issues of ideology there is the powerful impact of common sense which supports selective enforcement. It is argued that unless discretion is generously exercised the over-reach of the criminal-justice system would be such as to offend public expectations and to encroach on civil liberties. Discretion tends to modify the inappropriateness of the consequences of the law's application in a black and white (non-discretionary) sense. This line of thought has it that the purpose of the law is perhaps not always expressed in the letter of the law, but rather through the application of discretion. Discretion also provides an opportunity for rationalising police priorities on the street and giving individual police operatives some say in the way in which law enforcement police work is carried out.

Because of the immediacy of police interventions, discretion often provides the necessary adaptation of the law to changing circumstances. So the police through their discretion can extend their role as law enforcers to one of mediation and dispute resolution. In some situations the exercise of discretion can militate against the effect of bad laws or laws which are out of date or inappropriate to a particular context. In this respect discretion is an effective agent for law reform and may precede the slower and more deliberate mechanics of legislative change. Finally, public expectation, as well as the wishes of particular complainants, may be better reflected through the exercise of such discretion rather than through the blunt application of the law.

Discretion is essential for the individualisation of justice. Along with this, discretion is the mechanism for the individualistic application of police powers.

Police powers and discretion

The preconditions for the exercise of police discretion in many respects influenced the nature and functions of police power. Police powers themselves rely on discretion both in form and applications, therefore it follows that the nature of police powers and their impact is only to be fully understood against the context of opportunities for discretion.

As discussed above, selectivity is a crucial characteristic of police power and its applications. Selectivity in police work sets the tone for the progress for the rest of the system and the manner in which police powers can be viewed as an essential initiator of criminal justice.

As identified by the then Criminal Justice Commission in its discussion paper on police powers in Queensland: 'It should be a matter of concern to everyone in the community that the increased level of crime must be curtailed. Two essential elements in achieving this are the support of the community and the availability to the police of the appropriate tools to investigate, prevent and reduce crime.'[19]

The Royal Commission on Criminal Procedure in the United Kingdom proposed that the consideration of the appropriate police powers within a democracy involved balancing competing interests such as between:

• the individual and society
• offenders' rights and justice, and
• police duties and civil liberties.

The argument for democratic balance in the exercise of police powers is all the more complex in societies such as Australia where the community and its interests are not homogeneous. In addition, there is the reality that the police and the public may not relate to each other in a constant, universal, and harmonious state of *social contract*. The police may represent a form of power and authority which does not sit well with competing community demands or conflicting interest claims for negotiation. In their investigation encounters, for instance, the police and the suspect may not stand as equals in a debate over rights and responsibilities.

It would be cavalier to rely on police discretion alone as the way of resolving conflicting expectations for police powers and creating the necessary balance between competing interests within the community. The police are too close to the exercise of their powers, and in democratic government the responsibility for determining the appropriate exercise of police powers should rest with those more directly accountable to the community at large.

It is not our intention to discuss in detail the range of police powers available throughout Australia. Rather, we would like to examine the foundations of police powers in order to understand the way in which discretion becomes crucial to their exercise. In addition, it may be useful to look at the general arenas in which police powers are exercised in the operation of criminal justice. To do this we will focus on the pre-trial, trial, and punishment stages.

Before progressing to a discussion of police powers at various stages of the criminal justice process, a brief reflection on the importance of consent and tolerance is necessary. There are not enough public or private police in Australia to assert their authority or exercise their powers in the face of constant or widespread

---

19 Queensland Criminal Justice Commission (1991), *Police Powers in Queensland: An Issues Paper*, Criminal Justice Commission, Brisbane, p. i.

resistance. Policing by consent has been the historical guiding principle of the police service in most states and territories in Australia. If the police were to lose public support and goodwill to any significant degree, or at the very least were to see a shift in ambivalence towards policing into outright opposition, it seems clear that the traditional character of policing would change.[20]

It might be observed that in recent years public attitude to policing in Australia has often at best been one of ambivalence and significant sections of the community have reacted to the police presence with hostility. If in reality consensus policing is under challenge, this will substantially influence the police perception of their role and the development and exercise of police powers. The community's ambivalent attitude towards the police may be a reflection of a wider alienation from all aspects of the justice process. The exercise of police powers is more apparent and sometimes more confrontational than is the case with other agencies, and therefore public challenges to consent will significantly influence the exercise of police discretion.

The major stages of the criminal-justice process where discretion is exercised are:

- police pre-trial decision-making (e.g. apprehension, caution, arrest, diversion, charge, bail, and evidence gathering)
- prosecution pre-trial decision-making (e.g. *no bills*, alternate charges, plea bargaining, witness selection)
- defence pre-trial decision-making (e.g. plea bargaining, bail review, plea, witness selection)
- magisterial pre-trial decision-making (e.g. issue of warrants, *case to answer* determinations, committal for trial)
- judicial discretion at trial (e.g. acceptance of plea, admissions of evidence, jury instruction and direction, sentencing)
- decisions on appeal (e.g. granting leave, new evidence, conviction and sentence), and
- discretion during punishment (e.g. classification, variation, conditions, parole, executive release).

In their role as official *gatekeepers* of the criminal-justice process the police receive and interpret information in order that other stages can be invoked or avoided. In most crime situations, victims or other members of the public inform the police of the commission of an offence, of certain circumstances surrounding its commission, or of the parties involved in the offence. The police may then take charge of the crime investigation and the preparation of the prosecution case on behalf of the state. Rather than require any further initiative from the victim beyond presenting evidence, the police assume the role of the informant.

---

20   Critchley, T. (1978), *A History of the Police in England and Wales*, Constable, London, p. 328.

Diversion and cautions

Diversion is the process where the criminal-justice operative such as the police takes the decision to remove a suspect offender out of the criminal-justice process or to redirect the individual to other social agencies. Diversion therefore constitutes those resolutions at the pre-trial stage which avoid eventual recourse to trials. The police realise that an efficient administration of an already over-taxed criminal-justice system depends on diversion. They are also more able to transact these informal resolutions more easily than might be possible for other criminal-justice agencies at later stages of the process, because almost all crime-related matters must come first to police attention. They are also in a situation where informal resolutions are possible because of the general low visibility of their interaction with the public. Further, the practice of stereotyping, so essential to police investigation practice, means that many police decisions can be taken quickly on the basis of ready-made pre-judgments. Usually, also, the quicker the diversion the less publicly visible will be its consequences.

Provided the offence is not so serious as to require prosecution above all other interests, the police may decide not to proceed against the suspect despite their confidence that there would be a case to answer. Often it is the nature of the suspect and conditions of public interest which militate against the application of further steps in the criminal-justice process. This discretion to refrain from charging an offender has been formalised in some states and territories through processes such as the administration of juvenile cautions. Cautioning is a system (either formally or informally structured) in which the police admonish and discharge juveniles they have apprehended for criminal offences. These cautions are usually accompanied by a warning about the consequences of re-offending.[21]

Decisions on arrest or summons

Once the suspect has been identified and a reasonable suspicion exists in the mind of the police officer connecting the suspect with a particular offence, the officer in question has a choice of ways in which they may initiate proceedings.[22] The officer can either physically arrest the accused (or have a warrant issued for that purpose), or draft and serve a summons. The summons spares the accused from being physically restrained, but requires the accused to satisfy certain conditions including appearing at court on the nominated date.

---

21   For example, see Cunneen, C. (1988), 'An Evaluation of the Juvenile Cautioning System in NSW', *Proceedings of the Institute of Criminology*, 75, pp. 21–8.

22   The notion of 'reasonable suspicion' or 'reasonable belief' is a mechanism often employed in statutes in order to formalise the discretion of police in exercising these powers.

For offences of a minor nature and those where the security of appearance or the protection of witnesses is not required through bail procedures, the summons may be preferred as a way to proceed. In some jurisdictions, such as the Australian Capital Territory, police must determine that the summons route will be ineffective before they opt to arrest. The economic and resource incentives to summons have led to a new function for police—that of acting as punisher as well as investigator and prosecutor. Particularly with traffic offences, the police administer the infringement notice process right up to the collection of the penalty. Recently, similar infringement notice strategies have been used for minor drug and street offences.

Normally where the police officer reasonably suspects that an arrestable offence has been committed, they may arrest anyone reasonably suspected of the offence without first obtaining a warrant. To proceed *reasonably* appears to be the overriding determinate of the law of arrest, but as the determination of what is reasonable is in the mind of the arresting officer, its measurement is not objective. This is particularly so in relation to the use of force as part of the arrest process. In certain states and territories the police may proceed to detain a suspect after arrest in order to gain further information prior to charge.

Charges and 'bargaining'

The police do not only decide whether to initiate the criminal-justice process. They also predetermine to a large degree the future progress of the accused through the criminal-justice system since they are the investigators of an offence, the accumulators of evidence, and the initial interpreters and appliers of the law.

If charging a suspect is contemplated, then the initial collection of information sufficient to support a charge is regulated in various ways. These include the instructions or guidelines issued to police by commissioners and the adverse consequences for the rules of evidence and associated case-law related to inadmissible evidence.[23] From as early as 1975 the Australian Law Reform Commission has recommended some uniformity in the legislation which governs police practice at the investigation and charge stage.[24] One reason for resistance to this proposed change is the belief among police that they should retain extensive discretion over the initiation of consequent criminal-justice responses.

Once the decision to arrest and charge has been made, a presumption of guilt pervades the investigation process. This presumption is essential for all police involved at future stages of the prosecution of the offence, for its absence would undermine the justification in their own minds to initially arresting and charging

---

23   For a wider discussion of the relationship between the exercise of police discretion and the admission of evidence, see Findlay, Odgers & Yeo (1999), chapter 7.
24   See Findlay, Odgers & Yeo (1999), chapter 3.

the suspect. Such a presumption of guilt might be alleged right up until the com-mencement of the trial and the reading of the indictments. The charges can be amended, added to or dropped throughout the pre-trial process.

After arrest and charge the task for the police is governed by general crime-control concerns, considerations of organisational efficiency and individual notions of proper police work. Crime control is achieved, from the police point of view, by opposing bail and gaining convictions. The police have a vested interest in these convictions—they are a measure of their success. In addition, a conviction is viewed as a reaffirmation by other agencies that the police were right and that their efforts should be rewarded. Acquittals, on the other hand, can tend to fuel police suspicion concerning the competence and motives of other players and agencies in the criminal-justice process. Therein also lies motivation to divert or to plea bargain and avoid the perceived dangers of a committal hearing.

Charge bargaining in some jurisdictions in Australia has recently been recog-nised by the police, lawyers and magistrates as a legitimate means for expediting justice in an atmosphere of limited resources. Once admitted, however, the ques-tion of how such bargaining is to be regulated and by whom becomes pressing. In those jurisdictions which employ an independent prosecution service it might be deemed appropriate that the bargain process be theirs to monitor. However, this is rare.

Police and bail

Next to arrest and charge, the bail determination is one of the main ways in which police discretion affects the process of criminal justice and demonstrates the exer-cise of police power. Bail is a decision on the liberty or otherwise of the accused between the time of the arrest and the verdict. Where bail is considered by police following arrest, it is described as police bail.

Legislation governing bail throughout Australia provides both the police and the court with powers to determine bail entitlements, depending on the time and situation at which the determination is to be made. Police bail is a legislative crea-tion in all Australian jurisdictions and usually confers on police officers the power to release arrested people on bail on their undertaking that they will appear before court. Following the laying of charges the accused must be informed, in writing, as soon as possible, of their entitlement to bail and a determination must be made by the police, in writing. Whether it is police or court bail under consideration the same criteria apply.

There is no doubt that police opposition to the granting of bail is influential over a determination by a judge to refuse bail, and their opposition leading to refusal will affect impressions of the accused at trial and the eventual determina-tion of the sentences. Even something as simple as the accused being in custody during the trial may impact on the attitudes towards the accused. If the police oppose court bail, or resist appeal or review applications, bail is less likely to result.

Police and the court

In some jurisdictions in Australia police retain the responsibility for prosecuting cases in the lower courts. Traditionally this has demonstrated the close association between the police and the magistracy in Australia. The other roles of police in the court setting are to act as security providers, or as the principal witnesses in the prosecution case.

Police usually prefer to avoid their day in court. Trials are extremely disruptive of the normal police duties through the paperwork they generate and the uncertainty of their scheduling and duration. In addition, police are a class of witness facing attacks on their character in the witness box—this can undermine respect for police authority.

With the spectre of court delay hanging over much of the exercise of pre-trial and trial discretion, the motivation for efficiency is as important for pre-trial decisions as will be the concerns for justice. Police realise that pre-trial agreement with an accused party to plead guilty has advantages which directly impact on court delay. In addition, efforts to establish agreed facts and to rationalise the calling of witnesses will work towards a speedier trial and a lower level of police involvement.

Law-and-order politics: Calls for more police powers

A feature of contemporary criminal justice as displayed throughout Australia (*law-and-order politics*) has been the call for the increase and diversification of police powers. This comes against the recognised background that police powers are already extensive and largely discretionary throughout the nation. Even so, the calls for more powers remain constant.

The demand for increased powers is principally directed against those elements in society which are traditionally seen by the police as a challenge to their authority, and therefore, a threat to public order. For instance, in New South Wales the *Crimes (Amendment) Police & Public Safety Act* 1988 was introduced to provide police with search and confiscation powers for knives and other dangerous implements in public places and schools. The legislation built on existing wide powers for the police to stop and search in a street people whom they reasonably believed to be carrying offensive weapons. Somewhat like random breath-testing however, this legislation enables police to stop classes of people (usually young males) who might be deemed to be more likely to carry such weapons.

Also calls for greater powers have been connected with the desire to increase conviction rates and to make more balanced the prosecution of criminal offences. Again, for example, in New South Wales the *Crimes (Amendment) Detention After Arrest Act* 1997, had as its objectives 'to provide for the period of time that a person who is under arrest may be detained by a police officer to enable the investigation of persons involved in the commission of an offence and to authorise the detention of persons who are under arrest for such a period despite any requirement imposed by law to bring a person before a magistrate or a court without delay.'

The Act is innovative in that it is designed to defeat the common law principle against detention for questioning and the time-honoured requirement that a person arrested must be brought before a magistrate and charged without delay.

Essential to the understanding of police powers in Australia is the influence of law-and-order politics. The police themselves play a vital role in the expansion of police powers and the entrenchment of discretion, by supporting regular and constant calls for the expansion of police powers and thereby of police power.

Conclusion

As much as discretion in policing can be viewed as modifying the excesses of the law, it is also significant for the generation of tolerance as a feature of policing. Particularly in an atmosphere where *law-and-order politics* generate demands for mandatory law enforcement and sentencing in particular, police discretion may provide a counterpoint to conservative arguments about severity and certainty. For example, in the realm of drug-law enforcement several states in Australia have adopted a position whereby the police are largely responsible for the administration of cautions or infringement notices for minor drug use. This has not only avoided the difficulties involved in law reform but has also injected into this form of law enforcement a recognition of the ambiguity and inconsistency of community expectations in the field.

Additional reading

Reiner (2002), chapter 6.
Reiner (1997), in Maguire et al., pp. 997–1049.
Klockars (1985), chapter 5.
Findlay et al. (1983), chapter 14.
Eggar & Findlay (1988), in Findlay & Hogg, chapter 10.
Law Enforcement (Powers and Responsibilities) Act 2002 .
Haesler(2002).
McConville (1993), chapter 9.

NSW Ombudsman (2000), *Report on Policing Powers Introduced by the Crimes Legislation (Police and Public Safety) Act.*

Greer S. (1994), in *Modern Law Review.*

Walker & Starmer. (eds) (1999).

Freckleton & Selby (1988), part 3.

Finnane (1994), section 2.

Dixon (1997), chapter 7.

Police Accountability and Regulation

Introduction

The history of making police accountable in Australia has been both unsuccessful and characterised by compromise.[1] Distinctions have developed between account-ability in practice (largely internal organisations) and the legislative and institutional claims over accountability (often sitting outside police organisations). Recently royal commissions and commissions of inquiry have called for a heightening of the effectiveness and impact of accountability institutions for policing. This is at the same time that several of the more permanent bodies responsible for police accountability in Australia have recognised the impossibility of their task and are seeking compromises with the police themselves.[2]

This chapter examines the significance and dynamics of police accountability particularly in a community-policing climate. The purpose of the analysis is to reposition accountability away from a punitive paradigm, towards a process which can only improve police–community relations in the long term, through the promotion of respect and the development of informed consensus.

Accountability: The other side of discretion

For policing in particular, accountability may be viewed as the other side of the discretion equation. If one accepts that the legitimate operation of police discretion is premised on the assumption that it will be exercised responsibly (especially so

---

1   See Freckleton & Selby (1998), Part 5.
2   In the case of the NSW Ombudsman see Moss, I. (1998), 'Using Complaints to Improve Policing', *Current Issues in Criminal Justice*, vol. 10, no. 2, pp. 207–13.

when the powers it generates are so intrusive) then accountability is the essential balance and guarantee for police discretion.

It is not so simple, however. Unfortunately, there exists considerable definitional and perceptional uncertainty surrounding understandings and representations of accountability. For instance, the police image of accountability is generally punitive and seen as relating to complaints or criticisms about what the police did or did not do at any particular time. The institutions and machinery of accountability therefore, when confronted by the police, are considered to be a threat to the exercise of their discretion and a challenge to their independence. As such, accountability visualised as a threat to police is usually resisted or obstructed by them.

Some fallacies surrounding the punishment dimension of accountability are revealed when it is realised that:

1. Accountability facilitates the information flow which is at the heart of criminal investigation, and more generally community policing. If the public at large have confidence in the police reaffirmed through their openness and broad understanding of police work then the intelligence required to ensure the success of police investigations will be more forthcoming from the community.
2. Community policing and the actual face of police/public relations relies on the reassurance from accountability and mechanisms of review.
3. In confirmation of the police as an arm of democratic governance, police accountability needs to be more than merely a symbol.
4. Accountability, like delegation and responsibility, is at the heart of effective line management in a disciplined service such as the police.
5. Accountability is the real guarantee of any operational independence for police (for example, through the public confirmation of their impartiality).

When addressing accountability the complexity of police institutions provides some explanation of the difficulties encountered. For instance, the official processes of accountability for state-based police can rest with:

1. The police commissioner to administer authority and responsibility down the line of the disciplined service
2. The media to investigate policing activities and institutions
3. The public service structure to supervise police departments
4. General institutions which review the public sector, such as the ombudsman
5. Specialist institutions to examine policing activities based on integrity or the potential for corruption
6. Internal investigation agencies within the police
7. Interrelations between internal and external agencies
8. Special commissions of enquiry, and
9. The courts and the oversight of the law.

Unfortunately, some or many of these are merely management mechanisms or methods for identifying and regulating breaches of discretion in the exercise of police power. More wide-reaching attempts at accountability have failed to achieve long-term reforms because of their direction towards individual and organisational characteristics of policing, rather than occupational or ethical cultures. [3]

Concepts of accountability

Freckleton defined accountability as 'obligations to answer for a responsibility that has been conferred'.[4] This definition is one which relies on auditing[5] as its central component. Through the use of notions such as obligation and responsibility one needs to encounter the parties involved in any relationship where accountability is demanded.

• those who allocate responsibility
• those who accept responsibility
• those who give authority to allocate responsibility
• those for whom responsibility is exercised, and
• those against whom responsibility is exercised.

In auditing these individuals (organisations and operations) and their practices, if external review is preferred, then questions about the accuracy of that review, compliance with the review's objectives, and the efficient application of review resources need to be examined.

Reiner has taken a more conciliatory approach to police accountability.[6] When examining the utility of accountability he suggested that making institutions accountable will only be efficacious if those who seek accountability win over and work in conjunction with the internal disciplinary and self-regulating processes of that organisation. The organisation cannot be forced with a heavy hand, Reiner believed. This is, he argued, a recipe for balance when engaged in the debate about internal or external accountability mechanisms. Such mechanisms need to sponsor the development strategies which will see the police move in favour of, rather than resist, greater accountability.

Brogden proposed a narrower view of accountability and emphasised its political context.[7] For him, successful accountability involves 'institutional arrangements made to ensure that police do the job required of them.' This begs the question: what does control mean? Is it responsiveness to the law, an obligation to

---

3 For instance consult the Fitzgerald Inquiry in Queensland, and the Wood Royal Commission in New South Wales.
4 Freckleton, I. (1988), 'Police Accountability' in M. Findlay & R. Hogg (eds), *Understanding Crime and Criminal Justice*, Law Book Company, Sydney.
5 The audit concept of accountability can also be translated into considerations of compliance against an 'ethics and human rights' paradigm. See Meyroud & Beckley (2001), chapter 11.
6 Reiner, R. (ed.) (1993), *Accountable Policing: Effectiveness, Empowerment & Equity*, Institute for Public Policy Research, London, chapter 1.
7 See Brogden et al. (1988), chapter 7.

explain (retrospective accounting) or prospective control (where obligations to act impartially, efficiently and with consent are emphasised)?

Brogden's interpretation of accountability highlights public concern over arrangements for ensuring the police perform their functions and do so satisfactorily. This is a political issue at the heart of community policing.

In answering the question why is police accountability at issue, Brogden emphasised the community as the backdrop against which police work should be measured. Public expectations are crucial to this, along with ethical frameworks for the construction of accountability measures. However, to approach the controversy of accountability on the basis of political institutions alone is too limited, and fails to appreciate the important role that the community should play in making the state-sponsored police in particular more accountable.

To whom should police be accountable?

If we accept for state-sponsored police at least that the community and community interests are at the heart of their client base, then the community forms the primary arena for accountability. This, however, may be rather an idealised aspiration for democratic civil society as we accept that communities require representative institutions in order to ensure that their interests are guaranteed. This may not always be the case with policing as in certain communities a close relationship with their police has ensured a forthright and trusting exchange of responsibility and accountability at a local level. In general, however, it is for institutions which represent the interests of the community to demand the police are accountable, along with their political representatives.[8] These institutions sometimes correspond with state instrumentalities established for the purpose.

Even so, in heterogeneous communities such as those predominant in Australian society, representation is a complex and diverse issue. The task to make police accountable in terms which would satisfy a variety of representative community units with different and conflicting social agendas, may be indeed difficult. Further, within these community units, expectations for policing held by the young may vary considerably from those held by older citizens. The terrain for social accountability is complex and multifaceted.

Accepting that the police are accountable to themselves individually and their culture, the organisation for which they work, the community that they police, and the state, an integrated approach to answering the question to whom they should be made accountable is the most satisfactory. In addressing such a question in this context, consideration needs to be given to structural, internal and external

---

8   The relationship between police and political administrations is, as with the ideology of independence, problematic for clear lines of accountability.

determinants in order to integrate accountability. For instance, structurally, instructions and regulations covering state-based police are constructed so as to require some degree of daily operational accountability. Line management through the disciplined services examines accountability for the exercise of delegated powers. Courts should also have a role in reviewing the exercise of police powers and policing responsibilities discharged (or ignored) by law-enforcement officers. Internally, state police at least give the appearance of line responsibility, and paths for accountability should follow the hierarchy and vocational–cultural reasons (see chapter 8). Externally the bureaucratic motivations of the criminal-justice system require the police to account for shared goals and common functions. The state has expectations of the police and these can be measured both bureaucratically and against wider government considerations.

Accountability through discretion?

It might be said that while discretion fuels calls for accountability in policing, it enables contexts in which the exercise of police powers may occur largely unaccountable. Does police discretion in its conventional operations tend to deny accountability, and frustrate its institutions?

Sarre interrogated the denial of accountability.[9] In this denial he focused on:

- those who accept responsibility (individual, organisational, managerial, and political)
- those who ensure its existence (accountability as a natural result of certain mechanisms in place)
- those who refuse to countenance the knock-on effect it may have
- those who argue for balance, and
- those who represent the ideological significance of justice.

In any modern police organisation accountability needs to be seen as a transactional dynamic, one where responsibility is negotiated to suit certain contexts and against certain acceptable boundaries of permission. The exercise of discretion is a framework for the negotiation of police powers and authority, preferably governed by measures of responsibility which are accountable. At the same time police discretion can tend to conceal power and authority. It is through a reliance on accountability that discretion is opened up to such revelations. Therefore, the relationship between discretion and accountability may not always be adverse and dependent on degree. Rather it is a question of the manner in which discretion is exercised as to whether it will be reconciled with or opposed to accountability.[10]

---

9   Sarre, R. (1989), 'Towards a Notion of Policing by Consent and its Implications for Police Accountability', in Chappell & Wilson, chapter 8, p. 109.
10   For a critical discussion of discretion as it is regulated in justice (and sentencing) more generally see Lacey, N. (1987), 'Discretion and Due Process at the Post Conviction Stage', in I. Dennis (ed.), *Criminal Law and Justice*, Sweet & Maxwell, London.

Accountability too is best ensured through the widest notions of trust,[11] open-ness and communication. In addition, community consultation (through consent and not control) has the potential to guarantee accountability.[12]

Successful accountability within policing[13]

As was alluded to earlier, for accountability to take hold as a positive feature in Australian policing, it needs to move well beyond the notion of processes of punishment, complaint and discipline. In fact it requires a complete inversion of police operational priorities and cultural predispositions.

- moving away from isolation for police
- shifting from the predominance of force-based authority to client-centred service
- ditching the 'garrison mentality' towards the exercise of police function
- embracing the complexity of the community which the police serve
- anticipating cooperation and mutuality rather than resistance and confrontation
- developing flexible policing structures even within a disciplined service
- reducing the reliance on stereotyping and difference, and
- avoiding structural imperatives towards failure.

Accountability cannot be viewed in abstraction and with this in mind the application of broad accountability principles should be directed towards a critical study of policing. Before an exploration of accountability in context, however, the role of accountability in regulating police work should be specified.

Accountability as regulation

Requirements for accountability may be determined whether police authority is perceived as legitimate or otherwise. For instance, if the democratisation of policing is nominated by a community as a precondition for the legitimation of its authority then the participatory processes of accountability may be required in confirmation of police authority. In the case of communities where consent is withdrawn from police or a form of policing is deemed illegitimate these may be outcomes of a failure of accountability.

Mechanisms for requiring and measuring accountability usually possess some potential to regulate police practice. As is the case with most mechanisms of

11 Trust theory has not had a significant influence on writing about policing. If one reflects on the significance of consensus for policing this is perhaps surprising. In another context see Freiberg, A. (1995), 'Trust and Betrayal in Criminal Justice', in H. Selby (ed) *Tomorrow's Law*, Federation Press, Sydney, pp. 86–114.

12 In the context of private prisons see Frieberg, A. (1997), 'Commercial Confidentiality, Criminal Justice and Public Interest', *Current Issues in Criminal Justice*, vol. 9, no. 2, pp. 125–52.

13 Edwards (1999), Part 3 presents a comparison of accountability in policing Britain and the USA. Both operational and personal accountability are evaluated.

control in criminal justice, police accountability may not only support legality, it may also influence the nature and occurrence of malpractice.

Accountability is rarely a feature of the illicit policing relationship, except internal to deviant cultures of loyalty. Likewise it may be essential to control mechanisms directed against external accountability. For instance, police corruption thrives on anonymity while control agencies also rely on powers which grow out of autonomous authority. The appreciation of police malpractice or police deviance as a social threat or a community problem, however, is often constructed in very public–political dimensions. The genesis of police complaints' authorities and police community liaison committees as products of political rhetoric and community unease about the excessive or abhorrent use of police powers confirm the essential public dimension of accountability discourse and the community indebtedness to the institutions charged with its control.

Police deviance and its control may exist beyond public view while the deviance–control nexus relies on accountability in a variety of interesting *market* circumstances. These will go well beyond the obvious calls for open and responsible exercise of criminal justice, and may tend to explain the nature and progress of police deviance within certain *market* settings (e.g. the role sometimes played by state police operatives in the determination of drug markets).

There is no doubt about the significance of accountability for police power and authority as well as in the regulation of the police. This dual focus places accountability within opportunity structures that on the one hand regulate and on the other may promote malpractice.[14]

No matter what impression of accountability or its consequences we may settle upon, the application of accountability to police work reveals its complexity and tends to go well beyond punitive or regulatory intentions alone. In its broader sense accountability involves:

1. **Identification of responsibility.** Accountability is an expectation resulting from a structure of responsibility. With the requirement that accountability should be sheeted home to an individual, individualised responsibility goes beyond the apportionment of guilt alone and more towards the ramification of shared relationships and responsibility.

2. **Openness.** Requirements for openness in the exercise of investigatory and punitive powers have featured recently within debates about policing in Australia, particularly with respect to crime-control debates. Community interests are now more vocal in their expectations for liaison and consultation with crime-control agencies. These institutions, for their part, are expecting that communities should be openly implicated in the crime-control process through the provision of information and support.

---

14 See Findlay (1999), pp. 101–4.

3. **Popular participation.** Not so much as a characteristic of accountability but as a check on its dimensions, participation in criminal justice by a wide range of interests is advanced. If such participation is both popular and representative then claims for accountability appear more convincing.

4. **Audit**. Accountability relies on identifiable structures of responsibility and codes of conduct against which the behaviour of individuals and organisations might critically be reflected. The audit function of processes of accountability should not only expose individual shortcomings through this comparison but also inadequacies in these responsibility structures and conduct expectations.

5. **Compliance**. The proactive dimension of accountability arises out of the potential to combine responsibility, openness, participation, and audit into a motivation towards compliance. Effective accountability measures and mechanisms gain a functional credibility as much from their pressure to alter behaviours and relationships as they do from simply exposing impediments to good government.

6. **Complaints and discipline.** A common and unduly purgatorial conceptualisation of accountability is as a euphemism for discipline and penalty. The mechanisms for ensuring accountability, as so envisioned, are usually activated by individual complaints and therefore produce adverserial consequences. At least some of the participants in such accountability contests will only view accountability as something to be avoided.

7. **The background for stigmatisation and reintegration**. Where accountability does retain a cooperative image it still relies on processes of labelling and stigmatisation for its social impact. Whether such labels are eventually reintegrated or exclusionary will depend on a variety of environmental determinants which precede the behaviours and relationships under review.

Control dilemmas and accountability[15]

Good policing is traditionally only as strong as the mechanisms in place for controlling the exercise of police power. When considering the connection between police deviance and control, and the impact which accountability might have on this, the dilemmas which face control initiatives should not be overlooked. These dilemmas form boundaries around the control endeavour as well as the exercise of discretion. Such dilemmas in summary are:

- **Independence versus accountability**. How far can institutions of control such as the police, or accountability mechanisms over the police, be required to account for the exercise of their powers without compromising the legitimacy of their independence?

---

15   Edwards (1999), chapter 9 discusses the relationships between control, independence and accountability in policing.

- **Responsibility versus indemnity.** How can processes of accountability designed to control police power advance their legitimacy through the responsible exercise of accountable power while advertising individual indemnity as an investigatory tool?
- **Complicity versus secrecy.** How is the balance to be struck between the general community interest in seeing police power (and its abuses) controlled and the need to maximise efficient and specialist policing powers such as those which are investigative, requiring anonymity and individualised situations of discretion?
- **Anonymity versus exposure.** To what extent should the punitive consequences of controlling police power through the stages of accountability and exposure (sometimes involving public investigation) be balanced with the rights and reputation of the individual in the face of the ancillary effects of publicity?
- **Selectivity versus total enforcement.** If the ideology of controlling police deviance is of total prohibition then how can it sit with processes of specific accountability and selective enforcement?
- **Policing the police.** How are the abuses of police power sometimes present in the exercise of police investigatory powers to be avoided in accountability mechanisms directed against the police?

Accountability and structures of permission

So far we have considered police power relationships and their connection with responsibility and accountability. It is within specific structures of permission where these merge.

To some extent both police power and processes of accountability may be viewed within what we call *'perimeters of tolerance'*. Accountability connects with structures of permission in two principal ways. First, it forms an important part of the perimeters of tolerance. Requirements for accountability limit the nature and progress of relationships in society and require the establishment and operation of structures of responsibility. Second, accountability can become a positive link between opportunity, social relationships, and methods for their regulation.

Through focussing on relationships of deviance and control when looking at the need for accountability, while ignoring structures of permission within which they connect, an accurate appreciation of their impact on other social relationships becomes difficult, and a chance to expose and understand police power is perhaps squandered. Accountability has the potential to limit deviant police relationships and to activate the control of police power. This will occur whenever accountability influences deviant police power and control as they exist within structures of permission.

In order that accountability is instrumental in severing the connection between police deviance and the control of police power it needs to influence opportunities for police deviance, for control, and the resultant relationships between these entities. This positive and proactive influence of accountability must arise not only from a punitive dimension but also from the features of accountability that stimulate responsibility, openness, participation and compliance. Above all else, accountable police practice requires civil engagement. As Braithwaite wrote:

> Citizens cannot enjoy dominion if they feel powerless in the face of the coercive power of the police. Dominion does not require that citizens actually do participate in influencing the policies and practices of the police. It requires only those who have a subjective assurance of the opportunity to do so should they wish to.[16]

Whether effective engagement is to go beyond opportunity and assurances of participation to require actionable guarantees is part of the politics of police accountability. What is generally essential is that engagement progresses from the possible to the actual if community placing is to attain mutual interest.

New levels of accountability

Up until recently accountability within policing has been viewed as a distinctly jurisdictional process. The police are regulated by internal accountability cultures and structures. Outside this they are influenced by:

- specific institutions of accountability (such as complaints tribunals, integrity commissions)
- general institutions of accountability (such as ombudsmen, anti-corruption commissions)
- political institutions of accountability (ministerial, parliamentary)
- legal institutions of accountability (judges, rules of evidence, defence lawyers)
- community institutions of accountability (liaison committees, visitors), and
- inspectorates.

All of these were seen as jurisdictionally limited. The boundaries of permission tolerated by such accountability mechanisms rarely, if ever, extended beyond the operational limits of the police they covered. Regionalism and the internationalisation of criminal justice changed all that.

One of the recent debates about the introduction of a European arrest warrant covering the various jurisdictions of European Union member states related to the way in which you could make uniformly accountable the various police forces

---

16   Braithwaite, J. (1992), 'Good & Bad Police Services and How to Pick Them' in H. Eijkman & P. Moir (eds), *Policing Australia: Old Issues, New Perspectives*, Sydney, MacMillan, p 27.

responsible for the exercise of the warrant. Police in Europe have different powers and arrest conventions depending on their jurisdictions. Despite the uniform protection of rights to fair trial under the European human rights convention, there is still the view in Europe that the powers afforded police through a universal warrant would be a ticket for abuse under the confusion of jurisdictional difference.

At an international level, the Human Rights Act in the United Kingdom has forced British police services to measure the exercise of their discretion and its regulation through local legislation against supervening and more universal rights protections.

Positioning accountability: A case study on Aboriginal deaths in custody [17]

Aboriginal deaths in custody remain a significant cloud over the exercise of police powers in Australia. Despite recommendations of royal commissions and the best efforts of police administrations the terrible figures on Aboriginal deaths in police custody prevail.

An initial problem in dealing with deaths in custody for and by police was the absence of information relating to custodial policies and practices. The police themselves were suspicious about external investigations of the information which did exist, and of internal police practice, resisting the disciplinary dimension that obtained with any such external review. General bureaucratic pressures within the police service made internal investigation additionally difficult.

The political climate of criticism of police custody safety made the opening up of policing practice to community scrutiny only a matter of time. Even so, the state police as individuals and organisations were mesmerised by the possible consequences of openness, initially withdrawing from the exercise of accountability and consequential reform. This may explain the ultimate unsuccessful outcomes of investigation and reform in the area of police custodial practice and deaths in custody.

Following a range of inquiries a variety of recommendations were made to open up police custodial practice to reform and review. These included:

- alternatives to charge and police detention
- prisoner screening prior to and during custody
- inspection and supervision of prisoners' cells
- presumptions in favour of bailing prisoners
- prompt transfers to jails
- police education and training on safe custodial practice

---

17   For details of this study see Findlay, M. (1994), 'The Ambiguity of Accountability: Deaths in Custody and Regulation of Police Power', *Current Issues in Criminal Justice*, vol. 6, no. 2, pp. 234–51.

- the introduction of lay visitors' schemes
- the reform of cell design and construction, and
- a policy of working with others, involving police with other agencies and community groups to encourage a multidisciplinary problem-solving approach to prisoner safety.

In this regard, from a police perspective, accountability was not considered as enhancing policing opportunities, but rather curtailing the exercise of discretion by police in the custody and control of prisoners. The ambiguity of police attitudes to accountability and its position within police cultures became apparent when police authority was questioned by the community, and particularly by those with an interest in the safety of police custody. As with the ideology of community policing, accountable police practice is said to confirm the responsible exercise of police power. Abuses of power and malpractice, once identified at the community level, will stand opposed to police authority and be rejected by it.

The contradiction grows when this vision for police power is placed against the police view of their power and its appropriate exercise. Police occupational culture tolerates the abuse of power, or, on occasions, malpractice, so long as these conform to the precepts of the culture. In the case of Aboriginal deaths in custody the approach of 'keeping the lid' on incidents where a prisoner suicides in a situation of neglect or abuse was required by the ethic of unquestioned occupation solidarity.

Conclusion

Ede, Homel, and Prenzler have suggested that a strategic evaluation of complaints against police will reveal the connection between public dissatisfaction with policing and police misconduct.[18] More than this, however, their study challenges police management to look beyond the prosecution of individual police as an outcome of accountability through the complaints function. The challenge of police malpractice is for police administrations to address individual behavioural patterns along with a greater attention to effective supervision, and the promotion of positive police morale.

Where accountability takes police power beyond the occupational framework to expose policing to community ideologies places the mechanisms of accountability squarely outside boundaries of permission which prevail in cop culture. Resistance to these mechanisms from the police is a consequence of any such process of exposure.

---

18   Ede, A., Homel, R. & Prenzler, T (2002), 'Reducing Complaints Against Police and Preventing Misconduct: A Diagnostic Study Using Hot Spot Analysis', *Australian and New Zealand Journal of Criminology*, vol. 35, no. 1, pp. 27–42.

But what this simple oppositional view of policing and accountability ignores is the dynamics of the accountability process. In relation to police custody and safety, for example, accountability is as much concerned with the confirmation of appropriate police practice as it is designed to reveal malpractice or the abuse of power. In addition, accountability mechanisms may operate in ways which are supportive of both good and bad policing practice. An example is where the information on deaths in custody is only sought for the purposes of internal police disciplinary enquiries. In such situations the accumulation of information about custodial incidents is reluctantly and selectively facilitated by the police under investigation and closest to the incident, and as much malpractice may be concealed as is revealed.

Accountability mechanisms may also adopt or employ practices similar to those which they would otherwise expose to criticism. Investigations may be clandestine, coercive and unresponsive to independent inquiry. And the consequences of such practices may prove to be as unjust or abusive as those of the powers under review.

Policing is power; so too the relationship between police authority and accountability involves transactions of power. These transactions can minimise or propagate abuse and malpractice depending on the boundaries of permission they create and regulate and within which they operate.

Additional readings

For full reference details refer to the bibliography.

Brogden (1988), chapter 7.

Dixon (1999), chapters 3 & 4.

Findlay (1994), 'The Ambiguity of Accountability; Deaths in Custody and Regulation of Police Power', *Current Issues in Criminal Justice*, vol. 6, no. 2, pp. 234–51.

Reiner (1993), in Reiner & Spencer, chapter 1.

Findlay & Hogg (1988), chapter 11.

Wood. (1997), vol. 1, chapter 6; vol. 2, chapter 1b.

Chappell & Wilson (1989), chapters 2 & 7.

Edwards (1999), Part 3.

Prenzler (2000), 'Civilian Oversight of Police: A Test of Captive Theory', *British Journal of Criminology*, vol. 40, no. 4, pp. 659–74.

Biles & McDonald (1992).

Reiner (1992), chapter 6.

Goldsmith (1991), chapter 1.

Lewis (1999), chapters 3, 4, 5.

Dixon, Coleman & Bottomley (1990), 'Consent and the Legal Regulation of Policing', *Law and Society*, vol. 17, no. 3, pp. 345–62.

Goldsmith (1990), 'Taking Police Culture Seriously: Police Discretion and the Limits of the Law' in Reiner (1996), pp. 311–34.

8

Cop Culture, Police Malpractice and Prospects for Change

Introduction

The institutional ambiguity of the law (discussed in the preceding chapter), ena
bles cop culture as an interpretive context for law enforcement. Police discretion
empowers individual police and police organisations to play an active role inter-
preting the law though law enforcement. By exercising selective enforcement, the
police can introduce into the law a range of personal and institutional cultural
traits. These can influence the law to discriminate against those whom the police
identify as a threat to their culture, and in favour of those segments of the community which have consensual and respectful relationships with the police.

This chapter explores the construction of individual and organisational cultures
in policing. The potential for a perversion of moralities through the somewhat isolated and oppositional development of cop culture is seen as an explanation for malpractice and its rationalisation. In conclusion we speculate on the way forces for the
development of police cultures can be employed to promote best practice, through
transparency and accountability rather than secrecy and exclusion.

Cop culture?

It has been said of the culture of police work that it is predetermined by how police
officers view their social world and their roles within it. From a police perspective
this translates into questions of what is *'real'* policing, and the wider functions and
utility law enforcement.

Recently there has been some debate about whether a *police personality* exists.[1] Police organisations are dynamic and disparate despite the traditional demographic biases observed in their composition, which does not reflect the diversity of Australian society. The vibrant but conservative organisational culture of police services throughout Australia, while sharing essentially common values, norms, craft rules, and perspectives on justice informing the conduct of police work, also contains significant subcultures which maintain their own value structures in particular contexts.

Commissioner Fitzgerald[2] suggested that in their civilian lives most police share the same diverse interests, pleasures, standards, aspirations, problems, and faults as the bulk of their fellow citizens. At the same time, however, he suspected that as an organisational or occupational grouping police officers collectively form a strong bonded and separate social group with a unique culture. This culture of policing, for him implied that the occupation is essentially one with distinct values and norms at the organisational and individual level. Fitzgerald further speculated that these shared norms fostered and developed within a *brotherhood* which was often antipathetic to accountability and reforms.

Reiner argued that there are dangers involved of talking of police occupational culture as monolithic. For him the nature of police work and those involved in it are historically and socially variable. Reiner conceded that the culture of police— the values, norms, perspectives, and craft rules—are not monolithic, universal or without change. For him cultures of police work vary contextually while at the same time containing commonalties of outlook and attitude. These commonalties not only influence the nature of policing itself but also impact on the self-image of police officers and in so doing can stimulate both legitimate and illegitimate police practice. Further, Reiner identified cop-cultural characteristics as including:

- the tension between the ranks' sense of mission and their cynicism
- a hedonistic action orientation and the valourisation of masculinity
- isolation from society at large, but internal cohesiveness as a work unit
- an attitude of constant suspiciousness
- moral and political conservatism including prejudicial attitudes towards ethnic minorities, and
- an emphasis on pragmatism and police common sense which discourages innovation and experimentation.[3]

Among these traits the so-called *siege mentality* and *code of silence* have often been linked with the concealment and proliferation of police misconduct. Of all of these, cynicism appears to be a substantial element of the everyday attitude of individual police. This cynicism is more emergent throughout Australia as a negative

---

1 For a critique of cop culture as a monolithic notion see Chan (1997). For a discussion of definitions and characteristics of police culture see Dixon (1999), chapter 5.

2 Fitzgerald (1989).

3 Reiner (2000).

response to the realities of community policing and police operational policy. Further cynicism stems from the way in which the police perceive their power and its potential for exercise. While being endowed with significant powers over citizens, the police may perceive themselves as alienated from other structures of social control and access to them. Such limits on access tend to stimulate in the mind of the police a need to exceed or abuse power for the purposes of their own organisation. Fitzgerald recognised these reactions may be as much motivated by the police view of *noble cause* and a distrust of other forms of legitimate power and authority, as they may be by individual or institutional malpractice.

Reiner suggested that police cynicism, or what he refers to as 'unmitigated pessimism', can be extremely destructive in terms of the attitude of individual police officers towards their role, their functions, and their values. Conversely, cynicism often acts as a defence mechanism or 'is functionally analogous to the role of humour as a tension release'. Reiner envisaged the police as developing a thick skin and a tendency towards bitterness as a consequence of social isolation. Such isolation, as with all closed communities, breeds solidarity and solidarity in turn fosters secrecy and an inward-looking culture.

Cultures of masculinity and danger

Symbolically, cop culture and its prevailing masculinity are a function of the constant need for survival (individual and organisational, real and perceived) and the perception of prevailing threat. Solidarity within particular and defined limits is constructed around mutual reliance and the expectation of unquestioning support for survival and against threat. Threats can be about physical safety and challenges to authority, both being connected. The former is the most potent as a cultural consolidator in a culture such as policing where recourse to force is feared and revered. An example of police imaginings of threat (and its unreality) is the argument often presented by male police officers against women in the service. It is said that a female partner will not be able to respond as effectively against the threat of force as a male counterpart. The argument implies that such threats are constant, and the assumed deficiency of female police when security is challenged therefore is taken as a universal critique of their place within police culture.

The perception by police that they work under dangerous, unpredictable, and alienating conditions produces a reactive, sometimes negative foundation for the creation of occupational culture. Fitzgerald pointed out that police culture operates to the detriment of the disciplined service in a situation where cynicism, threat, and unquestioning solidarity are the argued and preferred response. The so-called 'police code' has in Fitzgerald's view helped produce forms of malpractice such as *verballing*[4] which flourishes in an atmosphere where wrongdoers are protected from detection and prosecution. This protection often goes beyond the ambiguous condoning of compromised behaviours and translates into a positive reinforcement for illegitimate practice when it is seen as supporting the prevailing interests of police codes. Fitzgerald's report also found that such a culture can extend to an atmosphere of contempt for criminal justice, disdain for the law, and a rejection of its application to police involving a disregard for the truth and abuse of authority. Fitzgerald emphasised that the 'unwritten police code' was a critical factor in the degeneration of police integrity.

Cultures within culture

The Fitzgerald explanation of cop culture reflects wider theories of subcultural criminality and differential association.[5] Despite the homogeneous and deterministic conception of cop culture promoted by critics such as Fitzgerald, which would have the police insulated from external environments, the reality is that the police throughout Australia have recently been exposed to environmental change and specific reform strategies.[6] These strategies have targeted recidivist culture and the malpractice that it has generated. At the same time remnants of police occupational culture as a powerful atmosphere for malpractice remain.

The *garrison* self-image of policing has made it difficult for reform which argues for individuality, accountability, and diversity to have a lasting influence on policing in Australia.[7] The significance of cynicism and suspicion, the climate of self-preservation, the morality of mateship, and the celebration of specialisation, has produced an attitude within policing that works against change.

Dixon[8] argued organisational codes of conduct and practice, and other police rules, while attempting to create a competing cultural consensus for policing, are 'open-textured and subject to interpretation'.[9] Because they are subject to discretion these normative frameworks do little to counteract problematic police cultures. In fact they may, if drafted in terms which are seen by their constituency as unrealistic or inaccessible, become a rallying point to endorse the occupational credibility of the competing counter-culture. Dixon concluded that normative

---

4   A practice where police fabricate evidence by alleging that an accused person or a witness has made admission or confessions to police, not usually confirmed by any independent record. See Fitzgerald (1989), pp. 206–7.
5   See Vold, G. & Bernard, T. (2001), *Theoretical Criminology*, Oxford University Press, New York, chapters 11 & 12.
6   See Dixon (1999).
7   See Dixon (1999), chapter 6.
8   (1999), chapter 4.
9   p. 97.

assaults on cop culture might only succeed if they are designed to produce a 'comprehensive reconstitution of the normative structure of policing by means of a review of current laws, rules and instructions'.[10]

A sense of mission

Police operational strategies to some extent add to the intransigence of cop culture. For instance, stereotyping in criminal investigation is an essential component of the process of definition and interpretation when police act as the front line in crime control. Through stereotyping the police designate potential encounters as dangerous, disorderly, disrespectful, or unpredictable.

Reiner viewed as an essential element of police culture the *sense of mission*. In this respect policing is *not just a job but a way of life*[11]. This chapter will examine the manner in which policing as a way of life represents individual and organisational attitudes to policing in Australia. Further, in the face of challenges to a monolithic culture and one which resists social change, the reality of police malpractice and the efforts at police reform will be touched upon.

What influences cop culture?

Chan in her discussion of multicultural policing and police racism[12] expanded on Bourdieu's[13] distinction between field (a social space of conflict and competition) and habitus (cultural knowledge), when re-examining the place of police culture. She suggested that changes in the field (i.e. in the formal rules and structures governing policing):

> inevitably alter the way policing is carried out since habitus interacts with the field but the resulting practice may or may not be substantially or even discernibly changed...It may be that it is easier to tighten the law (at least as it is 'in the books') than to change police culture but both can be unpredictable. Moreover, changing the field can be just as difficult as changing the habitus when the distribution of power and resources is the target of change.[14]

The creation of a police occupational culture is affected by individual, collective, and organisational variables. These include:

• individual personality

---

10   Dixon (1999), p. 97.
11   In police vernacular, policing is commonly referred to as 'the job'. Reiner (2000), chapter 6.
12   Chan (1997), chapter 4.
13   Bourdieu, P. (1990), *In Other Words: Essays Towards a Reflexive Sociology*, Polity Press, Cambridge.
14   Chan (1997), p. 92.

- the rank structure
- lines of responsibility
- career trajectory
- social isolation (both community and organisational)
- shared interpretations and values
- collective mythology
- 'enemy' stereotyping
- public and media expectations
- obsession with professionalism, and
- dichotomies inherent in policing.

Recent studies examining the relationship between police and ethnic communities in Australia have evaluated whether personal (individual) or institutional bias and racism predetermines the collective response of police to particular characteristics and challenges of policing ethnic communities. Chan[15] interpreted policing in a multicultural society as affected by police racism and attitudes to minority groups. It might be said that police racism, for example, only reflects the racist values held by a sector of the community in Australia which may be seen as sharing the wider values of cop culture and its interests. A problem with this interpretation, however, is that community policing intends state police to represent more than simply *the silent majority*, whether this is the case in practice or not. Police racism may be generated from, and evidenced by:

- an insensitivity to language and cultural difference
- prejudice and stereotyping
- over-policing—unfair targeting and harassment of minorities
- the abuse of power and the excessive use of force, and
- a distorted attitude to certain minority groups.

The example of police racism as characteristic of police culture indicates the way in which such cultural predispositions influence police work. Racism will lead to discrimination in policing. This in turn may reinforce the connection between social disadvantage, offending, and over-policing through discretionary and selective law enforcement, stimulated by discriminatory police stereotyping. American studies indicate that economic deprivation is strongly associated with the diminished regulatory capacity of a community which in turn has the strongest direct effect on delinquency.[16] Economic deprivation also has a significant direct effect on delinquency itself. Racial inequality and a concentration of underclass poverty in certain ghettos within cities influence the level of formal control exercised by agencies of the justice process such as the police. Add to this a personal or organisational predisposition against the groups concerned and over-policing will *confirm* the stereotyping directed towards minority groups by police.

---

15   Chan (1997).
16   See Braithwaite, J. (1979), *Inequality, Crime and Public Policy*, London, Routledge & Kegan Paul.

Institutional racism in policing is regularly demonstrated in Australia.[17] This can be witnessed as police carry out coercive, class-based, and *civilising* functions through intensive police operations in ethnic and minority communities in Australian cities.[18] In this respect racism can be seen as institutionalised oppression given the historical and structural positions of minority groups, especially Aboriginal people in Australian society. Of this Chan says: 'Inequality of power and opportunity is built into social and political institutions. Violence and abuses suffered by minorities have become part of life. Thus, while individual police officers may or may not be racially prejudiced they are inevitably part of the oppressive apparatus of the dominant classes of society. Examples of this type of interpretation can be found (in a number of government enquiry reports).'[19].

It is the institutionalisation of personal and operational prejudices such as racism, which produces a referential cycle that becomes the working personality of policing, wherein discrimination is seen as a legitimate determinant for the exercise of discretion. This takes the impact of police prejudice well beyond the predispositions of the individual and into the realm of a cultural characteristic, now unfortunately definitive of police work. Police may say that their survival depends on discrimination and selectivity. However, as the issue of police racism clearly demonstrates, this can be a smokescreen for the abuse of power centred around cultural prejudice.

Cop culture as a working personality

Cunneen[20] identified discretion and its selective exercise as the essential feature of police culture. He also established that police decision-making in all its occupational settings (from crime investigation to service provision) with a focus on discriminatory encounters, reveals the reality of the working personality. While the occupational culture of policing is complex, not monolithic nor immutable, this is a personality insulated from competing external influences and hence prone to rights abuses without much self-reflection.[21]

The working personality of police is more than an aggregation of individual personalities. Neyroud and Beckley have suggested that cultures of policing represent the following values which determine the working personality:[22]

• risk avoidance

---

17   See Cunneen (2001), chapter 2.
18   For an example of this in other contexts see Jefferson, T. (1991), 'Discrimination, Disadvantage and Police Work', in E. Cashmore & E. McLaughlin (eds), *Out of Order? Policing Black People*, Routledge, London; Brogden (1988).
19   (1997), p. 38.
20   (2001), chapter 6.
21   For a wider discussion of this theme see Neyroud & Beckley (2001), chapter 5.
22   (2001), pp. 80–1.

- comradeship
- search for positive policing outcomes
- professionalism
- opportunism, and
- community standing.

We would specify the last of these as the endless quest for respect within community identity.

Police culture is more than simply a reflection of the social or cultural background of individual police officers. The narrow socio-demographics of police organisations in Australia will obviously reflect and promote limitations of cultural experience and strains in cultural encounters. However, police culture is something which emerges from and moulds routine police work. It comprises informal occupational norms and values which exist within the strict ranks structure of the uniformed and disciplined service. In talking of the meaning of cop culture Manning[23] has identified these as including 'accepted practices, rules, and principles of conduct that are situationally applied and generalised rationales and beliefs'.[24] Skolnick[25] also has seen police culture as essentially the working personality of a police officer. Reiner too referred to the central feature of cop culture as the *sense of mission*, and this in turn gives legitimacy to the working personality. Police work influenced by such a culture becomes the preservation of a valued way of life. It is the *moralising* of the police mandate.[26] David Garland on institutions of punishment could have been commenting on police culture when he wrote about creating a 'sense of (its) own inevitability and the necessary rightness of the status quo'.[27] It is perhaps the settled, established and reproducing power relations on which the police working personality is founded that are self-confirming of it and tend to reproduce its legitimacy on a daily basis.

Grounding culture in a consideration of police work reduces the likelihood of discussing such culture in a rhetoric sense and requires that an analysis deals with actual self-image.[28] For instance, the inculcation of police pessimism about the operation of justice and their place within the community becomes the measurement of reality against which all *unreasonable* demands on police (even in terms of accountability and due process) can be considered. As mentioned earlier, the police themselves see the significance of cynicism and suspicion in terms of self-preservation and the need to stereotype. This for them is what criminal investigation, their pre-eminent and most imagined function, is all about.

---

23 Manning, P. (1977), *Police Work*, Massachusetts Institute of Technology Press, Cambridge, M.A., p. 143 refers to the 'core skills cognition and effect' which define 'good police work'.
24 Manning (1977), p. 360.
25 Skolnick (1966).
26 Mawby (2002), pp. 54–5 referred to this tendency as a natural reaction to diversity.
27 Garland, D. (1990), *Punishment and Modern Society*, Clarendon Press, Oxford, p. 3.
28 Mawby (2002), chapters 7 & 8.

Some have argued that police are not unique in having developed a distinctive culture particularly in closed and hierarchical occupations.[29] What makes police culture different is the manner in which it influences the exercise of considerable discretion-based power (see chapter 7). Another distinction from other forms of occupational culture is the fact that cop culture on the street may significantly differ from, or may be significantly opposed to management cop culture.[30] One may see the value of the past and the importance of comradeship against the management view of professionalism and procedural change.

As Chan suggested there are 'several assumptions implicit in most discussions about the police occupational culture: that there is a close relationship between the demands of police work and the existence of the culture; that the culture is relatively stable and uniform over time; and that the culture has a negative influence on police practice'.[31] The demands directed towards police work from a variety of quarters and interests no doubt exacerbate the intransigence of cop culture. These include:

- the necessity and encouragement of peer group solidarity
- conflict between the job as a profession (learnt) and a craft (trade skills)
- isolation within the criminal-justice process
- discretion as institutionalised within the law requiring constructions of attitudes about law and order (such as the reasonable police officer)
- internalised interpretations of who is policed and for whom, and
- a reliance on stereotyping within the investigation process which mutually reinforces the process and its meanings.

The 'them and us' mentality

One of the negative features of a police working personality is the overdevelopment of a commitment to solidarity in a climate of community isolation. This isolation exists police against the public, rank against rank, uniformed police versus plain clothes, operational police against management, and the individual officer against the organisation of policing.

Isolation in policing is exacerbated by the failure to address difficulties in translating the ideology of community policing into practice. At the heart of this are unrealistic expectations about policing and a misunderstanding of the place that police should rightly claim within diverse communities.

A way out of this problem is to recognise that police authority rests in community consensus rather than through the fear of force or external legal or state legit-

---

29 See Van Maanen, J. (1978), 'Kinsmen in Repose: Occupational Perspectives of Patrolmen', in P. Manning & J. Van Maanen (eds), *Policing: A View From the Street*, Goodyear, Santa Monica.

30 For a discussion of police managerial culture see Mawby (2002), pp. 28–36.

31 Chan (1997), p. 44.

imation. Authority, and indeed police efficiency, rests in community-consented respect. It is relationships of trust that underpin any successful police–community exchange. It is the activation of this trust in a climate of respect and consent that will tend to diminish police reliance on old stereotypes in culture. In addition, isolation which is amplified through distortion and stereotyping will diminish as the police confront the diversity of community interest and community needs. So long as the police choose to distance themselves from meaningful contact in the community then segregation, isolation and distortion will be a reactionary feature of cop culture.

Reintegrating police cultures

A homogeneous and determinist concept of cop culture, insulated as it is from external environmental pressures, may be considered to leave little scope for cultural change. This is not the way writers such as Dixon and Chan would have it portrayed. Recent reform strategies both within and external to state policing agencies throughout Australia (see chapter 12) have targeted the revision and recasting of police culture.

Brodgen and Shearing[32] suggest two ways in which 'orthodox' solutions for change in cop culture might be advanced: by *taking the police to the community*, and by *bringing the community to the police*. Further, they suggest that if cop culture is subject to continuing encounters with community sensibilities it is liable to undergo a positive modification. The significance of involving the community in partnership relationships in policing and de-emphasising the traditional police preoccupation with random patrols, fast car responses, and retrospective criminal investigation is implicit in any such shift. The effect of this is likely to improve police efficiency and lead to openness and accountability.

Attempts at the social reintegration of the police back into resistant communities will not come easily. An initially negative reaction to more transparent and engaged policing is to be anticipated in any strategy for reintegration when tried in the tougher community settings.

In the face of charges regarding corruption the police in New South Wales, Victoria, Western Australia and Queensland have recently attempted to clean up their image. Part of this has been a move towards merit-based promotion, away from the old system where officers moved up the ranks as a reward for years of loyal service. Radical organisational change has also been employed to break down resistant cultures and questionable work practices. Through the localisation of commands and through regionalisation, the specialist units have been broken down in an attempt to diversify the 'hot spots' for temptation and opportunities for

---

32   Brogden & Shearing (1993).

malpractice (such as drug law enforcement and criminal intelligence bureaus).[33] There has been a conscious expansion of the welfare and service function in policing, and specific attempts to address negative attitudes to the policing of domestic violence. In addition, the police have taken a more active involvement in law reform as they see it complementing police priorities.

Even so, the organisational impediments to social reintegration for police include:

- the disciplined service
- an antagonism individually and organisationally to accountability
- competing ideologies
- disproportionate allocations of police resources to areas of specialisation
- undebated police priorities, and external agenda setting
- stereotyping
- artificial social contract concepts of the community in community policing policy
- social imbalances in the demographics of policing
- institutional suspicions of other agencies and criminal justice, and
- failures in the diversification of police education and training.

Perception is essential in any consideration of culture and its recasting. Popular images of police and policing (see chapter 11) tend to distort police self-image and foster police conservatism. Many popular representations endorse the rogue-cop image (such as Dirty Harry), the male hero image (with its celebrations of violence and machismo), the preference for pragmatism over obedience to the law, and the inherent prejudice in policing through racism and sexism. Therefore the process of reintegration for police culture needs to be both actual and perceptual. In this a conscious redevelopment of police popular images is important as a context for reform.

Representing police malpractice

The relationship between police malpractice and cop culture is all about the creation of opportunity for deviant activity, and impediments to its disclosure. In a closed occupational culture such as police work, one in which the operational and individual ethic may at times differ from the procedures governing police work and the law that they enforce, such dilemmas will create situations where deviance may occur, may be condoned, its consequences neutralised, and its discovery unlikely.

Certain theories about malpractice tend to incorporate or ignore the significance of cop culture as a facilitating context. These include:

- the 'rotten apple' explanation for individual police deviance (where deviance as an organisational characteristic is normalised by identifying and exposing individuals rather than the systemic sites for opportunity)

---

33 Organisational change such as this can be short-lived and cyclical when police specialisation and the use of elite squads becomes a political issue.

- functional explanations of deviance (the latent result of trying to prosecute unenforceable or victimless crimes)
- opportunity explanations of deviance (where individual and organisational invitations are created through the nature and process of police work)
- occupational explanations (through such things as learning to be deviant and choosing to associate with those who are), and
- structural explanations of deviance (the consequence of suppressed or illegal and monopolistic markets as well as unbalanced regulation in which the police play a prominent part).

These explanations arise from a variety of situations in which police malpractice may occur. This malpractice may take the form of an abuse of power, extra-legal policing activities, violations of the law, or illegitimate or unjust results through the distortion of police power and its regulation.

Relationships between malpractice and cop culture are most clearly seen as:

- peer group support for occupational deviance and the rationalisation of rule violation
- distinguishing the nature of malpractice, being individual financial reward, individual self indulgence, or consequences directed towards specific interpretations of police priorities, and
- socialisation to malpractice through occupational experience.

Changing police culture

Unfortunately most representations of the solid, supportive and inward-looking police culture would paint it as negative and opposed to the legitimate priorities of police work. This is an oversimplification and fails to recognise the manner in which these cultural characteristics can also be used for good police work. In addition, the negative representations of police culture gloss over a variety of subcultures which have within them many positive characteristics, and may be required in order that particular police functions are achieved.

It is important, however, to convince the police along with the public that their working personality, and police cultures more generally, should be applied *to best practice policing*. Some ways of doing this would include:

1. **Recruitment.** Through affirmative action, positive discrimination, and a range of community-sensitive techniques the social demographics of policing should be opened up on the levels of age, gender, race, sexuality, education, and experience in order that the police, as a community, should better reflect the diversity in Australian society.

2. **Training**. While training standards throughout state-sponsored police organisations in Australia have improve markedly in recent years, they have also tended to narrow their realm of specialisation. For instance, fascination with management and organisational learning is a feature of police training programs. There is a need to raise the standard of education and training in policing as much in broad areas

of social understanding and critical analysis as is the case with the learning of spe-cialised skills. If the education experience is fostered outside police institutions it exposes the police to a range of knowledge and social encounters which is good for broadening the culture.

3. **Community policing.** Through an integrated approach to community policing where there is a greater emphasis on community and police interaction, police iso-lation will break down and the siege mentality essential for present police culture will dissipate.

4. **Special education on cultural change.** Police, through the exercise of signif-icant power, control a wide variety of community experience in Australia. It is nec-essary for the police, who may not emerge from a background which has otherwise understood community diversity, to be confronted specifically with community-sensitive priorities. An example of this is the gender issue at the heart of domestic violence.

Conclusion

In her detailed longitudinal study of police-recruit development in New South Wales, Chan[34] observed that a deeper understanding of the police socialisation process was required in order to understand the construction of police cultures. This socialisation process is more unpredictable than in the past, as a result of the changing social and political context of policing in contemporary Australia.

Through a variety of specific strategies, police organisations face the challenge of adapting culture to agendas for reform. The need for such reform to be compre-hensive and long-lasting is a substantial challenge to the individual officer and the police organisation, particularly in a conservative political environment of com-promise and concealment (see chapter 12). Deep-rooted operational culture needs to be confronted and redirected. As Chan and others have demonstrated, the coin-cidence of external and internal pressures for cultural change can be the stimulus for such cultural transformation.

An additional complication is that this cultural reform must occur on at least two levels simultaneously. The operational and ethical judgments of the individual officer must be influenced, along with the organisational decisions and decision-making frameworks of the institution. While the exercising of police discretion needs to be flexible and adaptive to complement the needs of diverse multicultural communities, it must also be governed by universal expectations for transparency and a fundamental acceptance of human-rights obligations. Finally, communities need to be involved in supporting and rewarding the transformation of the police working personality.[35]

---

34 Chan, J. (2001), 'Negotiating the Field: New Observations on the Making of Police Officers', *Australian and New Zealand Journal of Criminology*, vol. 34, no. 2, pp. 114–33.

Additional readings

For full reference details refer to the bibliography.

Reiner (2000), chapter 3.

Brogden (1988), chapter 2.

Barker & Carter (1994), chapters 1, 4, 5, 6, & 15.

Dixon (1999), chapters 1 & 6.

Klockars (1985), chapter 4.

Fitzgerald (1980), chapter 7.

Brereton & Ede, 'The Police Code of Silence in Queensland: The Impact of the Fitzgerald Inquiry Report', *Current Issues in Criminal Justice*, vol. 8, no. 2, pp. 107–129.

Chan (1997), chapters 4 & 10.

Chan (2001), 'Negotiating the Field: New Observations on the Making of Police Officers', *Australian and New Zealand Journal of Criminology*, vol. 34, no. 2, pp. 114–33.

Shearing (1995), 'Transforming the Culture of Policing: Thoughts from South Africa', *Australian and New Zealand Journal of Criminology* (special issue), pp. 54–61.

Dixon (1995), 'Change in Policing: Changing Police', *Australian and New Zealand Journal of Criminology* (special issue), pp. 62–6.

Manning & Redlinger (1977), pp. 279–310.

Brown (1998), 'The Royal Commission into the NSW Police Service: Process Corruption and the Limits on Judicial Reflexivity', *Current Issues in Criminal Justice*, vol. 9, no. 3, pp. 228–40.

Palmer (1992), 'Controlling Corruption', in Moir & Eijkman, chapter 4.

Wood (1997), vol. 1, chapters 2, 4, 5 & 6.

Shearing (1981).

Miller et al. (1997), chapters 7 & 9.

Bolen (1997).

---

35   See Neyroud & Beckley (2001), Part 2.

9

Policing Social Divisions

Introduction

Policing as a process of social differentiation comes with the territory of law enforcement. The notion of selective enforcement, which is generally accepted as essential for the efficient operation of criminal justice, relies on the discretionary exercise of police power usually based on determinations of respect and consensus. The disrespectful or the disobedient will be treated by the police in different ways from those who present as deferential and accommodating. Policing, therefore, can be seen as relying on and reinforcing the most obvious and visible indicators and determinants of social difference. They may also be the most problematic, loaded and conjectural.

This chapter goes beyond an exploration of the divisiveness of policing. It interrogates whether community[1] division and diverse communities also have an impact on the nature of selective law enforcement and service delivery.

Policing diversity, division and divisiveness?

Brogden confronts policing in society as having the potential for social division.[2] He suggests that a historical examination of the development of policing in

---

1   In this chapter, perhaps more than any other, we are mindful of the dangers of generalising or abstracting the notion of community. While a consistent application of the term is challenged by its diverse representations, it is useful at least to recognise that in this book the community is an actual, living, and dynamic entity. As Cohen (1985), p. 117 observed, nostalgic or entirely positive images of community are dangerous. Equally we are wary not to assume that policing is the same community to community.
2   Brogden (1988), chapter 6.

modern Western societies such as Australia shows a broad class bias in the form of police attention, albeit one mediated in particular ways. The mediation and concentration of police attention can be examined around the general socio-demographics of age, gender, race, class and sexual preference. These headings will locate the following brief examination of the potential for socially divisive police work. In particular, we will interrogate the importance of stereotyping among the techniques of social division, and use the examples of *Asian crime waves* as a case study.

It is important at the outset of an inquiry into policing social divisions that this consequence of police practice be deconstructed. At a superficial level, it may mean little more than recognition of the diversity of police work, and the essence of policing diversity. Earlier, we have emphasised that in Australian communities, cultural variance, and the spread of age and gender have meant that community policing is a complex endeavour (chapter 3). There can be no single form of polic-ing which adequately satisfies the expectations of a diverse community, or addresses the divisions which tend to stretch community consensus.

More than diversity, however, policing social division might be seen as a proc-ess for celebrating difference. Policing is about differentiating groups within society on the basis of public order, criminality, deviance, and often just plain difference. Police criminal-investigation practice works on the premise that difference is an initial indicator for police interest.[3] Suspects and offender populations are consid-ered to be physically, psychologically and experientially different from the law-abiding community, and thus visibly recognised as the *other*. Simple determinants of threats to police respect and public order are synonymous for police with fea-tures of age, gender, ethnicity, appearance, language, recreational preferences, and association. It is not coincidental that the relationship between police and young ethnic males in major urban centres in Australia is strained.[4] Police–Aboriginal relations in Australia have always been antagonistic and the police will often adopt condescending or stereotypical tones when dealing with women either as victims or in the rarest situations as offenders.[5] This is all about difference and the power of the police to declare it.

Along with diversity and differentiation is the suggestion that policing is essentially divisive. This implies that within the process of differentiation, the police will employ discriminatory agendas and frameworks in order to construct and maintain social difference. Further than this, the police may be accused of

---

3   Racial descriptors (such as 'Asian' or 'of Middle Eastern appearance') used by the New South Wales police in the face of their prohibition in national police guidelines are an obvious example of crude stereo-types regarding physical and cultural difference.
4   See Collins et al. (2000).
5   For an examination of the relationship between police and indigenous women see Gardiner, G. & Taka-gaki, T. (2002), 'Indigenous Women and the Police in Victoria: Patterns of Offending and Victimisation in the 1900s, *Current Issues in Criminal Justice*, vol. 13, no. 3, pp. 301–21.

forcing divisions within society. Private-sector policing, with its profit motive and its reliance on corporate interest, divides the propertied from those without sufficient capital or private property. Sometimes, police practice tends to support one side of the community against another in a most obvious and apparent way. Policing Aboriginal communities has often been criticised as a process whereby the interests of the white community are preserved against the interests of indigenous people. Certainly, policing youth in Australia is an exercise in maintaining the morality and interests of the older generation against the preferences and the recreation of the young. Policing sexuality, until recently in Australia, has championed heterosexuality against homosexual culture. Women, particularly as victims and in situations of domestic violence, have been typecast by police often in terms of their own domestic and sexual experience so as to render women powerless or unworthy of police protection.

Unfortunately, it is not difficult to expose policing social division as much more than just a recognition of diversity. Stereotyping and differentiation in policing goes well beyond the necessities of investigative practice. This is perhaps because the morality and culture on which policing relies tends to be discriminatory and to reflect the prejudices of white, middle-class, Australian society, and policing itself either as a public or a private-sector exercise often divides Australian societies down these lines. A reason why police prejudice more than general public prejudice is so damaging relates to the discretionary power with which the police can materialise discrimination. Recently, there have been some encouraging examples of where police have recognised this potential and against it have participated in reintegrative strategies in order to rehabilitate their presence within the wider communities.[6] If community policing in Australia is to become a process for reintegration and reconciliation, then it may be necessary to address the role of police in maintaining social divisions as well as the essential divisions of policing culture.

Social divisions confronting policing

As mentioned earlier, the main social divisions within the community enabling differential policing include:
- age
- gender
- race
- class
- sexuality, and
- selective and structural unemployment in terms of contemporary socio-economic discrimination.

---

6   See the role of police in restorative justice.

Each of these indicators forms a frame of reference for policing the community and community policing. They are obvious and consistent discriminators in all communities throughout Australia and, therefore, present important uniform qualifiers for police work and the behaviour of police individually and collectively. Each indicator, also, has been identified in contemporary Australian debate as an arena wherein discrimination may focus. Policing, as part of the process of discrimination, may endorse and enhance wider themes of discrimination throughout Australian society and give them real bite.[7]

Age

When confronting age in the context of policing social divisions, it is usually youth that is the concern.[8] Also, with age and gender, connections between these indicators represent more clearly the issue at hand whether it be social threats or the generation of crime fears. So, in the case of age and gender, the police focus their attention on young males, who are deemed to represent challenges to public order and to police respect. Police also take part in representing the threat posed by young males as most significant for women and the elderly. In fact, violence committed by young males is most likely to be directed against other young males.

Public space is an important territory for the young in Australia.[9] In particular, otherwise marginalised young males colonise public space either as a preferred territory for communication or recreation, or because they are excluded through policing and other forms of regulation from communal private space. It is also the communal use of public space which tends to exaggerate the representation of threat in terms of these discriminators. It is in public space where police and youth come into contact. The interface between the police and young males within public space has always been a site for struggle, as both the police and youth seek to establish boundaries of occupation and safety.

For young females, police have conventionally enforced morality which would see young women removed from public spaces for welfare motivations. Up until recently in most Australian jurisdictions, public-order legislation throughout Australia enabled police to remove young women from public space if it was deemed that their presence there placed them in moral danger. Today, homeless youth and young women who find their occupation on the streets as an escape from abusive domestic relationships or through their connections with drug abuse, regularly come into contact with police and their welfare services.

Encounters between police and young people also tend to evidence the inextricable connection between police and penalty.[10] Police–youth relations throughout

---

7 It would be wrong to leave the reader with the view that policing is the major irresponsible social discriminator in Australia. Public policing in the exercise of discrimination is far more accountable than biased media campaigns and irresponsible and racist political leadership.

8 White & Alder (1994).

9 Cunneen & White (2002), chapter 9.

10 Blagg, H. & Wilke, M. (1995), *Young People and Police Powers*, Australian Youth Foundation, Sydney.

Australia have recently relied upon interventions such as police cautioning, whereby the police take responsibility for many of the justice determinations which, for adults, would be in the hands of other agencies such as the courts. While police cautioning is seen by some as an example of society's preference for a welfare-based justice approach to juvenile offenders, others are concerned at the proliferation of police cautioning because of the power it gives police in situations where young people are uniquely different and particularly powerless. More recently police have adopted an active role in restorative justice interventions for juveniles such as family group conferences. With cautioning and some methods of conferencing the police have adopted a central position which sees the police function moving well beyond its conventional investigatory concerns towards mediation of penalty and conciliation of community interests.

In the policing of legitimate recreation, largely through licensing, the police also have an important role when it comes to differentiating the status and privileges, or otherwise, of young people. Many of the recreational environments for youth in Australia depend through licensing on approval and legitimation by the police. In some instances, the police, in fact, are responsible for differentiating those youths who may be allowed to participate in certain recreational activities while others are not. The use of motor vehicles, access to licensed premises, access to entertainment venues, and the determination of appropriate recreational drug use are examples of where the police maintain the boundaries between enjoyment and exclusion.

It is neither unique to Australia or to this social moment that generation gaps exist in communities between the young and the not so young. Police tend to represent the morality of adults when policing the behaviour of youth. Police, therefore, maintain the generation gap on behalf of the *silent majority* as they see it. In certain communities it is the view of the older generation which is sought out and publicised by the police often against the 'social threat' by young people in those communities. This has a tendency to alienate young people within their communities more than might be the case if the young and the old were required to mediate their understandings and disputes without the differentiation of policing.

As with domestic violence in Australia, concerns about child abuse have become a recent and potent inclusion in the policing function. Understanding and controlling domestic violence in large measure rests on the confidence of victims and others to report occasions of abuse. Such reports often are delivered first to the police and, in this respect, the reaction of the police to child victims in particular, is crucial for further intervention and successful prosecution.

As fathers and mothers, police officers carry with them into their engagement with young people their own morality about families and communities and the place of children within them. It is necessary for the police to appreciate children and young people are victims of violence, intimidation and harassment, as well as posing threats to social order and police consensus.

Gender

The masculinity of police culture means that encounters between male police and women may be unduly influenced by stereotypes and sexism.[11] Sexist police encounters with women will not be sufficiently militated against by police culture until police communities exist in a more gender-balanced state.

Women as offenders within crime and the criminal-justice process are rare. It has been said that, as a consequence of this, the criminal-justice process and the police in particular tended to treat female offenders either as bad or mad. This tends to produce a reverse sexism when the police approach female offenders. With an increasing involvement of women in violent offences, particularly in retaliation to abusive relations, police have been required to reassess their attitude to women and the context of their violent behaviour. Womens' victimisation and policing throughout Australia could not be understood in a contemporary context without appreciating the revolution in policing domestic violence. Until recently, many police took the view that the domestic environment (and private space) was no place for public policing. In addition, many male police experienced violent behaviour in their own domestic environments and were familiar with abused women in a domestic setting. Male domination and the occasional violent conse-quences of this were, for many male and female police, the natural order of things. This meant that it was even more difficult for women to assert their rights and require the police to act on their behalf in protecting their interests in a domestic setting.

The other inhibitor against a constructive, sympathetic and interventionist form of policing in the context of domestic violence was the notion that such vio-lence was not *real crime* and therefore did not create situations of *real policing*. It was only when police accepted that the majority of serious assaults and resultant hom-icides were a by-product of violent domestic relationships that the importance of domestic violence as a crime became clear. The government, women's groups, and police administrations were required to engage in re-education campaigns directed towards the understanding by police of the consequences of domestic violence in Australia. These campaigns, though hard to initiate, have generally seen a reap-praisal by police of their role in the control of domestic violence.

Another difficulty in convincing police to intervene in domestic violence situ-ations was the initially limited outcomes for them when such intervention took place. In particular, if successful prosecutions were the measure of a positive domestic violence outcome, then the police and prosecutors would need to rely on the courage of the victim-witness in order to achieve convictions. Unfortunately, the situation for many women was one of crucial dependency where they then

---

11   There is a deep history of this in Australian policing, particularly as it relates to the regulation of public morality. See Summers, A. (2002), *Damned Whores or God's Police*, 2nd edn, Penguin Books, Camberwell; Allen, J. (1987), 'Policing Since 1880: Some Questions of Sex', in Finnane, chapter 9.

believed that they could not afford to be without the support of violent partners. The cycle of fear and domination in which women victims found themselves was exacerbated by their own history of victimisation in abusive relationships, as well as the subjugative status of many Australian women. The police, on the other hand, would expect that female complainants would retain their commitment to prosecution right up to the date of the trial. Evidence of a reluctance on the part of women victims to continue in the prosecution process only produced a negative interpretation by many police who would then choose to punish this by a reluctance to intervene in further complaints. The creation of new intervention options available to the police and the victims (such as domestic violence orders) has tended to sensitise police to the situation of women in violent domestic relations and to broaden their attitude to appropriate policing in such situations.

Domestic violence tends to produce a range of stereotypes both for offenders and victims, which may be counter-productive to just outcomes. In certain situations, the nature of policing and the discriminatory views evidenced through the way police do business in domestic violence may only further discriminate against those who should be most reliant on police protection. The nature of the domestic setting and domestic relationships tend to cloud concepts of accountability both from a police and a community perspective which expects intervention in violent domestic settings. With police powers so heavily reliant on discretion, in areas such as domestic violence the personal prejudices of male police may tend to see discretion used in the manner which perpetuates the domination and subjugation so apparent in many violent domestic settings.

Racial divisions and ethnicity

When discussing policing histories in Australia (chapter 2), we touched upon the destructive reality of police–Aboriginal relations. Throughout Australia, police continue to exacerbate this reality through negative police encounters. The Aboriginal community, whether it be urban or rural, is unlikely to consider state police as engaging in police work on their behalf. In particular, young Aboriginal males and females, so heavily discriminated against in the criminal-justice process generally, find discrimination a constant feature of their dealings with the police.

Policing race in Australia, particularly when it relates to indigenous people, provides an interesting example of where the principal social discriminators touched on in this chapter interrelate. For instance, policing public space and young people presents a context in which the addition of a racial dimension increases the potential for policing to be divisive and discriminatory. In rural Australia in particular, Aboriginal people engage in recreation activity in public space. This may involve alcohol consumption and bring the individuals into contact with police over public-order issues. The visibility of indigenous people in public space, and their inability to access private-space alternatives, means that they are more likely to be the objects of police attention.[12]

Add to this police stereotyping in relation to indigenous people and alcohol consumption, and the selective and discriminatory nature of police encounters become apparent. Whether it is policing domestic violence in Aboriginal communities, or the regulation of public order and liquor licensing, police often demonstrate a tendency to be condescending and confrontational in their encounters. Police are less likely to caution young Aboriginal males and females for minor offences. These Aboriginal youths are less likely to have access to restorative justice alternatives and, due to the fact that a far greater number of Aboriginal juveniles have custodial histories, they are likely to be confined in police cells rather than to being given the benefit of bail. All these issues tend to conspire to produce a climate of discrimination and differentiation.

Recently, the debate in Australia regarding policing has tended to highlight other dimensions of police racism. Popular wisdom about Asian crime waves and ethnic crime gangs accord with police stereotyping and endorse police popular wisdom. Even the language of police investigation with its general references to Asian or Middle Eastern appearance descriptors ignores the ethnic and cultural complexity of Australian society for the sake of endorsing crude racial stereotypes.[13] These stereotypes then become the basis for policing practice as they directly challenge the operational reality of community policing.

In Australian cities, the apparent connection between certain cultural groups and drug trafficking forms the basis of policing operational practice. Members of Asian and Middle Eastern communities are rarely represented in Australian police services so positive association between the police and such community members is less likely and a more sensitive understanding of cultural and ethnic difference more difficult for police organisations to achieve. Differences in language, dress, appearance, and cultural predisposition tend to challenge uniform notions held by the police of *other* communities.[14] The masculine culture of policing with its associations and connections to certain forms of recreation, styles of language and particular family and domestic structures and histories means that police will feel more isolated and exposed in certain ethnic communities. This isolation and exposure increases the tendency among police to see ethnic or racial difference as an indicator of potential disrespect, a breakdown of consensus, and challenges to law enforcement. There may be something in these reservations when one reflects on the fact that many ethnic communities have a traditional aversion to the policing agencies of the states from whence they

---

12   Cunneen (2001), chapters 4 & 8.

13   Poynting, S. (2002), 'Bin Laden in the Suburbs: Attacks on Arab and Muslim Australians Before and After 11 September', *Current Issues in Criminal Justice*, vol. 14, no. 1, pp. 43–64.

14   Chan, J. (1994), 'Policing Youth in 'Ethnic' Communities: Is Community Policing the Answer?' in White & Alder.

came. However, there is never enough in these *cultures of disrespect* aversions to construct police–community relations. Police in Australia, therefore, carry the odour of negative encounters in other cultural settings and jurisdictions, but tend to reconstruct this into contemporary operational imperatives.

Organisational racism exists within most police services and styles in Australia. This is not limited to police–Aboriginal relations. Recent comments by senior police in Australia concerning crime and ethnicity, tend to demonstrate the ignorance or narrowness of police interpretations about the causes of crime as they relate to cultural difference. While it may be true that particular forms of violence seem to be more prevalent among certain groups within particular communities in Australia, it is misleading to see a causal connection between this and cultural or ethnic difference.[15] For instance, gang violence in certain Australian cities may occur when different groups of young males join together around ethnic symbols and come into contact with each other in ghetto environments. Yet these 'gangs' may be as much alienated from their cultural origins and communities as they are from the morality represented by police. It could be that young males such as these come together under ethnic symbols to which they relate no more than they would to American styles of dress and the demeanour determined by violent television or cinema. Therefore, in some respects, the ethnic communities from which these groups emerge may exhibit forms of alienation against their young people, simply taken up and exploited by styles of policing.

Class

Again, the historical origins of policing, particularly in the United Kingdom, were directed against working-class recreation and the public-space occupations of the unemployed. During the later stages of the Industrial Revolution, civil police in England, for instance, were stationed in certain sections of major cities, which were largely populated by what became known to the police as the *dangerous classes*.[16] Where these groups intersected with the activities and interests of the propertied classes, the police became a buffer to prevent any social unrest and tension which may have been generated. In addition, the police were blatantly employed to regulate the labour force for the benefit of capitalist economics. Policing the workforce is an area in which the early police were active and where they still tend to take a high profile. When this is incorporated with challenges to public space such as at the time of industrial unrest, then clashes between police and the working class are regular and constant.

In the early days of state policing, police both individually and organisationally may have been seen as class traitors working against, as they did, populations and

15   A recent report on crime and ethnicity in Australia advances issues such as unemployment and social marginalisation, features of urban ethnic ghettoes, as more significant explainers of youth deviance. See Mukherjee, S. (1999), 'Ethnicity and Crime' *AIC Trends and Issues*, no. 117.
16   See Silver (1967).

communities with which individual police officers would have greater association and more in common than those whose interests policing supported. In contemporary Australian society, police are also involved more and more with policing worklessness. Structural unemployment is the long-term lot of many young people in Australia. The relationship between unemployment and crime through social disorganisation and marginalisation is clear[17]. While structural unemployment and the rejection of conventional employment protection is a feature of modern labour-based economics, the negative social consequences of such social policy become the unfortunate responsibility of the police through consequential challenges to public order, drug abuse, and juvenile delinquency.

The association in Australia between particular forms of drug abuse, and worklessness has brought about a new class of repeat offender, and stereotyped suspects with whom the police have regular contact. This tends to further reinforce police attitudes to social morality as the *work ethic morality* which police themselves believe they exhibit, value and need to protect.

Unfortunately, the recognition by police of those determinants in society, which may be impossible to change without major structural alteration in the economies of Australian society, means that the real appreciation of crime and disorder seem to be beyond the operational understanding of the police community.

It is worth recognising that a number of socio-demographics causally connected with crime are more prevalent among the poor and the marginalised. Structural unemployment, low educational attainment, dysfunctional family histories, domestic violence, drug abuse, and custodial histories are characteristic of class division particularly in modern urban environments.[18] While there may be considerable debate about the criminogenic influences of poverty[19] and family breakdown[20] the connection between criminal and class division on a measure of economic advantage/disadvantage is hard to deny.

The apocryphal connection between crime and poverty is one explanation for histories of over-policing the poor and the socially disadvantaged. In this respect it is important to note migrant and indigenous communities in Australian society that bear the burden from over-policing have a high proportion of their members in what would be seen as the lower classes.

Sexuality

Gay liberation in Australia since the 1960s has meant that the homosexual community has become a powerful political force in Australian society. This has brought about a sea change in the policing of public morality in particular

17   Findlay (1999), chapter 2.
18   See Findlay (1999), chapters 3, 7 & 4.
19   Braithwaite, J. (1979), *Inequality, Crime and Public Policy*, Routledge & Kegan Paul, London.
20   Weatherburn, D. & Lind, B. (2001), *Offender Prone Communities: An Epidemiological Approach*, Cambridge University Press, Cambridge.

throughout Australia. Whereas more than a decade ago events such as the gay Mardi Gras in Sydney were the objects of confrontational policing, we now see the police organising public order and traffic regulations for such events in conjunction with the gay community. Recent initiatives by the gay community to protect their members against homophobic violence have also seen the cooperation of state police. Now it is common in most state police services to have gay liaison Officers charged with the responsibility of transmitting the expectation of the gay community into policing priorities, and making police themselves more aware of the needs and potential of the gay community.

The emancipation of gay communities demonstrates another important feature of the policing social division continuum. Essential for the maintenance of social divisions and the role of the police with it is the existence of social marginalisation. To this extent society is responsible through marginalisation for the divisions which the police police. As marginalisation is replaced with inclusion (and the development of rights and responsibilities associated with such transition) policing moves away from being divisive and the new constituency is given legitimate claims on police protection and support.

Even so, it would be incorrect to suggest that the homophobia which once characterised policing is a thing of the past. Macho police culture has little time for sensitivity when it comes to appreciating sexual preference difference.[21] While the politics of policing may require a degree of equanimity in policing gay communities, police themselves have a way to go in embracing more liberal recognition of cultural diversity in Australia at this level.

Stereotyping Asian crime

The suggestions which are advanced by certain media commentators in Australia that we are in the grip of an Asian crime wave present a picture of crime and expectations for policing which are instructive when looking at policing social divisions. The stereotyping of Asian crime, particularly as it relates to drug-law enforcement,[22] tends to feed off and promote the distortion of Asian communities and *Asianness* in a variety of settings.

The stereotyping of Asian crime advances a distortion of Asians as a homogeneous threat to Australia. The White Australia policy of the 1950s and 1960s provides a deep foundation for this distortion and apprehension in the white Australia psyche. By justifying reservations about the Asian community in terms of crime

---

21 Sharpe, A. (2002), 'Policing the Transgender/Violence Relation', *Current Issues in Criminal Justice*, vol. 13, no. 3, pp. 269–85.

22 For a discussion of racial stereotyping in the construction of drug-law enforcement policy within Asian communities see Maher, L. & Dixon, D. (2001), 'The Cost of Crackdowns: Policing Cabramatta's Heroin Market', *Current Issues in Criminal Justice*, vol. 13, no. 1, pp. 5–22.

and criminality, the police are able to build on the incipient racism against Asians widespread throughout Australia.

Recent interest among crime-control agencies in Australia about organised crime and drug trafficking perpetuates the Asian crime wave stereotype. It is not realised simply that certain drugs are produced and cultivated in Asia and, therefore, are imported into Australia through networks of Asian criminals where the economics of language, cultural similarity, and financial understanding means that the trade will be culturally specific. This is about conditions of enterprise rather than characteristics of culture. The economic reality of this is bypassed in an explanation which sees the drug trade as some form of Asian conspiracy and the nature of the exploitation inherent in drug trafficking as emerging from Asian cultural predispositions. This representation of foreign criminality introduced into Australia, also sits well with those who believe that the most serious crimes confronted by police today are *unAustralian*. The difference between the criminal activity of Asian Australians and wider fears held in the Australian community about specific crimes fuels the belief in an inherent connection between crime types and cultural origins. This, also, complements organised crime mythology promoted by policing organisations at institutions in Australia and overseas. For instance, organised drug crime is seen as gang-based, syndicated, and worldwide. Even the notion of gangs in Australian cities is now characterised as the province of particular ethnic communities. This ignores the historic reality that, at the turn of the last century, the gangs which terrorised Sydney and Melbourne came together around a range of general social determinants like religion, sport, urban territory, gambling, entertainment and other Anglo–Celtic cultural divisions.

This misunderstanding of the complexity of Asian communities encourages and is encouraged by the cult of difference. Stereotyping criminal activity as Asian, for instance, ignores the vast cultural differences which may exist between, say, Chinese and Vietnamese communities, which have been historically opposed to each other in their countries of origin. Australian Asian crime imagery completely ignores these realities.

By seeing organised crime and drug trafficking in particular as *Asian* rather than as an explicable style of trade-centred enterprise where identifiable trade links are preferred, renders the appreciation and policing of drug trafficking less effective. Misunderstanding the enterprise component of certain organised crime activity such as drug trafficking means that policing is distracted towards causal questions which may deny the supply and demand structure of this trade and its profit motive. In addition, concerns for ethnicity will deflect attention from the role that forms of regulation and policing may have when it comes to illicit drug commerce.

The *Asian crime wave* is sometimes masked by caveats that the Asian community at large is not criminal. It also glosses over those crime situations where Asian communities are uniquely victimised and often without the benefit of supportive and targeted policing. Therefore, similar to the interpretations of police corruption, a *rotten apple* theory of Asian crime is presented. This, however, coexists with associated pronouncements that the comparatively greater threat from this minority can only be understood in terms of ethnicity. The Asian crime-wave argument tends to associate crime control with immigration control and social engineering. Certain extreme political parties in Australia would have it that the inherent criminality of nominated cultures is an argument why they should not feature in our immigration strategy, or why the young male stereotype should be excluded on the basis of discriminatory measures.

As mentioned earlier this stereotyping further tends to deny the victimisation of certain Asian communities in Australia, along with the differential policing of their victimisation. For instance, the opportunistic nature of some crimes perpetrated against Asian communities (such as loan sharking in the Korean community) reduces the possibility of policing having a significant impact towards the safety and comfort of these communities. And poor relations between the community and the police, along with language and cultural barriers, will exacerbate the problems for effective policing. This may, therefore, promote the attitude that the community itself needs to take the law into its own hands in order to ensure its protection.

The nature of urban development in Australia and the consequence of immigration policy through waves of ethnic migrations has seen the development of cities in which ghetto communities intersect and violence among the young in those communities is a problem. This may have far less to do with the ethnic origins of these communities than with the nature of urbanisation and immigration policy, as well as consequent social marginalisation.

While Australia sees itself as an international crime destination and the crime problem is being globalised, Asian crime takes on an even greater threat in policing terms. The assumption is that Asian crime is the same in Australia as elsewhere and, therefore, the techniques adopted by other countries in its control should be translated without adaptation. Again, this tends to depreciate the cultural uniqueness of our community and the significance of multiculturalism for effective community-based policing.

The following identify the manner in which policing exacerbates Asian crime stereotypes:

1. Policing operates from an ill-informed popular bias regarding the threat of Asian crime, and the correlation between crime and ethnicity.
2. It specialises its reaction to the crime threat through a taskforce response where ethnicity is a discriminator and cultural difference is seen as criminal.
3. It perpetuates the notion of law-abiding communities under siege (from without and within).
4. It fuels a racist media image (for example, the recent observation of the Federal Police Commissioner in which he talked about 'particular sorts of people living in particular places, prone to particular crime').

5.   It fails to confront the non-ethnic or cultural characteristics of Asian communities which are criminogenic. These include unemployment, under-servicing
and marginalisation.

The example of policing Asian crime waves and the distortion through crude
stereotyping highlights the manner in which police culture and operational practice are imperatives in the division of Australian society. It also reveals the way in
which demonising a community has a powerful impact on policing community
fear, and the determination of risk.

Risk policing

A feature of modern operational policing is its mandate to regulate the unruly and
control the disorderly. To this extent policing is predictive of unrest and proactive
against perceived danger. The proactivity of policing advances the potential for
social division further into the realm of preparatory behaviours. The further subjugation of marginalised groups in society by police is justified by the risk they pose
along with the difference they represent.[23] The armoury of police powers has been
radically enhanced in Australia to confront the perceived risks posed by the young,
the mentally ill, the sexually aberrant, and the ethnically different. Risk is now the
justification, in an age of heightened community insecurity, for divisive policing
where once the presence of discrimination alone may have been justification for
police intervention.[24] Policing of this nature progresses beyond crime prevention
and into predictive social demarcation based on superficial and problematic measures of risk, by a front-line force ill-equipped to discriminate at such a level of complex social distinction.

Risk policing has the additional danger of making less likely what Bayley
advanced as a remedy for policing social divisions. Bayley[25] held out the potential
for a 'human rights based' approach in policing involving fairness, effectiveness
and openness to overcome tendencies towards social division. Yet risk motivations
in policing constructed in atmospheres of fear will provide just the justifications for
the denial of rights to marginalised suspects in situations where the police are
called upon to arbitrate over social safety.

Conclusion

In viewing the police as communities, their diversity also may produce both varied
and sometimes unpredictable policing responses. While in their more foundation

23   Ericson, R. & Haggerty, K. (1997), *Policing the Risk Society*, University of Toronto Press, Toronto.
24   In New South Wales law see the *Justice (Non-association and Place Restriction) Act* 2001.
25   Bayley, D. (2002), 'Policing Hate: What Can be Done', *Policing and Society*, vol. 12, no. 2, pp. 83–93.

forms, state-based police were largely comprised of young, fit, working-class males, this is not the case today. In recognising this, however, it would also be wrong to assume that the demographics of any police service reflect the age, gender, class, and ethnicity of the broad community; certainly not in Australia. The most obvious disparity is the gender of police officers. There has been significant success in moving away from single-sex policing in the state police organisations in Australia, however, gender balance is still a long way off. This is particularly the case in the higher ranks and in areas of police specialisation. While more women have entered police services in Australian jurisdictions, recent criticism by female police officers tends to suggest that macho culture prevails and works against job satisfaction and security for female police. Scratch the surface of any major police service in Australia and you will find discrimination and acceptance problems for officers coming from minority ethnic communities and from education and class experiences which are not well represented in the conventional police milieu. As our discussion of police culture in the preceding chapter established, the operational and vocational ethic which tends to bind police services is white, Anglo–Celtic, middle class and male. The culture does not sit well with diversity and change within the police service or as a feature of the communities in which state police in particular operate.

Additional readings

For full reference details refer to the bibliography.

Brogden (1989), chapter 8.

Chan (1997), chapters 1–3 & 5.

White & Alder (1994), chapters 6–8.

Crowther (2000), 'Thinking About the Underclass: Towards a Political Economy of Policing', *Theoretical Criminology*, vol. 4, no. 2, pp. 149–65.

NSW Anti-Discrimination Board (1982) *A Study of Street Offences by Aboriginals.*

Brittin (2000), 'Race and Policing: A Study of Police Custody', *British Journal of Criminology*, vol. 40, no 4, pp. 639–58.

NSW Law Reform Commission (1993), *People With Intellectual Disabilities and the Criminal Justice System: Policing Issues.*

Moir & Eijkman (1992), chapters 3, 9 & 10.

Hanmer, Radford & Stanko (1989), chapters 3 & 8.

Allen (1987), 'Policing Since 1800; Some Questions of Sex', in Finnane, chapter 9.

Prenzler (1995), 'Equal Opportunity and Policewomen in Australia', *Australian and New Zealand Journal of Criminology*, vol. 28, no. 3, pp. 258–77.

Burke (1994), 'Homosexuality as Deviance: The Case of the Gay Police Officer', *British Journal of Criminology*, vol. 24, no. 2, pp. 102–203.

Queensland Criminal Justice Commission (1993), 'Gender and Ethics in Policing', *Criminal Justice Commission Research Paper Series*, vol. 3, no. 3, pp. 1–8.

Heidensohn (1992), chapter 2 & 7.

Flynn (1982), 'Women as Criminal Justice Professionals: A Challenge to Change Tradition', in Rafter & Stanko.

Hunt (1990), 'The Logic of Sexism Among Police', *Women and Criminal Justice*, vol. 1, no. 2, pp. 3–30.

Walklate(1993), 'Policing by Women, with Women, for Women', *Policing*, vol 9, pp. 101–15.

Swivel (1991), 'Public Convenience, Public Nuisance: Criminological Perspectives on "The Beat"', *Current Issues in Criminal Justice*, vol. 3, no. 2, p. 237.

Baird (1997), 'Putting Police on Notice: A South Australian Police Study', in Mason Tomsen.

Allen (1990).

Police Professionalism

Introduction

Police services throughout Australia have identified professionalism as a significant corporate aspiration[1]. Police personnel individually seek recognition as professionals in order to ensure their status when confronting other professional groups within the criminal-justice system. An examination of the reality of police professionalism requires not only a consideration of what it means to be professional but also the manner in which police specialisation suggests a differential structure of professionalism within police services.

Traditionally, policing has been considered more a craft than a profession. Even the skill of criminal investigation has conventionally depended upon the involvement of external forensic personnel as well as specialists within the police service to analyse and explain crime scenes and crime scenarios[2]. Another field in which the police professional capacity has been challenged is in those jurisdictions where prosecution has been removed from the responsibility of police and given to specialist public prosecutors with legal qualifications.

State police services in particular now claim, through a specialist team approach in the exercise of principal policing functions, recognition as professionals and as a professional agency. This can be inferred from the development of the following:

1. The achievement of specialist scientific and forensic qualifications among police, and the institutional control by the police of forensic facilities and processes

---

1 For state-based police this is identified in strategic planning while private police are relying on training, certification and corporatisation.

2 In popular culture, this is how the private detective–superhero image incorporates the professional legitimacy of policing as both art and science.

2. The development of advanced intelligence techniques as well as information-gathering, incorporating modern and often complex information technologies
3. The employment of advanced crime-investigation techniques, such as crime mapping and 'hot-spot' policing
4. Cross-discipline team approaches to the exercise of specialist functions, particularly in areas of police investigation which have traditionally proved to be operationally insufficient (such as fraud)
5. Tertiary-level qualifications for police and graduate entry requirements[3]
6. A more sophisticated interaction with external agencies and experts which has been to some extent forced on conventional policing institutions by the emergence of new and powerful investigation–prosecution agencies
7. A hierarchy in the service and promotion based on expertise and not rank alone
8. The acceptance of complex measures of expertise and efficiency beyond conviction rates and the move towards proactive police practice.

Language of professionalism

Conventional policing ideologies (discussed in chapter 3) have developed a synthesis with the language of professionalism. For instance:

1. **Independence.** Through the claim to police independence, individual discretionary ability is recognised and relied upon. This stands against the position of the police as civil servants and officers in a disciplined service. Independence and autonomy are wider, recurrent themes within professionalism. However, for independence to appear convincing within police organisations it needs to be viewed as qualified. Distinctions are sometimes drawn between the administrative responsibility of police to government or to corporate employers as against their more universal law-enforcement functions.[4] Ministerial responsibility over policing and the separation of powers in democratic government make the analysis of police independence as a characteristic of professionalism, complex, and in a general-duties context, less than convincing.

2. **Responsibility to the community?** This is more than a question of the client focus of policing. It is argued by other professionals that they have grand and all-encompassing responsibilities to things such as the law, the courts, the preservation of life, and community welfare. By contrast, are the police simply an arm of government or is there some higher calling to which the police vocation might be seen as directed? Allied to this is the question of how police powers and police intervention might be directed towards the achievement of a higher occupational calling for the

---

3   The relationship between professionalism and education exposes a depth of tension in police culture over the pre-eminence of experiential knowledge (and the status measures it supports) and advancement on merit (which includes educational knowledge and attainment).

4   For a discussion of this relationship in the formalist legal discourse, see Lusher, J. (1981), *Report of the Commission of Inquiry into NSW Police Administration*, NSW Government Printer, Sydney.

police. Is the motivation for policing in the hands of the commissioner, politicians, the judiciary, the law at large, or the community? What is policing for?

3. **Authority.** Many professions claim their authority through the nature of their vocation, their ethical standing in the community, and the social value of the services they provide. Associated with this is a wider ascription to ethics which some professions expect to be worthy of respect and generating authority. The debate in policing is whether their authority is vested in original powers or is delegated from some source such as the Crown, the state, or the community itself. In addition, the reiteration of police authority is ultimately dependent on the consent of the communities. The construction of police authority, as with the authority of professions in general, raises the issue of accountability. If a profession is independent and benefiting from autonomous authority then how can it be made responsible to the communities in which it operates? For police, there is more intimate conflict between their immunity from executive control, and the supervision by superior officers as part of the disciplined service.

4. **Professionalism and specialisation.**

In the context of criminal-justice, professionalism is a comparative measure. The police work alongside lawyers and judges and would be alarmed at any suggestion that they are not part of a wider justice profession. Is it right therefore to measure the police in their claim for professionalism in similar terms to other criminal-justice professionals?

Theory of policing?

Professionalism for police is not only a novel claim but also one that can be viewed as part of the dynamic development of modern policing. Mawby identified the contemporary managerialist context predominating in policing organisations as promoting the push to professionalism. As part of the rationalist reconstruction of the public sector, consistent with conservative political theorising concerning bureaucracies, state policing has been consumed by public-sector management models which emphasise a transformational agenda triggered by:

- the appointment of professional managers held accountable for specific tasks, resources and results
- business-like operations management
- the setting of clear measurable standards and targets
- explicit costing activities
- development of performance indicators and league tables
- emphasis on outputs and results rather than processes
- rationalisation of purpose and scope of the organisation and the shedding of peripheral activities
- competitive environments—service contracts, client–contractor relationships, customer service

- reconfiguration of recipients and beneficiaries of public services as customers and consumers
- overhauling the working culture of organisations to improve productivity, and
- fragmentation—the monolithic state bureaucracy is replaced by local, flexible organisational configurations.[5]

Mawby also suggested that the intensification of media interest in policing in recent years and the compatible development of high-profile policing practices and personalities have meant that police *voices* and *processes of imagining* (self promotion) are engaging at a level of professionalism which previously was not a feature of police organisations.

To enhance notions of police professionalism it is right to search for occupational practice which is based on some systematic theory of policing. Today, that theory may locate in derivations of community-based policing. The degree to which occupational members, by virtue of their mastery of such a theory, are deemed by the community to have a distinctive authority on matters of practice should be a professional measure of police work. The degree to which the community affords the occupation legal control of its practice and institutions is implicit in the construction and maintenance of consensus on which policing relies. The interaction between the occupational members and their clients in policing as well as other professions should be governed by some explicit and binding notion of ethics and best practice. On this level at least police deviance and malpractice challenge any confirmation of police professionalism. The manner in which the culture of the occupation generally is a distinctive configuration centred on its importance to society through the services it provides (rather than through the satisfaction of a closed culture), and the respect for occupational members of that culture, again appears as a measure of police professionalism.

At the end of the day, for policing as with any other professional occupation, its identity relies on the management and dissemination of knowledge. Professions claim a monopoly over specialist knowledge as well as over the exercise of authority emerging out of such knowledge.

The meaning of professionalism

Cotterrell defines professionalisation as 'a process whereby producers of specialist knowledge and services seek to constitute and control the market for their expertise'.[6] Clearly in their role as the collectors, definers, maintainers, and disseminators of criminal-justice information, the police are able to enhance a specialist or

5   Mawby (2002), p. 29, summarising McLachlan, E. & Muri, K. (1997), 'The Future Lasts a Long Time: Public Police-Work and the Managerialist Paradox', in P. Francis et al. (eds), *Policing Futures: The Police, Law Enforcement and the Twenty First Century*, Macmillan, London, pp. 84–5.
6   Cotterrell, R. (1992), *The Sociology of Law*, Butterworths, London, pp. 194–200.

professional position by cordoning off crucial areas of knowledge[7]. Take, for example, the information produced through criminal investigation. Consistent with the essence of professionalism police investigators are able to:

1. Elevate their knowledge to the status of science
2. Neutralise competing and conflicting explanations of the social phenomenon which they investigate
3. Present themselves as the possessors of such knowledge, being disinterested, independent and objective regarding its use and outcome
4. Generate increased demand for services associated with this knowledge as a unique and specialist skill.

Particularly within criminal justice, the professions and professionalism, however, can no longer expect uncritical support from all communities, if in fact they ever could. Recent disillusionment with the legal and medical professions in Australia suggests how a critical community context for the operation of professions may produce tendencies to attack the status of the professional. Such attacks will be stimulated by:

- public alienation
- obvious divergence between the rules and practice of a profession
- breaches of ethics
- increasing social costs attendant on professional practice
- failure to address immediate social needs by the profession
- attacks generated from within the profession, and
- attacks from other professionals.

Law and justice professions in Australia have been recently criticised for their elitism and self-interest. Further, a lack of real accountability, particularly in terms of legitimate community expectations, also alienates these professions. And with groups such as the police, where the benefits of their practice may be unknown as a consequence of their negativity to transparency, then the tendency to criticise their general social utility is recurrent.

The social status and broad utility of professions relies on the continued construction of dependence. For policing it might be the participation of the police in the generation of fear concerning crime being evidence of the construction of dependence throughout the community[8].

As we will later discuss under the heading of reform (chapter 12), Australia has recently witnessed various processes of rehabilitating the image of the police as professionals. Specialisation and police services and the increased emphasis on the social utility of policing have played a crucial role in this rehabilitation of image.

---

7   Hogg (1983).
8   Grobosky, P. (1995), 'Fear of Crime and Fear Reduction Strategies', *Current Issues in Criminal Justice*, vol. 7, no. 1, pp. 7–19.

What model of professionalism is relevant for the police?

The following are models particularly relevant for consideration against claims of police professionalism:

1. **Specialist knowledge model.** Here the police elevate their operational knowledge, through terminology such as *intelligence*, to the status of science. At the same time, within the criminal-justice process as a whole, knowledge becomes dependent on police operational practice and it is the police who create and control the knowledge about other aspects of criminal justice. Through this process the police can create and regulate increased demand for knowledge and services.

2. **Specialist skills model.** The police claim and promote a monopoly over criminal investigations. This requires a strict and status-oriented division of labour, particularly as far as the investigation goes. Recently, many police have developed a team-tasking approach to criminal investigation as well as accepting the need to interact with external agencies and experts. The particular skill and expertise of police investigators are now capable of external comparison through the acceptance by them of the relevance of tertiary qualifications.

3. **Specialist service model.** Since the identification of community policing as a central ideology for policing function in Australia, the significance of the community focus and its co-option into policing has reinforced claims for professionalism. The reliance on crime prevention and the advancement of proactive policing has tended to sophisticate and diversify the police vocation. Now that policing is integrated within other service dimensions and institutions, even beyond criminal justice, the reflected professional status back on to policing as an occupation is worthy of notice.

4. **Status model.** Status as a key to the evaluation of professionalism sits well with the concept of a disciplined service. Status also recognises the structure and sources of police authority. Status can be confirmed by the monopoly over the legitimate use of force, as well as the access police have to unique information sources. Finally, the status model identifies the essential importance of the police maintaining respect and consensus.

The development and marketing of police functions as a profession

The gradual shift away from *avocational* policing was clearly function-driven. The more the police became relied upon by the state and its agencies as a front-line social-control provider, and service deliverer, the more the need for policing as a vocation was galvanised. The same could be said about the growth of private contractual policing to complement the security and property needs of corporate communities. Regarding the conventional and original functions of state police, the concentration on prevention, public space and public order has given way in modern policing towards the specialised management of crime prevention and control technologies. Private police now share information technology and electronic funds transfer as well as patrolling property and regulating the workforce.

In many aspects of social regulation such as licensing, the police require control over time and space. Through these wide social regulation functions the police determine the fundamental rights of access by citizens to a wide array of services and benefits. In contrast, technologised policing may invade and challenge these rights.

The police have moved their function from the public to the private domain and now intervene into essential relationships. Their welfare function also sees them colonising other professional situations and provisions. Modern policing functions are essentially implemented and maintained as a factor of domain. The wider the police domain, the greater the claim to professionalism. Domain determines and delimits persons who become the subject of police attention and allows for the determination of professional space. However, as domain increases in its intangibility (such as across the Internet) police are forced to rely on the assistance of ancillary professions to achieve even conventional functions.

With the activation of police function affected by the police working personality it becomes essential to locate that personality within claims for professionalism. In order to convince the community that professionalism is a feature of policing, accountability is crucial.

To whom should police be accountable?

As discussed in chapter 7, accountability and policing can be viewed either institutionally or individually. In a structural sense state police have a line-management system which, in theory at least, invites a determined hierarchy of responsibility. Besides by media and community opinion, this in turn is regulated by laws, court decisions, and instructions and regulations. Within the system of policing there are a range of checks and balances on policing which emerge from this structure of line responsibility. Externally community expectations, media review, and bureaucratic motivations from other aspects of the criminal justice system provide opportunities for accountability. With private police, accountability issues are on a commercial footing and therefore more direct, privileged and transparent.

Notions of professionalism throughout Australia have become more dependent on effective structures of accountability. It is no longer sufficient, for instance, that doctors or lawyers retire behind their status, or expect review through professional associations to satisfy community demands for accountability. This is particularly so where professions are provided with authority and influence through the wider consent and respect of the community. With policing, consent and respect are essential, and therefore accountability becomes a foundation for these along with broader notions of professionalism.

The reality of professional accountability within policing is a matter regularly tested through the exercise of discretion. Discretion is crucial to the existence and operation of police power and provides the mechanism for authority to be endorsed. However, as with all discretion-based power in a democracy, it requires regulation, and the processes of accountability in policing established boundaries of permission for the exercise of discretionary power. Tolerance in this regard becomes the balance to power, and the context for authority.

When examining the relationship between accountability and police claims for professionalism there is some debate as to whether more or less discretion advances any such claim. On the one hand it might be said that binding rules of professional behaviour limit individual discretion. On the other hand, a feature expected of professions and professionals is that their special skills and knowledge put them in a position of trust where independent discretionary decision-making is acceptable and anticipated.

Like most things in policing, accountability as an indicator of professionalism goes back to an issue of balance. The responsible application of discretion, and openness as a context for its exercise, will mean that claims to professionalism by the police are easier to sustain more generally, and more convincing.

Identifiers of professionalism

Further in his discussion of the legal profession, Cotterrell distinguished professions from vocations or occupations. The following identifiers of professionalism provide additional measures when evaluating the reality of claims by police to professional status.

1. **Professionalism is all about guardianship**. The police represent themselves as the 'gatekeepers' to the criminal-justice process in that through law enforcement and the selective application of discretion, all later phases of criminal justice are dependent on police authority. Particularly in respect of public order and personal safety, as well as the maintenance of private property, the police could be seen as the front-line guardians of community interest. Further, the selective exercise of police discretion will identify the directions and limitations of police interest in community guardianship.

2. **A profession is for service**. In policing, the shift to a service function means much more than simply a change of name. It is a recognition that the significant majority of police functions and responsibilities relate to the provision of

community services. Problematic here are the interests which again designate the provision and nature of such service delivery, its direction, and who may lay claim to it.

3. **Professions rely on ethics.** In policing, the oath of office, and the ongoing dedication to law enforcement should mean that the ethical atmosphere of policing in Australia is unquestioned. However, police culture and the ambiguities present in selective law enforcement, mean that the ethics of policing can sometimes appear equivocal. If ethics are seen simply as part of the process of accountability and therefore designed to penalise malpractice alone, then the important relationship between professions and their ethical base will be misunderstood in policing. At least in an ideological sense the ethical base of professions is intended to inform the performance of their duties and to ensure these are done with a *best-practice* commitment.

4. **Professions have a monopoly over specialist knowledge and practice**. As mentioned earlier, the police are the producers, recorders, negotiators, and evaluators of criminal-justice knowledge. They control the meaning of crime and law enforcement in an official sense, and enable access to this meaning.

5. **Professions rely on self-regulation.** Much of the debate about police accountability pragmatically returns to the realisation that no mechanisms for reviewing police discretion will succeed without the goodwill of police organisations themselves. Therefore, with policing more than any other profession perhaps, regulation and accountability require an even-handed approach, incorporating external review and internal or self-regulation.

6. **Professions have a particular mandate.** With the police in Australia, community policing represents an integrated and co-optive mandate. Along with this, however, there exists a changing world of police functions. Political expectations for policing in particular require that police work be dynamic and responsive. Therefore, the mandate for policing, beyond general aspirations for personal safety, the protection of private property, and the maintenance of civil order, will always be socially and contextually relative.

7. **Professions generate status.** The reward of status delivered through the determination as a profession is even more significant in policing than most other vocations. This is because of the essential importance of community consensus generated through respect for police. In recent years, throughout Australia there has been a loss of public confidence in state policing and this has brought with it a reduction in public confidence, a deterioration of the status of policing as an occupation in the eyes of many within the community.[9]

---

9   Interestingly at a recent seminar on crime and ethnicity a representative of the Ethnic Communities Council explained as a reason why it was difficult to recruit law enforcement officers from their communities as being related to the perceived low status of the job.

8. **Professions are autonomous.** The ideology of state policing celebrates the individual independence of the police officer, as well as the organisational independence of policing from government. Whether this holds in practice is as problematic as with the claimed autonomy of many other professions.

9. **Professions control the market for their services.** The extent to which particular policing styles can control the market for their services depends on the nature of the market and the services to be provided. A feature of contemporary policing in Australia is the integration between private and public-sector policing in the provision of services, particularly for the private sector.

10. **Professions generate 'folk' concepts representing their organisational entity.** The mysticism of policing and its powerful prevailing ideologies give significant authority to police work.

11. **Professions exist within unified but stratified regimes of service delivery.** The strength of policing culture, and the diversity of policing functions, sit well with such characteristics.

It is said that a merging of client interests and public agendas is crucial to the conceptualisation of the profession as a social benefit. Associated with this are competing claims for privilege advanced by professions dependent on which interests their work reflects. For policing, there exist particular interests well beyond the notion of privilege associated with the status of being a profession.

Policing and professional interest

Cohen, in his discussion of criminal justice as a profession, explores the concept of expertise as it rests in the management and use of specialist knowledge[10]. The autonomy of criminal-justice professions in the exercise of power emerging from this specialist knowledge is an important determinant of their authority and its scope. For instance, the police through their power and ability to classify, stereotype, screen, select, and to diagnose the community in contact with criminal-justice rely on and reiterate a largely autonomous police authority. Further, the power of the police to intervene in the whole range of different criminal-justice situations and to exercise control, treatment, punishment, as well as a variety of other outcomes, strengthen police professional authority and the powers arising from it. The police are facilitators of criminal justice and in large measure determine the issues for debate regarding law and order and the reform process.

As initiators of the criminal-justice process, the police represent a significant professional class, while claiming to share and employ the cognitive systems of the wider society, and at the same time having a significant impact on the way in

---

10   (1985), chapter 5.

which those cognitive systems develop. Our discussion of policing diversity is evidence of this (see chapter 9).

Police as a profession enjoy the logic and the language of control. They are part of the management of what Cohen refers to as 'crisis talk'. Allied to this is the power of the police to determine the individual and process measures of success or efficiency in the early stages of criminal justice, as well as regulate the information flow which is applied to such measures. The ambiguity of criminal justice *facts* and measures of efficiency can be seen in the way in which the police use the crime rate either to justify successful operational policing, or at the same time to claim a need for greater resources.

Overall the police as a criminal-justice profession carry a predominant role in the process of crime classification and the maintenance of difference. They determine what is orderly and disorderly, who is criminal and who is not, and the circumstances in which deviant behaviour is allowed or regulated. As the primary profession in criminal justice the police are open to confrontation with other professional groups, and with their interpretation of how justice is to be ensured.

Professionalism in criminal justice: A struggle between professions

Criminal justice is clearly divided by professional participants and lay involvement. At all levels, criminal-justice professionals interact in either a cooperative or antagonistic environment while distancing themselves from the lay participants for whom the system is said to function[11].

The debate about whether criminal justice is a system or a process is well known[12]. What is beyond 'question relates to the significance of decision-making (individual and collective) in order that the process operates through its various stages[13]. This decision-making tends to be both exclusive and exclusionary. The language of criminal-justice decisions and the interpretation of evidence to support them are the province of the professional practitioner and rarely is the accused person, the witness or the victim able to penetrate the professional *club* which is made up of justice professionals.

Criminal justice is a continuum, predetermined by rules, and reliant on the exercise of professional discretion. Those professions who manage the rules, and their interaction, are influenced by competing realities of independence, competing client interests, and competing measures of success in the outcome of their

---

11   McBarnet, D. (1981), *Conviction: Law, the State and the Construction of Justice*, Macmillan, London.
12   Findlay (2001), Part 2.
13   Findlay (1999), chapter 4.

interventions. The police in particular have a well-determined view of their place in the process and often see themselves as separate from the *illegitimate* (as the police determine them to be), interests of all other professional participants.

The importance of delegation is a feature of police professionalism within the criminal-justice process. It is counterbalanced by the contest over accountability, and operationally evidenced through selective law enforcement. Therefore, the role of the police in criminal justice, as professionals, is heavily reliant on the exercise of discretion and the manner in which the police can manage claims over accountability.

Conclusion: A principled approach to criminal justice[14]

In his book *The Criminal Process* Andrew Ashworth[15] proposed a rights-based model for criminal justice.[16] The emphasis on rights in the determination of the justice process has an important meaning when evaluating the police as a profession. Should the police stand outside the process of protecting and ensuring rights in criminal justice (particularly if other professions do support the rights imperative) then this will challenge police professionalism. Neyroud and Beckley have suggested that the ultimate measure of the relevance of police ethics is their confluence with human rights protection. They offer out the opportunity for change and renewal of policing in the context of a rights-based ethical commitment on which its claims to professionalism can be argued, noting '...the negotiation of a new broader mission linked to human rights may offer policing a new basis for legitimacy and authority.'[17]

Inevitably this will lead to a reconsideration of the role of police within a system where the common language can only be professionalism, and where the acceptance of rights and access is crucial to such a classification.

A rights-based interpretation of criminal justice has important significance for the construction of ethical policing. In fact many of the debates about the protection of the rights of the accused in pre-trial and trial settings go back to appropriate policing practice. The challenge for policing is to recognise this in a positive fashion and to go forward to ensure that competing rights in criminal justice merit equal efforts at protection.

---

14 For a wider discussion of these themes see Edwards (1999), chapters 7 & 8.
15 (1994).
16 For policing, and in relation to ethical dilemmas this has been advanced by Neyroud & Beckley (2001), particularly Part 2 & chapter 11.
17 (2001), p. 17.

One of the fundamental themes of criminal justice is that the innocence of the accused is to be protected against wrongful conviction. Associated with this is the requirement for consistent treatment within declared policies of fair trial or a balanced investigation process. More recently the rights of victims for protection against harm have become more apparent and more persuasive within criminal justice. Even so, the push by police for a more *balanced* interpretation of investigation, prosecution and trial process will inevitably lead to a repositioning of these accused-based rights which are at the heart of conventional common-law criminal justice.[18]

General integrity in the operation of criminal justice also presents a rights dimension. Should the rights of the accused, the victim, and the system be recognised, through the exercise of integrity, then these will necessarily impact on, and be reflected in, our criminal-justice decision-making. In drawing the connection between ethics and best-practice, Goldsmith indicated in his study of police integrity (in the context of leadership and governance)[19] 'Police forces must become more transparently ethical at all levels as well as democratically accountable, so as to ensure a broad representation of interests in police decisions on matters affecting the integrity of police organisations.'[20]

The widest respect for rights is a potent performance indicator of the integrity of police practice. Police professionalism will enhance rights protection if it advances openness and ethical ascription at all levels of practice.

If the police are to join other criminal-justice professions in ensuring the advancement of legitimate rights within the criminal-justice process then the functional interdependence of criminal-justice professionalism, at the level of service, will become a feature of Australian policing in future.

Additional readings

For full reference details refer to the bibliography.

Brogden (1988), chapter 5.

Klockars (1985), chapter 4.

Cotterell (1992), chapter 6.

Kleinig (1996). Davids (1998), 'Shaping Public Perceptions of Police Integrity: Conflict of Interest Scenarios in Fictional Interpretations of Policing', *Current Issues in Criminal Justice*, vol. 9, no. 3, pp. 241–61.

Finnane (1994), chapters 7 & 8.

---

18 Reflect on reforms such as the abolition of the dock statement, restrictions on the right to silence, the institution of detention before charge, and the pressure on the defence to disclose prior to trial, which are all part of the police package against an accused-based interpretation of criminal-justice rights.

19 Goldsmith, A. (2001), 'The Pursuit of Police Integrity: Leadership and Governance Dimensions', *Current Issues in Criminal Justice*, vol. 13, no. 2, pp. 185–202.

20 Goldsmith (2001), p. 198.

Chan (1997), chapters 6 & 10.

Wood (1997), chapters 7 & 8.

Bayley (1994), chapters 7 & 8.

Lewis (1999), chapter 1.

Squires (1998), 'Cops and Customers: Consumerism and the Demand for Police Services', *Policing and Society*, vol. 8, no. 2, pp. 169–88.

Police and Popular
Culture

Introduction

The place of policing in popular culture essentially depends on two significant themes: processes of representation,[1] and the *entertainment* dimension of policing.[2] This chapter therefore is divided into a consideration of representations about policing (which will interrogate the relationship between the police and the media), and a discussion of the manner in which policing has assumed the status of entertainment iconography, and what this means for policing and its communities. These two parts inform each other insofar as representations of policing are vitally dependent on popular understandings of police work. These understandings, while being influenced by media representation, are more significantly dependent on entertainment imagery.[3] In addition, the entertainment value of policing is an important reason why the media dedicates so much of its attention to police activity.

Policing as a feature of popular culture also has influence over the development of police culture. As we indicated in chapter 8, cop culture is reliant on self-imagery and like others in the community police officers themselves create expectations about policing, its motivations, and the measures of the success of their work from media reporting as much as any other source.[4]

Film, television and paperback presentations of policing are dependent on fashions in popular culture. For instance, television shows about police may focus on the mystery of criminal investigation, conflicts of interest in small-town

---

1   For a wider discussion of the essence of representation in criminal justice see Findlay (1999), chapter 1.
2   This was the object of interesting analysis in Davids, C. (1998), ' Shaping Public Perceptions of Police Integrity: Conflict of Interest Scenarios in Fictional Interpretations of Policing', *Current Issues in Criminal Justice*, vol. 9, no. 3, pp. 241–61.
3   Sparks, R. (1992), *Television and the Drama of Crime*, Oxford University Press, Buckingham, chapter 6.
4   Mawby (2002), chapter 8.

policing, or on the personal relationships in the policing unit. The morality exhibited in media portrayals of policing is unique in that it overtly adopts the rhetoric of justice and can exhibit very simplistic, comic-style scenarios of the struggle of right against wrong. Whatever the purpose behind popular representations of policing, they say much about the positioning of police within their communities.

Representations of policing

In chapter 10, we discussed the manner in which the police represent themselves as professionals. Third-party representations of policing, heavily reliant on news and entertainment media, have a more ambiguous record when it comes to representing policing. This may be due to the fact that the intentions at the heart of such representations are dependent on the context in which the image may be created, and the audience for which it is intended. In any case, the representation of policing by the media is largely symbolic, and the language of representation demonstrates this constantly through the manner in which complex issues such as the use of force are reduced to black and white concerns.

In exploring representations of policing, as they are part of popular culture, it is necessary to go beyond impressions and even popular wisdom. This analysis of policing and its representation needs to examine relationships at the heart of image-making, such as the symbiotic connection between particular media outlets and police public-relations organs. Along with the consideration of such relationships, thought needs to be given to the significance of triggering events which transform representations of policing, and ignite the context in which such representations will be deemed credible. Later in this chapter we will look at media representations of police shootings as an example of the way in which a triggering event can compel the conclusion of a representation as positive or negative.

The relationships which formulate representations of policing in popular culture are dynamic even though they may rely on established and long-lasting institutional connections. For example, a newspaper police reporter may develop a cooperative and supportive working relationship with a police spokesperson, and yet the manner in which that reporter represents the official account of policing activities (from the mouth of the spokesperson) is not insulated from wider attitudes to policing which exist in popular culture at that time.

The police themselves are instrumental in creating popular-culture contexts for their representation and the marketing of their priorities. An example of this is the manner in which popular impressions determine climates of fear about crime and the inadequacies of law enforcement.[5] In addition, these popular

---

5   See Grabosky, P. (1995), 'Fear of Crime and Fear Reduction Strategies', *Current Issues in Criminal Justice*, vol. 7, no. 1, pp. 7–19; Gunter, B. (1987), *Television and the Fear of Crime*, John Libbey, London.

impressions may identify areas of risk within the community which suit policing operational objectives and support demands by police for resourcing to achieve those objectives.

Recently, law-and-order politics in New South Wales have meant that the representation of policing is determined by surrounding misleading political discourse, and media equivocation.[6] In such an atmosphere the police have found themselves caught up in crime-and-justice campaigning, where the interests of the police may be directly pitted against those of other criminal-justice professions such as the judiciary. The police have argued that the exercise of their legitimate function in the detection, apprehension, and prosecution of criminals has been made more difficult by the leniency of judicial officers. Media sources have been complicit in broadcasting this view to the public and creating an atmosphere in which wider criminal-justice objectives are balanced against the partial understandings and imperatives of the police organisation.

As the emphasis on crime and the fear of crime shifts in communities, or preferred explanations about crime and justice prevail in popular culture, the public sense of the reality of crime becomes dependent on those justice institutions with the closest and most effective relationships with media outlets. The police therefore can create their own representations of crime and justice, transfer these to preferred media outlets, and have some say in the way in which these images are translated into popular culture.[7]

Both the media and the police have interests in the representation of crime and justice within popular culture. Analysis of crime in context has the potential to unmask these interests and thereby challenge misconceived stories about crime by examining crime relationships in actual settings.[8] These settings, being actual communities themselves in states of change, mean that the context of crime in question is tangible and dynamic, not just represented and symbolic from a media voice. By appreciating the place of crime and justice within social change, and the influence of social change on the development of crime and crime control, the understanding of law enforcement and the police in particular will depend, more appropriately, on the contexts from which popular-culture representations of policing are grown.

Media representations of policing

The literature on crime, criminal justice, and the media, is replete with examples of the symbiotic relationship between the police and media forms.[9] The interde-

---

6 Hogg & Brown (1998), chapter 2.
7 For a discussion of the political savvy of police media units see Mawby (2002), chapter 6.
8 A study into policing riots achieved this. See Cunneen, Findlay, Lynch & Tupper (1989).
9 See Ericson, R., Baronek, P. & Chan, J. (1987), *Visualising Deviance: A Study of News Organisations*, University of Toronto Press, Toronto.

pendence between the police and the media impacts on the visualisation of deviance. For instance, the official account of a crime occurrence emanating from police sources can be translated down a tree of media sources and relationships whereby impression becomes fact and all other stories and accounts are excluded.[10] In their discussion of the media construction of public disorder, Cunneen et al. have chartered the manner in which television and newsprint methodology transformed an official police account from a wire service summary into a total-event scenario. The representations here, and the new meanings they presented for popular wisdom about the challenge to public order, were advanced and confirmed by the presentation in dramatic form of law-and-order images through television, newspaper headlines, and pictorials. These representations supported a range of conclusions complimentary of the police position. For example, the public-order challenge was a surprise, the police response was restrained, and the reaction of the crowd was unpredictable and dangerous in its collective form. In this respect Cunneen et al. questioned whose interest the news stories and media reporting served and went on to explore the manner in which the media was implicated in the process of public disorder and policing.

It is important to examine the presentation of the official account by police when considering the process of media–police interaction.[11] This is not about conspiracy theory, but rather an instance of where the police can control access to a news story in return for sympathetic representations. The media, on the other hand, is given easily digestible content, in return for representing a complimentary view on public-order policing. It appears in such circumstances that it is the role of the media to identify the policing issue. However, it may in reality be more likely that the police have determined the direction of media reporting.

Through the employment of the official account by the media it is not difficult for the police to reinforce their preferred self-image. In this process the media becomes compromised in the task of making a public institution such as the police accountable for the exercise of their powers. In addition, the media becomes the mechanism for broadcasting favourable representations of the police and making these visible through popular culture.

It might be said that the media and the police share realities when it comes to crime and law-enforcement. To some extent the media might argue that it is the social conception of its clients and the wider understanding of the community they service which determine representations of crime as rational, crimes as serious, crime scenes as dangerous, and cops as crime solvers. In fact, certain media outlets in Australia would confound this view by the campaigns in which they have engaged to the benefit or the detriment of the police in order to push a particular attitude to crime and justice.[12]

---

10   See Cunneen, Findlay, Lynch & Tupper (1989), chapter 6.
11   Burton, F. & Carlen, P. (1979), *Official Discourse: On Discourse Analysis, Government Publications, Ideology and the State*, Routledge & Kegan Paul, London.
12   See Mawby (2002), chapter 3.

Mawby[13] has identified the *staged media event* as a feature of modern police–media relations. Police press officers and *set-piece promotions* have now become an acceptable way in which the police can broadcast operational priorities and lay claim to successful strategies. In return the police grant the media concessional access to crime events and are not beyond creating representations and opportunities for the media to visualise crime and law-enforcement in an entertainment–news context.

The dangers associated with this relationship between the police and the media are not only that news is no longer objective and vulnerable to distortion. Also, the closer the media and the police are in the business of representing crime and law-enforcement, the more likely it will be that accountability will be mediated, communications between the police and the community will be mediated, and police–public encounters will rely on media reinterpretation for their reality. Mawby argues that:

> Face to face interaction involves the actors being present in the same place at the same time. Mediated interaction introduces a technical medium such as the telephone, email, or letter and the actors can be divided by space and time. … Mediated quasi-interaction is one directional, mono logical and oriented towards an indefinite range of potential participants. It is the type of interaction which involves watching television, listening to the radio and reading books and newspapers.[14]

For policing, this type of interaction, more than personal contact or individual experience, creates and translates the images about their work far more than the product of real operational relationships.

Marketing the police perspective: Media reporting on use of force

Police continue to shape the crime problem in the public imagination while the media supplies the public with the visualisation of deviance. This is particularly the case with television and radio reporting where television pictures are the community's window onto crime, and radio reporting is the voice of control responses. In this respect the media enables the many to see the few. First-hand understandings of crime within the community are rare and therefore issues such as victimisation, threat, fear, and retaliation are largely third-party constructs presented to the community through the media.

The symbiotic relationship between the police and the media is most clearly tested in the terrain of reporting police violence. While police continue to control

---

13   (2002).
14   Mawby (2002), pp. 73–4.

media access to stories about crime, this control will be at its greatest when the story relates to the police use of violence. The media, on the other hand, can manipulate public interpretations of crime and deviance, and in the case of the police use of force, media reports can carry justifications or condemnations. Rarely, if ever, will media accounts of police violence be equivocal. Even when such accounts are directed from a state perspective, police may be criticised if their actions stand well outside justifications by the law or the state for the exercise of force.

Media accounts of police shootings[15] move from one of two themes: (1) The killing is justified because of the crime allegedly committed by the victim or the dangerousness they represent. In this case, if there is criticism it will be of poor training, ineffective leadership, panic, or in some cases malevolence. (2) The force or violence represents a specialised police power. Criticisms in this context relate to structural failure (the wrong use of violence) or subcultural failure (a police sub-culture committed to the use of force).

The media tends to represent shootings by police as (1) self-defence or rough justice (and in this case, tends to support such an outcome), (2) individualistic behaviour by police officers (support here is provided by the police culture and to a limited extent, policing organisations), or (3) a structural problem (where the media may launch an individual or management critique).

Each of these representations possesses the potential to neutralise the consequence of the violence to the victim and its inherent dangers to the wider community against counterbalanced concerns provoked by the fear of crime and the necessity for tough responses to criminal violence. The role of the media in representations such as these moves well away from social commentary and into the realm of institutional apology. This response and the associated representations of violence will only shift when, as with the shooting of Ronald Levi on Bondi Beach in 1997, the officers involved are exposed as deviant, and significant community opinion challenges the necessity of the response. Here too, the context of the event, occurring as it did on one of Australia's most recognised tourist spots, highlights the community danger dimension and thereby makes the necessary justification more difficult to maintain.

Organising the spectacle: Media fascination with violence

Media representation of violence in general is problematic in contemporary society. When such violence emerges out of police practice the media faces the dilemma of sensationalising violent behaviours on the one hand and attempting to

---

15 It is instructive to compare such representations against actual categories of police shootings. See Harding, R. (1970), *Police Killings in Australia*, Penguin, Ringwood.

present a moral evaluation on the other. Overall it is common for the media to neutralise the significance of police violence through the use of comparative justifications such as self-defence, and the necessity of police operations. Even the nature of the violence and its context can be inverted by media reporting and the victims of violence invested with responsibility for the violent outcome. For instance, when deaths arise as a result of police vehicle pursuits, the media tends to focus on the dangerous behaviour of the victim driver. This is particularly the case in situations of joyriding where juveniles are seen as at fault. The inherently dangerous nature of the pursuit tends to be ignored, particularly when other media representations of appropriate police behaviour include fast cars and dangerous chases.

Tangentially, it is worth mentioning that much of the popular culture about policing in Australia is flavoured by American news reporting, reality-television broadcasting, and entertainment programming. Particularly when police use force, the apparent prevalence of violent encounters in American police work will influence the attitude of Australian communities as to the inevitability and appropriateness of police violence. Such misapprehensions are not countered by Australian police dramas which also have an unrealistic and excessive concentration on violence as entertainment.

The recognition by the police of media representations about their use of force as being both acceptable and justified, may have a reciprocal impact on police culture and its perpetuation of violence. Where police see themselves as driving fast cars in the process of apprehending dangerous suspects who themselves carry responsibility for the pursuit then the real danger inherent in the situation will not be brought home to the police involved. If a contrary interpretation was presented to them concerning potentially dangerous driving behaviours involving a risk to the safety of inconsiderate and inexperienced juvenile drivers, then perhaps their interpretation of their actions and consequences would be very different. Where is the role of the media in such a reality check? The image of the chase, which ranges from the comic to the sexy in entertainment contexts, is pregnant with justification for the police when imagining their relationship with violence. The pointless death of a young joyrider as a result of a high-speed police pursuit does not merit the same coverage.

The partial interpretations by police of dangerous force-centred scenarios is hard to counteract when the media, in its reporting of police violence, is reluctant to challenge the independence of the police or to insist on their accountability.

Media as control

It is unrealistic to anticipate that the media will provide an effective break on police malpractice if the media sources are so heavily implicated in the promotion of compromised representations regarding such behaviour. In addition, reporters and journalists will seem contrary should they on the one hand justify the excessive use of force by police while on the other calling into question the impact of external controls over police practice. However, this is just what is done in many cases. The media may shift the wide position of support to a position of criticism depending on public reaction and the production of new evidence in the description of police violence.

The media is responsible for systematic under-reporting or non-reporting of deaths and injuries arising out of police violence. The tragic history of Aboriginal deaths in custody throughout Australia, which preceded the establishment of royal commissions into the subject, is a catalogue of media failure to report a national disgrace.[16] Explanations for such under-reporting find root in the relationship between the police and the media, and the reluctance of reporters and journalists in general to threaten that relationship by championing an unpopular cause such as the custodial safety of Aboriginal suspects.

As mentioned earlier, the media is heavily reliant on the privileged accounts of state personnel such as police spokespeople. As the police themselves have proved reluctant to address candidly their responsibility for violence against citizens, the media has in turn preferred the official account as satisfaction of the problem. In this the media propagates the fault of the victim, focuses on the presumed danger of the situation, emphasises police force as last resort, identifies the inevitability of violence, and excuses the outcome in terms of mistake or misfortune.

The reason why it is appropriate to call the media into account when examining effective controls over the exercise of police violence is not only because of the mutual relationships between the police and the media. More significant is the manner in which film and television in particular rely on violence as a focus for entertainment. Because of this, it is both unlikely and improbable that the media will adopt and maintain a principled position in the regulation of the police use of force.

To understand the relationship between the police and the media, as well as the way this connection has a crucial impact on popular-culture representations of policing, the wider representations of policing and violence demand analysis. Television has recently indulged in *reality* programming where participation in police operations (often violent) is a staple. Policing series rely on homicide, sexual assault and assault, domestic violence, and personal injury as essential building blocks in story lines. Investigating police officers are represented as dedicating much of their time to hunting and chasing equally violent offenders. Police biographies celebrate the *rogue cop* who through the indiscriminate use of violence ekes out just results that the more professional institutions of justice are represented as incapable of attaining. The place of police in movies resonates with justice outside

---

16   See Cunneen (2001), chapter 9.

the law. Individual police win against the odds and their battle is not simply against crime but bureaucracy, institutional corruption, moribund legality, and the forces of evil. The human interest in many policing movies focuses on comradeship and celebrates cop culture as an alternative morality.

Police as the *authorised experts* on crime and justice

The media as a purveyor of perceptions about policing is often the willing tool of police image-makers. In modern police organisations police media liaison units tactically disseminate information about policing and police operations to media outlets in the form which will predetermine the media's treatment of the story. In addition, as mentioned previously, the police may invite preferred media commentators into their operations on the condition that the representations of police work in these instances is sympathetic and controlled. The wider relationship between politicians, the police and the media provides an opportunity for setting law-and-order agendas through staged broadcasting at times of particular public sensitivity such as during election campaigns.

The police, like any modern major organisation in the public or the private sector, employ proactive public relations as a justification for organised change and the resource and requirements that this may present. Following the recent Royal Commission into the New South Wales Police (the Wood Commission), for example, the then Police Commissioner used a variety of media set pieces to promote his policies for reform, and to attempt to turn the tide of public opinion which was then against the police. Reform agendas throughout Australian policing have historically demonstrated a primary public-relations motivation (see chapter 12).

The police in their connections with the media may establish and transfer a range of meanings associated with their work. Through the media the police can locate the causes of crime in simplistic and redeemable terms. Such representations of the causes of crime and its control are complemented by cinema and television diets of criminal investigation and detective stories. Television can create primary images about the causes of crime by focusing on suspects delivered to the courtroom and victims at crime scenes. Such pictorials have direct impact on the emotions of the community and tend to maintain non-problematic differentiations between good and evil, the police and the criminal.

One-dimensional views of crime and punishment support the images of policing that the media broadcasts in news commentary and entertainment. From the reliance on the first report of the official account in news broadcasts through to its reinterpretation in dramatic dialogue for a television series or a film, the police maintain an instrumental influence over the representations of both their lives and actions.

Police heroes: Machismo and the media

Moving from the news-reporting genre, popular-culture representations of policing in film, television, and the novel, focus heavily on the place of the hero. In the creation of the *rogue* cop, representations have an economy of imagery and meaning. In this style of popular-culture presentation, narrative and imagery imbue the hero with grandeur. There is a concern to dignify the hero through cop movies in particular, within a more complex narrative. That narrative focuses on struggles for justice where the law and due process are often portrayed as inadequate to the task. As a result, police are individualised as the last defence against crime as evil. In such cinema the representations of policing to some extent are constrained by reality and the need to locate the hero within recognisable contexts. Now however, these representations are so common they seem more real and recognisable than everyday experience.

The police as heroes to be convincing need to establish a *moral fit*. In this, subliminal representations of justice place the police hero above the law. The law is often external to his actions or resistant to his intentions. The hero is represented in relief, outside a corrupt or inefficient system. The vision of the hero is one which primarily addresses social and political frustrations with the criminal-justice process. The tone is often one that fluctuates from sophisticated and disillusioned scepticism to almost comic-book parody.

The representation of the individualised police officer in such a context is to some extent subservient to the celebration of heroic masculinity. He is an anti-establishment hero. He will always appear masculine, and the issue of gender goes beyond sexuality towards strength, courage, and daring. The creation and maintenance of the hero as the *star image* often is achieved through exaggerated masculinity, or masculinity in excess. The brave man representation is hyperbolised and represents a potent strain of resistance to establishment incapacity.

These heroic figures presuppose some failure of human social arrangements. They are often located in apocalyptic scenes which invite the superlative, while encouraging the viewer to barrack for the hero. However, at the same time the hero might be portrayed as an outcast, unattached to decaying or weakening social relationships.

Consistent with our earlier concerns is the place of violence in such representations. Violence has no separate or identifiable existence from the hero story and is regularly embedded in the narrative. Violence is not simply meaningless and is invested with an atheistic concern, at the same time laden with moralities.

Recently there has been considerable debate about the effect of such imagery on the behaviour of young males. Violence in the media and video games dominates young male entertainment in a constant and disturbing fashion. While there may be a denial of causality between such representations and the violence of a young male audience, there appears to be little doubt that either investing violence with moral significance or removing it from its more negative responsibility can tend to confuse those who see violent reactions as normal and appropriate.

Some would argue that in these representations of police there is a distinction between violence as a creator of fear and victimisation, and violence as a component of entertainment. The credibility or validity of screen violence remains dependent on the role of the police in such films or television series. The distinction between good and bad violence is important even in the entertainment setting. However, self-perceptions of violence by police will be distorted as they too, like others in the community, are regularly offered the suggestion that force is a preferred method to ensure justice rather than the systems and institutions of due process.

The entertainment value of these representations of policing is recognised by the constancy of this film and television product. The audience is engaged and enthralled through knowing the hero and enjoying with him the thrill, the risk-taking and the pleasure of violence. It is an example of experiencing third-hand what is forbidden in more regulated social life. The audience gives permission to the hero to engage in violence but to no-one else.

Representations of crime and violence: Where do the police sit?

Popular culture as demonstrated in film, television, radio, novels, comic strips, magazines, and the Internet, is fascinated with violence and disorder. Whether this ranges from international conflict through to lonely individual homicides, the focus on violence and disorder is disproportionate to its impact on communities.

Perhaps an explanation for this focus is the human desire to represent order through the exposure of disorder. Popular culture constitutes an active discourse about the ordering of activities of the people and agencies such as the police, who manage crime and law-enforcement. In this respect the media takes on a role of delineating through reporting, serialising, and dramatising the order of things, the procedures by which that order is accomplished, and the preferred organisational arrangements through which the procedures are invoked. The specific legal and policing provisions for the reproduction of social order, and the identity of human agents responsible for this reproduction is either critiqued in popular culture through anti-hero imagery or becomes the substance of political representations about preferred policing and law-enforcement methods.

News agencies and institutions help articulate morality and order through the sharing of tragedy. Violence and disorder is brought to the viewers' dinner table through television, and thereby the audience is able to face disorder and violence cinema-style. Generally the representation of the role of policing in these situations has police involved in the stability of meanings about order, and essentially responsible for combating disorder with which the viewer or the reader has no familiarity.

Crime as a challenge to institutional morality and order, as viewed through the media, becomes symbolic of the dangers of modern society. Police are shown as both eager and capable of confronting disorder and violence on behalf of a community, with force when necessary. In this respect the actual function of policing is distorted and the justifications for police in society become confused and unbalanced. The police themselves adopt such irregular notions of police function, and this can lead to their own dissatisfaction with the reality of police work. Flowing on from this, community encounters between the police and the public may be strained by a shared confusion and mutual disappointment which arises from the imbalance between popular-culture representations of policing and police work in practice.

Popular-culture representations of policing are now well established as part of a wider morality play about the consequences of violence and disorder. In this context the police play a facilitating role in maintaining social outrage, but also providing the lighter relief when policing becomes entertainment.

Conclusion

This chapter might be criticised as overstating the influence of the police on the media and understating influence in the opposite direction. It was a conscious intention not to portray the police as victims of media impression, and without responsibility when it comes to creating popular wisdom about policing. In any case, it seems that on issues of high media interest, the police may be no more likely to adopt media impressions of policing and criminal justice than others in the audience.

A more important project for this chapter was to explore the mutuality of interests in representations about crime and justice from the police and the media. The importance of a symbiosis between the police and the media in the creation of popular culture about policing is, of course, not simply in the province of these mutual interests. The manner in which the community responds to, or 'buys', these representations is also crucial for the perpetuation of police popular culture. Interestingly it would appear from Dowler's work[17] that positive personal contacts with police are as significant as hours in front of the television watching sympathetic representations of policing. It also appears that the relationship between citizen attitude to police effectiveness and the media is reciprocal. A sobering finding is that the greater the media consumption, the worse will be the citizen's appreciation of police effectiveness. The determinant of public confidence in the police as

17   Dowler, K. (2002), 'Media and Citizen Attitudes about Police', *Policing & Society*, vol. 12, no. 3, pp. 227–38.

individuals appears to be real community satisfaction levels rather than perceptions of effectiveness.

Additional readings

For full reference details refer to the bibliography.

Sparks (1996), 'Masculinity and Heroism in the Hollywood "Blockbuster"' *British Journal of Criminology*, vol. 36, no. 3, pp. 348–60.

Moir & Eijkman (1992); chapter 6.

Miller et al. (1997), chapter 8.

Ericson, Baranek & Chan (1991), chapter 4.+ Brown & Hogg (1996), 'Law and Order Commonsense', *Current Issues in Criminal Justice*, vol. 8, no. 2, pp. 175–91.

Hatty (1991), Police, crime and the Media: An Australian Tale, *International Journal of the Sociology of Law*, pp. 171–91.

Young (1996), chapter 4.

Smith (1992), 'Tabloid television', *Polemic*, vol. 3, no. 2, pp. 120–3.

Schlesinger and Tumber (1994), chapter 4.

Putnis (1996), 'Police–Media Relations: Issues and Trends', in Chappell & Wilson, chapter 11.+ Chan (1997), chapter 8.

Kasinsky (1994), 'Patrolling the Facts: Media, Cops and Crime in Barak.

Clarke (1986), 'This is Not the Boy Scouts: Television Police Series and Images of Law and Order', in Bennett, Mercer & Woollacott.

Sparks (1992), especially chapter 6.

Klockars (1980), 'The Dirty Harry problem', *The Annals* 452, pp. 33–47, reprinted in Klockars & Mastrofski.

Agendas for Reform: New Policing?

Introduction

In his article *Truth in Policing*[1] Sturgess asked why it is that police reform has become a political mantra throughout Australia, and how in fact police reform can be possible. As essential preconditions for reform he suggested that politicians, the community, the media, and the police hierarchy need to reach agreement about what it is that we want the police to do. In this context our considerations of both policing and reform are taken back to the first chapter of this book, with its reflections upon the idea of the police and normative expectations about policing.

Perhaps the most significant reform to police operations throughout Australia in recent decades has been the commitment to community-based policing, and the attendant focus on crime prevention (see chapter 3). These developments have been successful or otherwise, depending on the extent to which police are involved in the communities they serve. Police alone cannot stop crime. In order that crime prevention achieves its broadest aims, community responsibility for policing requires constant recognition and commitment.

Organisational reform focus

The discussion of police reform in Australia has, however, focused much more on structural and institutional change in police organisations, rather than strengthening police–community engagement. Royal commissions have detailed the revision of management strategies to overcome police misconduct, and to improve the

---

1   Sturgess, G. (1996), 'Truth in Policing', *Current Issues in Criminal Justice*, vol. 7, no. 3, pp. 382–7.

delivery of policing services.[2] Education has been identified as a way in which basic operational policing can be improved, and negative and limited police cultures may be broadened. The structure of the disciplined service has been identified as an impediment to reform, and its rehabilitation has been suggested through a 'bottom up' approach to police accountability and responsible management.

Regarding accountability, the problematic challenges of police reform in Australia are well identified (see chapter 7). Senior police managers have argued that their fundamental functions are thwarted by the incessant and burdensome requirements to be accountable across the community and government. While there are calls for more and more detailed rules requiring police accountability these are met with the argument that legal regulation provides an unnecessary brake on dynamic policing.

Dixon[3] has hope for the prospects of legal regulation as a tool for police reform provided that the law can:

- give clear expression to desired standards of conduct
- ensure effective training in order to modify police culture
- complement favourable political circumstances for reform
- enjoy the backing of effective sanctions for non-compliance, and
- rely on public knowledge of their rights and the limitations of police power.

Police reform depends on a community involved in the process, and knowledgeable about police powers and responsibilities (see chapter 1). The other side of this is that the police need to realise the exercise of their powers is not always ultimately justified in crime-control terms. In many respects, for the reform process to be more than window dressing, or a quest for the re-establishment of police legitimacy, the relationship between the police and the community, established as it must be on viable processes of accountability, is the essential context for reform.

There is a new tone in recent writing on police reform that speaks about the potency of a commitment to ethical standards, and *best-practice policing*.[4] Accepting that the context of policing Australia is changing, as are the challenges it confronts, for police to retain the respect of the community and its consensus about their claims for professionalism, clear ethical standards require enunciation in the language of police management (see chapter 10). These standards must be more than expressions of ideology, or normative aspiration, if they are to be adopted into policing practice. Police ethics need operational as well as moral legitimacy.

In addition to this, any new ethical underpinning for policing should recognise developments in the wider conceptualisation of criminal justice. Movements in police ethics should not be jurisdictionally bound. Today, for maximum relevance

---

2   For instance see Fitzgerald (1980); Lusher (1981); Wood (1997).
3   Dixon, D. (1996), 'Reform of Policing by Legal Regulation: International Experience in Criminal Investigation', *Current Issues in Criminal Justice*, vol. 7, no. 3, pp. 287–301.
4   See Neyroud & Beckley (2001).

these codes of conduct for police need to contemplate the emergence of an international criminal justice and the principles on which it is based.[5]

Human rights and their maintenance through the process of criminal justice have become an important paradigm in international criminal justice. Neyroud and Beckley argue that in an international atmosphere where human rights have been given clear standing by regional and international criminal-justice institutions, the police cannot fail but to be influenced by such developments. The consequence will be that police take a proactive role in the enhancement of their individual, organisational, and operational ethics, towards specific and more universal human-rights solutions. There should be nothing esoteric and detached about this aspiration. Rather, when it is presented in the context of *best-practice policing* it will enable a variety of policing agencies to appreciate the benefits of transparency for the generation of community consent and respect, so crucial to the continuation of legitimate police practice (see chapter 3).

What is reform?[6]

Police reform is directed down three principal pathways:

1. Changes in the structural and organisational components of policing
2. The imposition or revision of a policing ethic
3. Individual, institutional, or systemic change in operational practice and procedure.

These tend to produce their own unique aspirations for reform outcomes. As noted above, the resilience of reform rests as much on expectations and their generation, as it does on the constant achievement of new outcomes.

For the police to retain an important position in the symbolism of justice ideology it is necessary to legitimate police authority regularly (see chapter 1). In recent years, Australian police practice, and community reaction to it, have tended to undermine this authority. Political imperatives to restore the authority of police, and through this its legitimate place in the bureaucracies of the state, has required a reliance on reform cycles (see chapter 8). In this the political practice has initially been to alter the mechanisms internal to policing which achieve discipline and accountability. If and when these fail, resort is had to external and independent commissions of inquiry with a brief in particular to examine the more obvious examples of police malpractice. These investigations reveal to the public whether police are living up to their own ideologies or corporate ethics. Unfortunately (and

---

5   For a discussion of these principles in the context of sentencing see Henham, R (2003), 'The Philosophical Foundations of International Sentencing', *Journal of International Criminal Justice*, vol. 1, pp. 64–85.

6   Prenzler, T. & Ransley, J. (eds) (2002), *Police Reform – Building Integrity*, Hawkins Press, Sydney.

consistently) the result has been disappointment against the underachievement of such measures.

Recent reform initiatives have provided an opportunity for both government and the community to evaluate their satisfaction with policing outcomes. In particular, community-based policing offers the measures of community responsiveness and client satisfaction as appropriate evaluators for reform.

To ensure police reform is long-lasting, the strategies for its realisation must go deeply into human interaction between the police and the public. Whether the police treat communities differentially, yet their members with uniform dignity and with equality, is another measure of public satisfaction (see chapter 9). Particularly for police interaction with minority communities, client satisfaction may require determination in each selective context. The comparisons of policing in these different contexts offers up the opportunity to criticise bias and discrimination in police practice more universally.

Why reform police?

A constant objective during the reform process is to redefine the police mandate. Community-based policing, for instance, would have that mandate located within an atmosphere of sensitivity and responsibility to community needs (see chapter 3). To some extent this explains the essence of resistance that operational police have shown to community-policing ideology. The suggestion that community policing creates greater demands for police accountability has tended to colour such policing strategies from a police perspective, with a confrontational or isolationist potential (see chapter 8).

In an effort to ensure the centrality of state policing within democratic values, police reform seeks the achievement of:

- equity
- service delivery
- responsiveness
- openness
- equality in the distribution of power, and
- transparency in the provision of information.

Concerns for equity in policing focus on selective enforcement (see chapter 6). The need to make law-enforcement strategies dependent on the actual quantity and severity of offences committed within particular communities may come from a desire for more equitable discretion in law enforcement. While the broad ethic covering police-investigation practice, for instance, requires of the police respect for due process, police are encouraged to discriminate against individuals and groups within the community on the basis of sometimes lopsided crime stereotyping.[7] This clearly results in particular social or ethnic groups and certain kinds of crime being over-policed.

The way in which such dilemmas can be accommodated within uniform and equitable expectations for reform is through the universal improvement of police service delivery. The evaluation of a service delivery function is governed by expectations about more equitable and harm-driven law enforcement. The improvement of managerial controls and supervision within police organisations is essential to reform in service delivery.

Accountability as evidence of reform, in part requires redress from the police for those in the community who believe they have been unfairly targeted by selective policing policy. Not only should compensation be available, but also reform here requires the potential to have offending policies reversed. In individual cases it should be possible for citizens who have been wronged by the police to have their complaints investigated and gain compensation if they are upheld. These expectations are recurrent in reform discourse. The complaints function, even more crucially, should provide a framework for institutional as well as individual reform practice (see chapter 8).

Community-based policing as a reform strategy has required greater participation in the policing process, and more constructive participation by the police within community needs and interests. Democratic accountability will depend on information being more widely available about service delivery, about decision-making and about policy development for policing, particularly in a community-based management model. This in turn requires increased openness and independent media involvement to promote critical capacity in the community concerning policing.

Connection more generally by the police with other agencies and organisations in the criminal justice process is evidence of addressing those isolationist police cultures resistant to reform. On the basis of participation, performance measures should not be simply indicators of crime control, but have the potential to generate understanding about how police services really operate within the criminal-justice community. Information access and client responsiveness provide a platform for greater understandings, and give potency to the possibility of citizen redress. By constantly reviewing standards of service it is possible for police to remove incompetent and malevolent management behaviours and thereby enhance the possibility for redress. Redress will also be achieved through independent management of complaints against police. However, complaint-centred reform developments have the potential to retard the reform movement because of their interpretation as punitive intervention, and the resultant resistance by police in practice.[8]

---

7   Street violence rather than domestic violence, individual rather than corporate crime.
8   For a discussion of the reasons for reform in more detail see Jones, T. et al. (1996), 'Policing and the Idea of Democracy', *British Journal of Criminology*, vol. 36, no. 2, pp. 182–98.

Pressures for reform

The reform of policing in Australian jurisdictions has largely been the consequence of political initiatives. Obviously these are favoured by a climate of popular opinion which is critical of policing, or believes that in relation to certain problematic issues, police practice needs to be investigated and called into account. The principal forms that such reform pressures take are (1) corruption-led reform, often forced on police by external sources like the media and political opposition, and (2) incompetence-led reform, usually internally driven and motivated by essential restructuring for increased efficiency.

Pressures for reform manifest themselves in routine reform cycles. An example of this is the regularity with which royal commissions in Australia have examined policing and police practice (see chapter 8). The Wood Royal Commission in New South Wales was recently given the obligation to determine what needed reforming in policing in that state. The Commission initially identified:
• inadequate leadership
• lack of direction
• lack of openness
• inadequacy of focus on staff
• insularity of education and training
• inability to implement change, and
• negative police cultures.

Along with this, the reform practice has been to identify individuals appropriate for castigation and removal. Through this process of attrition the reform agenda is purgative of policing and thereby supportive of police legitimacy, which is seen as renewable through the heat of public investigation.

Having addressed the identified deficiencies, the Wood Royal Commission focussed its reform recommendations on the following:
• a move to a flatter management structure
• the devolution of responsibility and accountability down the management line
• the introduction of wider service provision
• the improvement of criminal-investigation skills
• the re-ordering of occupational cultures, and
• the enhancement of institutional education.

Such reforms could be described as organisational priorities to answer identified management failings. They left open the questions of how reforms could be achieved with regard to ethics and cultural issues (see chapter 8).

Is the police service capable of moving in the reform direction?

Organisational structures reflect a mode of policing (for example, responsive policing as opposed to proactive policing) to which reform may be directed (see chapter 4).[9] Central innovations in policing policy, such as community-based policing, can be criticised in reform terms for not having the power to change the 'ethics' of operational policing.

Police reform initiatives throughout Australia have identified two orthodox directions for changing police culture. These involve taking the police to the community (community policing) and bringing the community to the police. The notion of community policing may be linked in reform terms to the idea of policing by consent. In this respect reform initiatives are best essentially directed towards the generation and maintenance of community respect for the policing task. Reform with this purpose in mind will shore up the legitimacy of police authority, as a consequence.

Central to the process of reform as identified by the Wood Royal Commission is the enhancement of professionalism. How can professionalism assist the reform process? To answer this question one needs to consider the essential and internal ethics of professionalism as claimed by policing. On this issue the Wood Royal Commission stated that 'professionalism calls for the peer group to drive out the corrupt and the wilful non-performer'.[10]

The *best-practice* professionalism espoused in the Royal Commission indicated a movement to a *high-trust* model and increased self-regulation. However, this may be both consistent with and endangered by low-level visibility of police decision-making in one-to-one discretionary encounters (see chapter 6). It is right to question whether professionalism can coexist here with such anonymous decision-making encounters, where in other contexts professionalism relies on openness and transparency (see chapter 10).

Recent reform initiatives have questioned whether police professionalism means different things to different parts of the organisation, for instance, between management and street-level operations. Chan considered professionalism to be an ideal in the absence of models of *best practice*.[11] Essential to her arguments about professionalism and its reform potential is the existence of realistic codes of ethical conduct (i.e. mechanisms which do not involve the punishment of honest mistakes). Codes of conduct in the process of professionalism therefore should move to positive reinforcement rather than the anxiety avoidance involved in a punitive model of police accountability (see chapter 7). This is not to suggest that accountability in policing can be appropriate if removed from disciplinary processes in a general form.

With the identification of ethics as important to police professionalism and contributing to pressures for reform, which professional standards require, it is appropriate to question how such ethical standards might be endorsed. Is it necessary that police ethics should have a legal basis, and what is the form that such reform should take?

---

9   Palmer, D. & Cherney, A. (2001), ''Bending Granite?' Recent Attempts at Changing Police Organisational Structures in Australia: A Case of Victoria Police', *Current Issues in Criminal Justice*, vol. 13, no. 1, pp. 47–59.

10   Wood (1997), p. 214.

11   Chan (1997), chapters 9 & 10.

One of the reasons argued against detailed and comprehensive legal regulation of the exercise of police power is the suggestion that it will unfairly and inappropriately limit police discretion (see chapter 3). There is also the danger that legal reforms may simply do little more than legitimate existing police practice. It has been argued that law reform in the field of police powers has failed because of its segmented and partial application. Recently, in most jurisdictions in Australia, the direction of law reform in police powers has been largely about empowering the police rather than calling them to account for the exercise of already existing powers (see chapter 6).

Legislative change, as a pressure for the reform of policing in general, cannot be considered in isolation from other legislative initiatives in the criminal-justice system. Indeed, transforming police behaviour in an atmosphere of criminal-justice reform should not be understood in terms of law alone. Policing operates in the discretionary paradigm of criminal justice, as its principal discretionary institution, within broad situations of tolerance, determined by the community and the judiciary, rather than tight boundaries of permission designated by legality (see chapter 6). A good example of this is the multifaceted role of police as investigators, accusers, and prosecutors in the adversarial trial process. Our expectations for the achievement of these functions are often contradictory, requiring an open and dispassionate investigator who can also be partisan and selective in the investigation and prosecution of a particular crime. Community demands on the police as crime investigators sometimes place them both inside and outside the adversarial process. This creates a significant dilemma for the police, as the adversarial process is the context in which the police themselves measure their success.

Hogg identified the role of police in routine evidence gathering as being legitimated by the courts, the media and *popular common sense*.[12] The courts are said to overlook police improprieties and illegalities in the gathering of evidence if they can be justified as contributing to successful apprehension and prosecution of suspects. In collusion with lawyers who encourage guilty pleas or inappropriately plea bargain, and with judicial officers who through concessional sentencing options put pressure on the accused in the plea process, the police simply become contributors to any ultimate miscarriage of justice which may result.

It would be wrong to imply that the police alone provide resistance to pressures for reform. Politicians, lawyers and the judiciary are also resistant to changes in criminal justice, particularly those in which they are directly implicated. Judicial officers commonly present a complacency about the failings in the operation of the criminal-justice process.[13] Further, a cynicism may prevail within the community that victims of miscarriages of justice do not deserve better treatment or that in fact the compromise of due process and the abuse of power may be justified by the risks

12   Hogg & Brown (1998), chapter 1.
13   For a discussion of this see Walker, C. & Starmer, K (eds) (1999), *Miscarriages of Justice: A Review of Justice in Error*, Blackstone Press, London, chapters 10 & 18.

that certain criminal activities pose for the community at large. The media may collude in the view that due process simply hampers appropriate policing behaviour and that the police need more powers rather than the restrictions imposed by reform agendas. When the debate about justice versus control degenerates into one about being soft on crime, politicians will come behind the resistance to reform.[14]

Reform agendas

Reform agendas for policing in general, and in particular in Australia, can be divided into four broad categories:

1. Style and approach to policing
2. Structures of police organisation
3. Police powers, and
4. Aboriginal issues.

Much of the recent pressure for reform has stemmed from adverse community perceptions of police. These perceptions have emerged from the confusion about the role of police and produced a decline in community trust.[15] The authority of the police has been challenged across classes and communities throughout Australia. This has led to negative atmospheres in which the police case against reform has been exposed as self-interested and reactionary.

Policing approaches and styles

Recent royal commissions have criticised cop culture (see chapter 8). Despite rather simplistic appreciations of the culture of policing, these commissions have moved to reconceptualise police culture and have recommended a reconsideration of the interpretation of its relationship with political and legal imperatives.

Multicultural policing has been a focus for reform discourse. The identification of a need for greater cultural awareness and cross-cultural communication has dominated reform recommendations.

Community policing has been confirmed as the preferred ideology for policing in reform agendas. Therefore, the foundations of reform must rely on an understanding of the nature of police organisations, their communication pathways, and the manner in which structures of police responsibility operate, each in essential community contexts. Partnerships and support mechanisms from the police and the community, along with discriminatory and targeted police priorities, provide a

---

14 Hogg & Brown (1998), chapter 1.
15 The crucial importance of trust in the reformulation and perpetuation of productive police–community relations cannot be understated. A useful review of the 'trust' literature is Cherney, A. (1997), 'Trust as a Regulatory Strategy: A Theoretical Review', *Current Issues in Criminal Justice*, vol. 9, no. 1, pp. 71–84.

reform context in which the interaction with other policing and community agencies is a priority.

Training is identified in part of police-reform agendas, as essential for the transformation of negative police cultures. Discussions about broad-based tertiary educational opportunities versus specific in-service and field training provide the substance of the debate around the relevance of education as a reform facilitator. Continuing police education and professional development is also identified as important.

New strategies for recruitment, incorporating more egalitarian selection procedures reflecting equal opportunities and multiculturalism, are at the heart of this agenda. Recruitment should facilitate the introduction of assistance measures to provide access to minorities in meeting general entrance requirements. Associated with this is the need to change constructively attitudes towards the gender of policing. Physicality, exclusion, ambivalence, and negative coping strategies or mechanisms have been identified as problems.

When dealing with the reform of policing styles, comparative analysis of overseas models is common and instructive (see chapter 5). In addition, reference to other reform initiatives which succeed in criminal justice situations outside policing (such as juvenile justice models) is instructive when measuring the capacity and achievement of police reform initiatives.

Reform agendas need to be mindful of what has become known as *change fatigue*. The routine reform cycle could be criticised for generating just such problems for police management and morale in policing.

Police organisational structure

As indicated earlier, much of the recent evaluative literature on police reform in Australia has focused on concerns of organisational structure. For instance, as part of reform agendas there has been suggestion that productivity issues, and in particular measures of policing effectiveness, require sophistication. In the context of community-based policing, the argument has been for a shift from simple crime-control measures, such as clear-up rates and successful prosecutions, to more general concerns about client satisfaction and measures of community response (see chapter 1). The area of productivity measurement has, however, highlighted competing expectations for police reform. On the one hand those who advocate community-based policing argue for improvement in response, and greater accountability, while on the other the media in particular presses the police for more significant crime-control results and in this respect values convictions and clear-up. To some extent this sends mixed messages to the police as they interpret reform of their own managerial structures.

Management disciplines have become a fascination for police institutional hierarchies in recent decades. This is revealed by the way police organisations have valued management training above all other professional development avenues for their middle-order and senior staff. Management language has governed the discourse of police strategic planning. Total quality management for instance, has become an aspiration for police organisations. Police budgetary planners are now attracted to the recent public financing doctrines of 'user pays' and private/public partnerships (PPP).

Even in reform discourse there has been a shift away from singular support for external regulatory bodies to govern the work of the police and to order and expose corruption and misconduct. Even in the face of critical royal commissions the conventional external-review agencies (particularly those with complaints functions such as ombudsmen) have an operational dependency on the police internal disciplinary structure. In addition, some of the more general agencies of police accountability are becoming progressively more reliant on the policing bureaucracy as a realistic and essential conduit to investigate complaints. For example, in New South Wales the office of the ombudsman has openly declared its reliance on the police to investigate themselves. Whether this is recognition of police professionalism, or rather of the inevitable, is debatable.

Self-regulation and review strategies in Australian policing are developing in parallel with a more critical confidence in external regulation. Again, in New South Wales, arising out of the Wood recommendations, the Police Integrity Commission has subsumed the work of a number of other external agencies while at the same time directing its attention to the internal operations of police institutions. The anticipation is that the PIC will act as a litmus test for the adequacy of self-regulation and review within police management.

A common and uniform reform trend across police organisational establishments throughout Australia has been civilianisation. State police services have a new look brought about as a consequence of the injection of civil administrators, specialists, and volunteers. The introduction of *non-warranted* or even volunteer personnel into state policing organisations has allowed for function change. On the one hand new initiatives in the areas of information management, forensic sciences, community liaison, and interdepartmental task-forcing are possible as a result of the diversification of the police occupational community. On the other hand, important and conventional components of police function (such as traffic and licensing as well as crowd control in public events) has been given over to non-state police institutions. Outsourcing to private agencies has also produced a repositioning of policing within the finance-generating networks of government.

Consistent with civilianisation, management structures within policing are gradually moving away from the 'militaristic model' where responsibility relied on the disciplined service, more to standard corporate management design. This may be a natural consequence of the increased desire on the part of police organisations to put forward a professional image. Such management reforms continue to present difficulties in responsible governance, however, when the police as a disciplined service translate corporate management models within the rigid and competing context of traditional hierarchical leadership.

A way around problems of modern policing management is through a revision of the police promotion structure. It may seem strange to those outside conventional police occupational culture that merit-based promotions programs would be both novel to many police organisations and resisted by police from 'old-school' backgrounds. The reconstruction of police promotions schemes has also been employed as a tool to ensure that reform is transferred more effectively down the management and discipline lines, and that those pockets of resistance to reform are broken and dispersed through the use of employment strategies. Associated with merit-based systems is the notion of interdisciplinary resourcing in policing. This reform strategy has been achieved through lateral transfers where professionals with experience outside policing have been inserted into the structure at middle and higher management levels in order to add to the skills base of a police organisation, along with broadening its social experience.

Reform has also been promoted by the creation of alternative career structures within policing institutions, so that police personnel get the widest exposure to all aspects of the police function. It is now widely accepted that to break the close connection of rank with status and pay in policing is a positive step towards the production of a more flexible institutional and professional service. The move away from the positioning of police officers for long periods in static units has assisted in this development. In some police organisations in Australia, specialist units and elite squads have also been dismantled in favour of a more strategic, taskforce and skills-based delivery of omnibus policing services.

There is no doubt that the success of the reform agenda depends heavily on acceptance by the lower ranks. In order to improve the legitimacy of such reform initiatives and their applicability at all occupational levels the involvement of *rank-and-file* police in the decision-making process and at various stages of policy development is productive. This, however, poses a challenge to the disciplined, uniformed (military-style) force and invites police management to give meaningful consideration and the reward of implementation to ordinary police initiatives and concerns. These potential outcomes are particularly significant where police institutions wrestle with operational accountability and its application down the line of the disciplined service.

The organisational structure of policing in its operational roles has diversified in Australia in recent decades. Regionalisation is a common technique to reconstruct the delivery of policing services and to broaden lateral access to policing skills. In addition to this the devolution of command responsibilities down to more localised situations and structures has tended to encourage the development of management expertise across police services, and the appropriate diversification of structures of responsibility. Another technique has been to develop flexible and empowered teams around particular functional issues rather than the more conventional approach of organising police against operational skills and general functions.

Organisationally, a shift in functional focus for policing (such as the move toward crime prevention) can bring about significant changes in the manner in which the police carry out their work. This is not merely a consequence of management reform agendas, but can come about as a result of the valuing of different indicators of expertise and efficiency. A crime-prevention focus, for instance, has tended to more easily expose dishonest law enforcement by questioning the application of selective discretion (see chapter 8). Honest law enforcement is more consistent with a crime-prevention agenda as crime prevention relies heavily on community consent and the respect of those in the community who are involved in the prevention initiatives. A crime-prevention functional focus will produce better policing provided it is built on transparency, a transparency essential for the generation of community confidence on which crime prevention relies.

Police organisational concerns within reform agendas rely on the responsible and informed exercise of discretion. Against this is the realisation that police discretion, where exercised to shore up corrupt police cultures, will act as a significant impediment to the achievement of reform agendas (see chapters 6 & 8).

Police powers

We have mentioned earlier in this chapter the arguments in favour of the legal regulation of police practice in order to ensure reform, and the difficulties associated with this approach. Even so, most states and territories in Australia have introduced police powers legislation designed to clarify and codify the relationship between the police, their powers, their responsibilities to the community, and the obligation of policing to the political process. Such legislative development will at least lead to a standardisation of the reform process through the mechanism of legislative change.

In jurisdictions outside Australia (such as England and Wales) there has been significant development in the area of police law reform. This has not simply involved a process whereby police powers have been expanded without complementary requirements as to the exercise of police responsibility. The pressure for police to recognise their role in the protection of human rights is tending to reinterpret radically the notion of police responsibilities for due process and criminal justice. International criminal justice experience is revealing the future need for the police to redefine their place in the adversarial system against more uniform and detailed requirements for the protection of human rights and access to fair processes of criminal justice. With the breaking down of jurisdictional divisions between police, both nationally and internationally, the push for a more uniform commitment to rights-based policing will increase. It should also be anticipated that the routine and recurrent exposing of bad practice in policing will be a product of this opening up of police jurisdictions.

In Australia, the reform interest in the exercise of police power has focused on the detention and the questioning of suspects, the powers in relation to entry search and seizure, public order powers such as information gathering and compulsory relocation, and the expansion of electronic or forensic surveillance.

The exercise of police powers in a critical context is also a natural result of concerns about police malpractice. Therefore, for example, the exposure of police involvement in the fabrication of evidence, and the abuse of criminal informants have provided a range of opportunities for investigation and reform recommendations impacting on essential elements of police operational culture.

Aboriginal issues

As we discussed during chapter 2 (Police Histories), Aboriginal–police relations throughout Australia remain at poor levels. This historical division between the police and indigenous communities has translated itself into urban environments and strained modern police practice. Discriminatory policing, particularly in custodial environments, has remained central in reform agendas for police–Aboriginal relations.[16] Cultural sensitivity and awareness, cross-cultural communication, access to the service function provided by police, and the dismantling of destructive stereotypes all make way for change in the area.

Particular legislative initiatives to protect Aboriginal people who are vulnerable when in contact with the police have produced a greater awareness among policing organisations of their specific responsibilities to Aboriginal people, and to improve police–Aboriginal relations. Unfortunately in Australia this has not emerged within a wider human-rights context, but more as a perpetuation of paternalism, and therefore some would argue that these developments can be no more than piecemeal and patronising.

The over-representation of Aboriginal people in the criminal-justice process is a challenge for policing. Police organisations need to realise that their selective policing of Aboriginal people has a unique influence over the reality of Aboriginal criminalisation in all its discriminatory manifestations.[17] There is no doubt that the development of diversionary alternatives for Aboriginal people from policing should be a priority in the reform of police–Aboriginal relations.

Reform beyond organisational priority

Having listed the organisational issues predominant in the police reform debate, it is worthwhile considering wider or higher-level concerns for the reform of police practice. Police ethics are essential considerations for this purpose.

16 Cunneen (2001), chapters 5 & 9.
17 Brown et al. ((2001), *Criminal Laws*, Federation Press, Sydney, paragraphs 2.2.9–2.3; 12.10.2.

These would canvass the following questions:

1. What is the ethical model of policing to which we aspire?
2. What relationship between the police and the community do we wish to foster?
3. What community do we want to see created by policing?

Answers to each and all of these questions connect back to the debate about police professionalism (chapter 10). A model of professionalism relevant for policing must rely on a realistic operational context for drafting and broadcasting ethical standards. These standards should designate the nature of relationships between the police and the community, as well as forming the foundation for appropriate professional police cultures.

Professionalism has a central position within the reform agenda. Claims for police professionalism require openness and honesty in police operational practice as much as they do the support of strong and enunciated normative frameworks. The relationship between legal regulation and ethics also depends for its potency on specific translation into police operational practice.

If the reform agenda is reliant on claims to professionalism and evidence of their substantiation, then reform will possess a legitimating potential beyond symbolism.

It is clear that for police reform to be long-lasting and influential over police work, the system which manages reform initiatives must be endorsed by the widest possible police constituency. To obtain this confidence the reform process needs in fact to produce reforms, which police can see, can appreciate, and from which they can benefit. If this occurs then the legitimation of police authority will be publicly enhanced through community awareness of the relevance of reform, identifying its outcomes through popular common sense.

An unfortunate consequence of the cycle of reform in policing has been a cynicism, a complacency and a resistance to change among the police and other criminal-justice operatives, impugning the sincerity of reform strategies. The success of reform and the need for changing the context of policing is the challenge for those with the responsibility to reform policing.

The success of police reform

In the face of regular cycles of police reform in Australia the community might be forgiven for doubting the capacity and the impact of the next reform waves. It was noted during the Wood Royal Commission in New South Wales that similar reforms had been introduced by Commissioner John Avery over a decade before, as a result of the Lusher Inquiry. In short, these reform decades focused on a push for more accountable, community-centred policing. Organisational reforms followed with changes to recruitment and training. Community-based initiatives were developed on a regionalised management basis. But what happened with policing in New South Wales necessitating it to be again subject to a major critical and independent review so soon after the Avery reforms had been implemented? Were the changes following the Wood Royal Commission more likely to be successful than earlier reforms to the police service in New South Wales and why?

Chan[18] has stated that reform efforts prior to Wood did not work because they were concerned with changing the habitus rather than the context of police work. Habitas refers to the police sense of mission about being crime catchers, using selective law enforcement and stereotyping, relying on police common sense, and operating within a culture of secrecy. The context or field in which policing takes place includes the specific structural conditions of police work such as political context, social and economic status, the treatment of visible minorities, discretionary powers in police practice, legal protections against police abuse, and the internal organisation of the police force. Chan considered that little has changed in the field of policing since earlier reforms. In her view, sustainable change requires a permanent source of pressure for change, and this needs to be much more that simply the piecemeal reaction to complaints against policing.

A new culture of policing requires development. Such cultural change must be facilitated by law reform, external and internal monitoring, quality reviews, reward for best practice policing, and positive accountability structures.

The field of policing may be difficult to change unless there is a change in attitudes both within policing, and from the legal profession, the judiciary and other criminal-justice professionals intimately connected with police practice on a daily basis. Political support for change must also go beyond the identification of a need for reform and the celebration of its success. Significant financial investment should precede obtaining and maintaining changes in police culture. Unfortunately, the fickleness of political will has meant that as law-and-order political agendas become more conservative and control-focused, the commitment to essential police socialisers, such as investment in broad-based education and the improvement of the service function, are sacrificed in the name of tougher crime-control programs. This is music to the ears of those who would resist the reform and resocialisation of policing. It leads to the reinvention of feudal police organisations and the stratification of negative police cultures around the predominance of a criminal investigation and crime-control function for policing.

As policing diversifies and the structures of policing become more varied, transparency and accountability are more difficult to enforce. Australian communities experience more and more policing. There are very few situations left in community life where policing does not have a direct impact. As this diversification process continues and the shape of policing in Australia changes, the need for a common and comprehensive code of ethics for policing is more apparent.

---

18   Chan (1997), chapter 6.

Police have important decision-making powers over the lives of citizens, and even other justice professionals. At best, codes of ethics acknowledge this power is dynamic and address how it should be appropriately employed. Police codes of ethics are a public commitment to normative boundaries within which police power should be negotiated. They provide a frame of reference for the measure of malpractice and the abuse of power. However, they are not empowered by a reliance on enforcement or redress. Ideally, codes provide guidance for the individual and the organisation regarding the values of their profession and the positive consequences of their ascription, or at least the negative results of their violation.

On the one hand a code of conduct for policing comprises a public set of constraints under which police are pledged to operate, and is intended to provide a tangible basis for public trust to mediate between the providers and users of services. The context of community policing is compatible with ethical engagement. Service delivery is the function which supports and is complemented by the social values most supportive of professionalism, even more than crime-control imperatives and the ethical compromises they invite.

Kleinig argues that the purposes of police codes of conduct centre on two main issues: (1) external regulation through a visible frame of reference for the mediation between providers of policing services and the public they service, and (2) internal regulation making possible mediation between the providers themselves.

What is at stake in the violation of a code is both the external loss of trust and the internal compromise of individual and organisational integrity. There need 'not be any conflict between these two ends, for maintaining the integrity of the professional activity will generally contribute to the public good and thus sustain public trust'.[19]

The functions expected of police conduct codes include:

External
- assurance
- improved public relations, and
- limited liability

Internal
- individual personal standards, and
- an organisational ethos
  Their contingent problems are:
- enforceability, and
- cynicism.

Ethics at the heart of policing codes of conduct go beyond a management strategy for best practice: '...Good policing in the twenty first century requires more

---

19   Kleinig, J. (1996), *The Ethics of Policing*, Cambridge University Press, Cambridge, p. 123.

than good performance. It needs a renewal of the contract between police officers and the citizen, which in turn requires greater openness and scrutiny, continuously improving professional standards, and a new commitment to ethics at the core of policing.'[20]

Conclusion

As an intention of this book has been to clarify an understanding of the idea of police and policing, it is incumbent on us to make some projections about an institution which is neither perfect, nor immune from change. In recent times, policing throughout Australia has dropped low in public opinion, and the essential foundations of community-based policing, respect and consensus, have lost public confidence. As Wright indicated in his discussion of the politics of policing,[21] a new paradigm for policing is necessary, one which is based on reciprocity and communication. Policing needs to develop:

> ...beyond the crass managerialism that marks power relationships to a more explicit and authentic adoption of the idea of working in and with a diversity of communities. It implies a diffusion of power and a balance between the concepts of social control and social care. At best, policing becomes part of society at every level whether working on transnational organised crime or in highly localised surroundings. Inevitably the immanent relationship between the concept of reciprocity and policing practice will mean that policing will need to look to these communities for support and legitimation.[22]

The generation and preservation of a climate of trust by the police with their communities cannot be overstated as essential for policing, which is inclusive and reciprocal. The mechanisms (ethics or otherwise) put in place to promote these aspirations should recognise 'The aim of a regulatory strategy designed upon the dynamic mechanisms of trust engender greater compliance through the development of confidence and obligation. It is a consequentialist theory identifying the option that promises the achievement of goal maximisation, that option being a trust-based strategy the goal being maximum adherence to regulatory standards.'[23]

If these standards are rights-based then the ethics central to policing and their regulation can rely on themes of trust and compliance, wherein the police are protectors rather than violators of essential rights in civil society.

It is the ethics of inclusion, which reciprocity and communication demands, that should be the focus for the reform of contemporary police practice in Australia, otherwise the challenge for policing a multicultural society will be lost.

---

20   Neyroud & Beckley (2001), p. 220.
21   Wright (2002), p. 177.
22   Wright (2001), p. 178.
23   Cherney (1997), p. 80.

Additional readings

For full reference details refer to the bibliography.

Dixon (1999), chapters 1, 4 & 6.

Edwards (1999), Part 4.

Neyroud & Beckley (2001), chapter 1.

Hogg(1991), 'Identifying and Reforming the Problems of the Justice System', in Carrington et al., chapter 12.

Dixon (1996), 'Reform of Policing by Legal Regulation: International Experience in Criminal Investigation', *Current Issues in Criminal Justice*, vol. 7, no. 3, pp. 287–301.

McConville et al. (1991), chapter 10.

Jones et al. (1996), 'Policing and the Idea of Democracy', *British Journal of Criminology*, vol. 36, no. 2, pp. 182–98.

Chan (1997), chapter 10.

Moir & Eijkman (1992), chapter 13.

White & Alder (1994), chapter 10.

Chappell & Wilson (1989), chapter 8.

Brown & Hogg, (1996), 'Law and Order Commonsense', *Current Issues in Criminal Justice*, vol. 8, no. 2, pp. 175–90.

Findlay, Odgers & Yeo (1994), chapter 10.

Brown (1987), 'The Politics of Reform', in Zdenkowski et al., chapter 13.

Brown (1976), 'Criminal Justice Reform: A Critique', in Chappell & Wilson, pp. 471–91.

Alder & Polk (1986), 'Criminal Justice Reform in Australia', in Chappell & Wilson, chapter 16.

Polk, (1994), 'Criminal Justice Reform in Australia', in Chappell & Wilson, pp. 291–314.

Brereton (2000), 'Policing and Crime Prevention: The New Product', in Chappell & Wilson.

Ericson & Haggarty (1997).

Marks (2000), 'Transforming Police Culture From Within: Dissident Groups in South Africa', *British Journal of Criminology*, vol. 40, no. 4, pp. 557–73.

Bibliography

AG for NSW v. Perpetual Trustee Co. [1952] 85 CLR 237.

Alder, C. & Polk, K. (1986), 'Criminal Justice Reform in Australia', in D. Chappell & P. Wilson (eds), *The Australian Criminal Justice System: The Mid 1980s,* Butterworths, Sydney, chapter 16.

Allen, J. (1987), 'Policing Since 1880: Some Questions of Sex', in M. Finnane (ed.), *Policing in Australia: Historical Perspectives,* University of NSW Press, Sydney, chapter 9.

Allen, J. (1990), *Sex and Secrets: Crimes Involving Australian Women since 1880,* Oxford University Press, Melbourne.

Ashworth, A. (1998), *The Criminal Process: An Evaluative Study,* Oxford University Press, Oxford.

Avery, J. (1981), *Police – Force or Service,* Butterworths, Sydney.

Baird, B. (1997), 'Putting Police on Notice: A South Australian Police Study', in G. Mason & S. Tomsen (eds), *Homophobic Violence,* Hawkins Press, Sydney.

Baldwin, J. & Bottomley, K. (eds) (1978), *Criminal Justice,* Martin Robertson, Oxford.

Baldwin, R. & Kinsey, R. (1982), *Police Powers and Politics,* Quartet, London.

Barak, G. (ed.) (1994), *Media, Process, and the Social Construction of Crime,* Garland Publishing Inc., New York.

Barker, D. (2001), 'Barricades and Batons: A Historical Perspective of the Policing of Major Industrial Disorder in Australia', in M. Enders & B. Dupont (eds), *Policing the Lucky Country,* Hawkins Press, Sydney, chapter 15.

Barker, T. & Carter C. (1994), *Police Deviance,* Anderson, Cincinnati.

Bayley, D. (1986), *Community Policing in Australia – An Appraisal: Working Paper Report Series,* Australian Centre for Police Research, Paynehan.

Bayley, D. (1988), 'Community Policing: A Report from the Devil's Advocate', in J. Greene & S. Mastrofski (eds), *Community Policing: Rhetoric or Reality,* Praeger, New York.

Bayley, D. (1986), *Patterns of Policing: A Comparative International Analysis*, Rutgers University Press, New Brunswick, N.J.

Bayley, D. (1989), 'Community Policing in Australia: An Appraisal', in D. Chappell & P. Wilson (eds), *Australian Policing: Contemporary Issues*, Butterworths, Sydney, chapter 4.

Bayley, D. (1994), *Police for the Future*, Oxford University Press, New York.

Bayley, D. (2002), 'Policing Hate: What Can be Done', *Policing and Society*, vol. 12, no. 2, pp. 83–93.

Biles, D. & McDonald, D. (1992), *Deaths in Custody in Australia 1980–1989*, Australian Institute of Criminology, Canberra.

Bittner, E. (1980), *The Functions of Police in Modern Society*, Oelgeschlager, Gunn & Hain, Cambridge, MA.

Blagg, H. (1977), 'A Just Measure of Shame: Aboriginal Youth Conferencing in Australia', *British Journal of Criminology*, vol. 37, no. 4, p. 481.

Blagg, H. & Wilke, M. (1995), *Young People and Police Powers*, Australian Youth Foundation, Sydney.

Bolen, J. (1997), *Reform in Policing: Lessons from the Whitrod Era*, Hawkins Press, Sydney.

Bottomley, K. (1973), *Decisions in the Penal Process*, Martin Robertson, Oxford.

Bourdieu, P. (1990), *In Other Words: Essays Towards a Reflexive Sociology*, Polity Press, Cambridge.

Bowden, T. (1978), *Beyond the Limits of the Law*, Penguin, Harmondsworth.

Bradley, D. & Walker, N. (1986), *Managing the Police, Law, Organisation and Democracy*, Wheatsheaf, Brighton, U.K.

Braithwaite, J. (1979), *Inequality, Crime and Public Policy*, Routledge & Kegan Paul, London.

Braithwaite, J. (1992), 'Good and Bad Police Services and How to Pick Them', in P. Moir & H. Eijkman, *Policing Australia: Old Issues, New Perspectives*, Macmillan, Melbourne, chapter 1.

Brereton, D. (2000), 'Policing and Crime Prevention: The New Product', in D. Chappell & P. Wilson (eds), *Crime and the Criminal Justice System in Australia: 2000 and Beyond*, Butterworths, Sydney, chapter 8.

Brereton, D. & Ede, A. (1996), 'The Police Code of Silence in Queensland: The Impact of the Fitzgerald Inquiry Report', *Current Issues in Criminal Justice*, vol. 8, no 2, pp. 107–29.

Brethnach, S. (1974), *The Irish Police: From Earliest Times to Present Day*, Anvil Books, Dublin.

Briody, M. (2002), 'The Effects of DNA Evidence on Sexual Assault Cases in Court', *Current Issues in Criminal Justice*, vol. 14, no. 2, pp. 159–81.

Brittin, N. (2000), 'Race and Policing: A Study of Police Custody', *British Journal of Criminology*, vol. 40, no. 4, pp. 639–58.

Brodeur, J. (1983), 'High Policing and Low Policing: Remarks about Policing of Political Activities', *Social Problems*, vol. 30, no 5, pp. 507–20.

Brogden, M. (1981), 'All Police is Conning Bastards: Policing and the Problems of Consent', in B. Fine et al. (eds), *Law, State and Society*, Croom Helm, London.

Brogden, M. (1987), 'The Emergence of the Police: The Colonial Dimension', *British Journal of Criminology*, vol. 27, no. 1, pp 4–15.

Brogden, M., Jefferson T. & Walklate S. (1988), *Introducing Police Work*, Unwin Hyman, London.

Brogden, M. & Shearing, C. (1993), *Policing for a New South* Africa, Routledge, London.

Brown, D. (1976), 'Criminal Justice Reform: A Critique', in D. Chappell & P. Wilson (eds), *The Australian Criminal Justice System*, 2nd edn, Butterworths, Sydney, pp. 471–91.

Brown, D. (1987), 'The Politics of Reform', in G. Zdenkowski et al. (eds), *The Criminal Injustice System*, vol. 2, Pluto Press, Sydney, chapter 13.

Brown, D. (1993), 'Notes on the Culture of Prison Informing', *Current Issues in Criminal Justice* vol. 5, no. 1, pp. 54–71.

Brown, D. (1998), 'The Royal Commission into the NSW Police Service: Process Corruption and the Limits of Judicial Reflexivity', *Current Issues in Criminal Justice* 9/3: 228–240.

Brown, D. et al. (2001), *Criminal Laws*, Federation Press, Sydney.

Brown, D. & Hogg, R. (1996), 'Law and Order Commonsense', *Current Issues in Criminal Justice* vol. 8, no. 2, pp. 175–90.

Brown, M. & Sutton, A. (1997), 'Problem Oriented Policing and Organisational Form: Lessons from a Victorian Experiment', *Current Issues in Criminal Justice*, vol. 9, no. 1, pp. 21–33.

Burke, M. (1994), 'Homosexuality as Deviance: The case of the Gay Police Officer', *British Journal of Criminology* 24/2: 102–203.

Burton, F. & Carlen, P. (1979), *Official Discourse: On Discourse Analysis, Government Publications, Ideology and the State*, Routledge & Kegan Paul, London.

Carrington, K. et al. (eds) (1991), *Travesty*, Pluto Press, Sydney.

Carson, W. (1970), 'White Collar Crime and the Enforcement of Factory Legislation', *British Journal of Criminology*, vol. 10, no. 4, pp. 383–98.

Carson, W. (1984 & 1985), 'Policing the Periphery: The Development of Scottish Policing', parts 1 & 2, *Australian and New Zealand Journal of Criminology*, vol. 17, no. 4, pp. 207–32; vol. 18, no. 1, pp. 3–16.

Cashmore, E. & McLaughlin, E. (eds) (1991), *Out of Order? Policing Black People*, Routledge, London.

Chambliss, W. & Mankoff, M. (1976), *Whose Law? What Order? A Conflict Approach to Criminology*, Wiley, New York.

Chan, J. (1994), 'Policing Youth in "Ethnic" Communities: Is Community Policing the Answer?', in R. White & C. Alder (eds), *The Police and Young People in Australia*, Cambridge University Press, Melbourne.

Chan, J. (1997), *Changing Police Culture: Policing in a Multicultural Society*, Cambridge University Press, Melbourne.

Chan, J. (2001), 'Negotiating the Field: New Observations on the Making of Police Officers', *Australian and New Zealand Journal of Criminology*, vol. 34, no.2, pp. 114–33.

Chappell, D. & Wilson, P. (eds) (1976), *The Australian Criminal Justice System*, 2nd edn, Butterworths, Sydney.

Chappell, D. & Wilson P. (eds) (1986), *The Australian Criminal Justice System: The Mid 1980s*, Butterworths, Sydney.

Chappell, D. & Wilson, P. (1989 & 1996), *Australian Policing: Contemporary Issues*, 2nd edn, Butterworths, Sydney.

Chappell, D. & Wilson, P. (eds) (1994), *The Australian Criminal Justice System: The Mid 1990s*, Butterworths, Sydney.

Chappell, D. & Wilson, P. (eds) (2000), *Crime and the Criminal Justice System in Australia: 2000 and beyond*, Butterworths, Sydney.

Cherney, A. (1997), 'Trust as a Regulatory Strategy: A Theoretical Review', *Current Issues in Criminal Justice*, vol. 9, no. 1, pp. 71–84.

Clarke, A. (1986), 'This is Not the Boy Scouts: Television Police Series and Images of Law and Order', in T. Bennett, G. Mercer & J. Woollacott (eds), *Popular Culture and Social Relations*, Open University Press, Milton Keynes.

Clarke, C.M. (1962), *A History of Australia: From the Earliest Times to the Age of Macquarie*, vol. 1, Melbourne University Press, Melbourne.

Coady, T., James, S., Miller, S. & O'Keefe, M. (2000), *Violence and Police Culture*, Melbourne University Press, Melbourne.

Cohen, S. (1985), *Visions of Social Control*, Polity Press, Oxford.

Collins, J., Noble, G., Poynting, S. & Tabar, P. (2000), *Kebabs, Kids, Cops and Crime*, Pluto Press, Melbourne.

Connell, R. & Irving, T. (1980), *Class Structure in Australian History: Documents, Narrative and Argument*, Longman Cheshire, Melbourne.

Cotterrell, R., (1992), *The Sociology of Law*, Butterworths, London.

Cowdery, N. (2001), *Getting Justice Wrong: Myths Media and Crime*, Allen & Unwin, Sydney.

Crimes (Forensic Procedures) Act (2002) NSW.

Critchley, T. (1978), *A History of the Police in England and Wales*, Constable, London.

Crowther, C. (2000), 'Thinking About the Underclass: Towards a Political Economy of Policing', *Theoretical Criminology*, vol. 4, no 2, pp. 149–65.

Cunneen, C. (1988), 'An evaluation of the Juvenile Cautioning System in NSW', *Proceedings of the Institute of Criminology*, no. 75, pp. 21–8.

Cunneen, C. (1990), 'Aboriginal–Police Relations in Redfern: With Special Reference to the "Police Raid" of 8 February 1990', *Report Commissioned by the National Inquiry into Racist Violence*, Human Rights and Equal Opportunities Commission, Sydney.

Cunneen, C. (1991), 'Problems in the Implementation of Community Policing Strategies', in S. McKillop & J. Vernon, *The Police and the Community in the 1990s,* Australian Institute of Criminology, Canberra.

Cunneen, C. (1991), 'The Historical Development of the Special Weapons and Operations Section of the NSW Police Service' (unpublished paper).

Cunneen C. (2001), *Conflict Politics and Crime, Aboriginal Communities and the Police,* Allen & Unwin, Sydney.

Cunneen, C., Findlay, M., Lynch, R. & Tupper, V. (1989), *Dynamics of Collective Conflict: Riots at the Bathurst Bike Races,* Law Book Company, Sydney.

Cunneen, C. & White, R. (2002), *Juvenile Justice: Youth and Crime in Australia,* Oxford University Press, Melbourne.

Darcy, D. (1999). 'Zero Tolerance—Not Quite the Influence on NSW Policing Some Would Have You Believe', *Current Issues in Criminal Justice,* vol. 10, no. 3, pp. 290–98.

Davids, C. & Hanack, L. (1988), 'Policing, Accountability and Citizenship in a Market State', *Australian and New Zealand Journal of Criminology,* vol. 31, no. 1, pp. 38–68.

Davids, C. (1998), 'Shaping Public Perceptions of Police Integrity: Conflict of Interest Scenarios in Fictional Interpretations of Policing', *Current Issues in Criminal Justice,* vol 9, no. 3, pp. 241–61.

Davis, K. (1969), *Discretionary Justice,* University of Illinois Press, Urbana.

Davis, K. (1975), *Police Discretion,* West Publishing, St Paul.

de Lint, W. (2000), 'Autonomy, Regulation and the Police Beat', *Social and Legal Studies* 9/1: 55–84.

Dixon, D. (1995), 'Change in Policing: Changing Police', *Australian and New Zealand Journal of Criminology* (special issue) pp. 62–6.

Dixon, D. (1996), 'Reform of Policing by Legal Regulation: International Experience in Criminal Investigation', *Current Issues in Criminal Justice,* vol. 7, no. 3, pp. 287–301.

Dixon, D. (1997), *Law in Policing,* Clarendon Press, Oxford.

Dixon, D. (ed.) (1999), *A Culture of Corruption: Changing an Australian Police Service,* Hawkins Press, Sydney.

Dixon D., Coleman, C. & Bottomley, K. (1990), 'Consent and the Legal Regulation of Policing', *Law and Society,* vol. 17, no. 3, pp. 345–62.

Dixon, D. & Maher, L. (2001), 'The Cost of Crackdowns: Policing Cabramatta's Heroin Market', *Current Issues in Criminal Justice,* vol. 13, no. 1, pp. 5–22.

Dowler, K. (2002), 'Media and Citizen Attitudes about Police', *Policing & Society,* vol. 12, no. 3, pp. 227–38.

Ede, A., Homel, R. & Prenzler T. (2002), 'Reducing Complaints Against Police and Preventing Misconduct: A Diagnostic Study Using Hot Spot Analysis', *Australian and New Zealand Journal of Criminology,* vol. 35, no. 1, pp. 27–42.

Edwards, C. (1999), *Changing Policing Theories for Twenty First Century Societies,* Federation Press, Sydney.

Eggar, S. & Findlay, M. (1988), 'The Politics of Police Discretion', in M. Findlay & R. Hogg (eds), *Understanding Crime and Criminal Justice*, Law Book Company, Sydney, pp. 209–23.

Emsley, C. (1996), *The English Police: A Political and Social History*, Longman, London.

Enders, M. & Dupont, B. (eds) (2001), *Policing the Lucky Country*, Hawkins Press, Sydney.

Enever v. R [1906]3 CLR 969.

Ericson, R. (1981), *Making Crime: A study of Detective Work*, Butterworths, Toronto.

Ericson, R., Baranek P., & Chan, J. (1991), *Representing Order: Crime, Law and Justice in the News Media*, Open University Press, Milton Keynes.

Ericson, R., Baranek, P., & Chan, J. (1987), *Visualising Deviance: A Study of News Organisations*, University of Toronto Press, Toronto.

Ericson, R. & Haggarty, K. (1997), *Policing the Risk Society*, University of Toronto Press, Toronto.

Evans, D. et al. (1992), *Crime, Policing and Place*, Routledge, London.

Findlay, M. (1990), 'The Tactical Response Group: Some Notes on its History and Organisational Development'(unpublished paper).

Findlay, M. (1992), 'Police Authority, Respect and Shaming', *Current Issues in Criminal Justice*, vol. 5, no. 1, pp. 29–41.

Findlay, M. (1994), 'The Ambiguity of Accountability: Deaths in Custody and Regulation of Police Power', *Current Issues in Criminal Justice*, vol. 6, no. 2, pp. 234–51.

Findlay, M. (1994) 'Breaking the Crime-Control Nexus: Market Models of Corruption and Opportunity', in D. Chappell & P. Wilson (eds) *The Australian Criminal Justice System: The Mid 1990s*, Butterworths, Sydney, pp. 270–82.

Findlay, M. (1999), *The Globalisation of Crime: Understanding Transitional Relationships in Context*, Cambridge University Press, Cambridge.

Findlay, M. (2001), *Problems for the Criminal Law*, Oxford University Press, Melbourne.

Findlay, M., Egger S. & Sutton, J. (eds) (1983), *Issues in Criminal Justice Administration*, George Allen & Unwin, Sydney.

Findlay, M. & Grix, J. (2003), 'Challenging DNA in Court', *Current Issues in Criminal Justice*, vol 14, no. 3, pp. 269–82.

Findlay, M. & Hogg, R. (eds) (1988), *Understanding Crime and Criminal Justice*, Law Book Company, Sydney.

Findlay, M., Odgers S., & Yeo S. (1999), *Australian Criminal Justice*, 2nd edn, Oxford University Press, Melbourne.

Findlay, M. & Zvekic, U. (1988), *Informal Mechanisms of Crime Control*, UNISDRI, Rome.

Findlay M. & Zvekic U. (1992), 'Analysing Alternative Policing Styles' (unpublished conference paper).

Findlay, M. & Zvekic, U. (1993), *Alternative Policing Styles: Cross-Cultural Perspectives*, Kluwer Law & Taxation Publishers, Deventer.

Finnane, M. (1987), 'The Politics of Police Powers: The Making of Police Offences Acts', in M. Finnane (ed.), *Policing in Australia: Historical perspectives*, University of NSW Press, Sydney, p. 88.

Finnane, M. (1987), *Policing in Australia: Historical Perspectives*, University of NSW Press, Sydney.

Finnane, M. (1994), *Police and Government: Histories of Policing in Australia*, Oxford University Press, Melbourne.

Finnane, M. (1999), 'From Police Force to Service? Aspects of the Recent History of the NSW Police', in D. Dixon (ed.), *A Culture of Corruption: Changing an Australian Police Service*, Hawkins Press, Sydney, chapter 2.

Finnane, M. (2002), *When Police Unionise: The Politics of Law and Order in Australia*, Institute of Criminology, Sydney.

Fitzgerald, G. (1980), *Report of a Commission of Inquiry Pursuant to Orders in Council*, Government Printer, Brisbane, Qld.

Flynn, E. (1982), Women as Criminal Justice Professionals: A Challenge to Change Tradition, in N. Rafter & E. Stanko (eds), *Judge, Lawyer, Victim, Thief: Women, Gender Roles and Criminal Justice*, North Eastern University Press, Boston.

Francis, P. et al. (eds) (1997), *Policing Futures: The Police, Law Enforcement and the Twenty First Century*, Macmillan, London.

Freckleton, I. & Selby, H. (1988), *Police in Our Society*, Butterworths, Sydney.

Freckleton, I. & Selby, H. (1988), 'Police Accountability', in M. Findlay & R. Hogg (eds), *Understanding Crime and Criminal Justice*, Law Book Company, Sydney, chapter 11.

Freiberg, A. (1995), 'Trust and Betrayal in Criminal Justice', in H. Selby (ed.), *Tomorrow's Law*, Federation Press, Sydney, pp 86–114.

Frieberg, A. (1997), 'Commercial Confidentiality, Criminal Justice and Public Interest', *Current Issues in Criminal Justice*, vol. 9, no. 2, pp. 125–52.

Gans, J. (2000), 'Privately Paid Public Policing: Law and Practice', *Policing & Society*, vol. 10, no. 2, pp. 183–208.

Gardiner, G. & Takagaki, T. (2002), 'Indigenous Women and the Police in Victoria: Patterns of offending and victimisation in the 1900s', *Current Issues in Criminal Justice*, vol. 13, no.3, pp. 301–21.

Garland, D. (1990), *Punishment and Modern Society*, Clarendon Press, Oxford.

Gill, M. & Hoot, J. (1998), 'Exploring Investigative Policing: A Study of Private Detectives in Britain', *British Journal of Criminology*, vol. 37, no. 4, pp. 549–67.

Glare, K. (1991), 'Community Policing in a Multicultural Australia', in S. McKillop & J. Vernon (eds), *The Police and the Community in the 1990s*, Australian Institute of Criminology, Canberra.

Goldsmith, A. (1990), 'Taking Police Culture Seriously: Police Discretion and the Limits of the Law', *Policing and Society*, vol. 1, no. 3, pp. 190–214.

Goldsmith, A. (1991), *Complaints Against the Police*, Clarendon Press, Oxford.

Goldsmith, A. (2001), 'The Pursuit of Police Integrity: Leadership and Governance Dimensions', *Current Issues in Criminal Justice*, vol. 13, no. 2, pp 185–202.

Grabosky, P. (1989), 'Efficiency and Effectiveness in Australian Policing: A Citizen's Guide to Police Services', in D. Chappell & P. Wilson (eds), *Australian Policing: Contemporary Issues*, Butterworths, Sydney.

Grabosky, P. (1995), 'Fear of Crime and Fear Reduction Strategies', *Current Issues in Criminal Justice*, vol. 7, no. 1, pp. 7–19.

Greene, J. & Mastrofski, S. (eds) (1988), *Community Policing: Rhetoric or Reality*, Praeger, New York.

Greer, S. (1994), 'Miscarriages of Criminal Justice Reconsidered', *Modern Law Review*, vol. 57, no. 1, pp. 58–74.

Griffiths v. Haines [1983] ALJR 108.

Gunter, B. (1987), *Television and the Fear of Crime*, John Libbey, London.

Haesler, A. (2002), *An Overview: The Law Enforcement (Powers and Responsibilities) Bill 2001*, Public Defenders Office, Sydney.

Hall, S. et al. (1978), *Policing the Crisis*, Macmillan, London.

Hanmer, J. et al. (eds) (1989), *Women, Policing and Male Violence*, Routledge, London.

Hanmer, J., Radford, J. & Stanko, E. (1989), *Women, Policing, and Male Violence*, Routledge, London.

Harding, R. (1970), *Police Killings in Australia*, Penguin, Ringwood.

Hatty, S. (1991), 'Police, Crime and the Media: An Australian Tale', *International Journal of the Sociology of Law*, vol. 19, no. 2, pp. 171–91.

Hay, D. & Sneider, F. (eds) (1989), *Policing and Prosecution in Britain*, Clarendon Press, Oxford.

Heidensohn, F. (1992), *Women in Control?: The Role of Women in Law Enforcement*, Clarendon Press, Oxford; Oxford University Press, New York.

Henham, R. (2003), 'The Philosophical Foundations of International Sentencing', *Journal of International Criminal Justice*, vol. 1, pp. 64–85.

Hogg, R. (1983), 'Perspectives on the Criminal Justice System', in M. Findlay, S. Egger & J. Sutton (eds), *Issues in Criminal Justice Administration*, George Allen & Unwin, Sydney, pp. 3–19.

Hogg, R. (1987), 'The Politics of Criminal Investigation', in Wickham G, (ed.), *Social Theory and Legal Politics*,Legal Consumption Publications, Sydney, pp. 120–40.

Hogg, R. (1991), 'Identifying and Reforming the Problems of the Justice System', in K. Carrington et al. (eds), *Travesty*, Sydney, Pluto Press, chapter 12.

Hogg, R. et al. (1994), 'Counting Crime: Are victim surveys the answer', (unpublished conference paper).

Hogg, R. & Brown, D. (1998), *Rethinking Law and Order*, Pluto Press, Sydney.

Hogg, R. & Brown, D. (1990), 'Criminal Justice Policy in Australia', in I. Taylor (ed.) *The Social Effects of Free Market Policies*, Harvester, London.

Hogg, R. & Hawker, B. (1983), 'The Politics of Police Independence', *Legal Services Bulletin*, vol. 8, pp. 160–65 & 221–23.

Holdaway, S. (ed.) (1979), *The British Police*, Edward Arnold, London.

Humphries, S. (1981), *Hooligans or Rebels: An Oral History of Working Class Childhood and Youth 1889–1939*, Blackwell, Oxford.

Hunt, J. (1990), 'The logic of sexism among police' *Women and Criminal Justice*, vol. 1, no. 2, pp. 3–30.

Innes, M. (2002), 'The Process Structures of Police Homicide Investigations', *British Journal of Criminology*, vol. 42, no. 4, pp. 668–88.

Institute of Criminology (2001), *Use of DNA in the Criminal Justice System*, Institute of Criminology, Sydney.

James, S. & Sutton, A. (1998), 'Policing Drugs in the Third Millennium: The Dilemmas of Community Based Philosophies', *Current Issues in Criminal Justice*, vol. 9, no. 3, pp. 217–27.

Jesilow, P. & Parsons, J. (2000), 'Community Policing as Peace-making', *Policing & Society*, vol. 10, no. 2, pp. 163–82.

Johnston, L. (1991), 'Privatising and Police Function: 'New Police' to New Policing', in R. Reiner & M. Cross (eds), *Beyond Law and Order*, Macmillan, London.

Johnston, L. (1992), *The Rebirth of Private Policing*, Routledge, London.

Johnston, L. (1993), 'Privatisation and Protection: Spatial and Sectoral Ideologies in British Policing and Crime Prevention', *Modern Law Review*, vol. 56, no. 6, pp. 771–92.

Jones, D. (1982), *Crime, Protest, Community and Police in Nineteenth Century Britain*, Routledge & Kegan Paul, London.

Jones, T. et al. (1996) 'Policing and the Idea of Democracy', *British Journal of Criminology*, vol. 36, no. 2, pp. 182–98.

Justice (Non-association and Place Restriction) Act (NSW) 2001.

Kasinsky, R. (1994), 'Patrolling the Facts: Media, Cops and Crime', in G. Barak (ed.), *Media, Process, and the Social Construction of Crime*, Garland Publishing Inc., New York.

Kelling, G. & Coles, C. (1996), *Fixing Broken Windows*, Free Press, New York.

Kleinig, J. (1996), *The Ethics of Policing*, Cambridge University Press, Cambridge.

Klockars, C. (1980), 'The Dirty Harry problem', *The Annals* 452, pp. 33–47; reprinted in C. Klockars & S. Mastrofski (eds), *Thinking About Police: Contemporary Readings*, 2nd edn, McGraw-Hill, New York.

Klockars, C. (1985), *The Idea of Police*, Sage, New York.

Klockars, C. et al. (1991), *Thinking About Police: Contemporary Readings*, McGraw Hill, New York.

Kratcoski, P. et al. (1995), *Issues in Community Policing*, Anderson, Cincinnati.

Lacey, N. (1987), 'Discretion and Due Process at the Post Conviction Stage', in I. Dennis (ed.), *Criminal Law and Justice*, Sweet & Maxwell, London.

Law Enforcement (Powers and Responsibilities) Act (NSW) 2002.

Leaver, A. (1997), *Investigating Crime*, Law Book Company, Sydney.

Lewis, C. (1999), *Complaints Against Police: The Politics of Reform*, Hawkins Press, Sydney.

Lurigio, A. & Rosenbaum, D. (1997), 'Community Policing: Major Issues and Unanswered Questions', in M. Dantzkler (ed.), *Contemporary Policing: Personnel Issues and Trends*, Butterworth Heinemann, New York, pp. 195–216.

Lusher, J. (1981), *Inquiry into NSW Police Administration - Parliament of NSW, 29/4/81*, NSW Government Printer, Sydney.

MacIntyre, S. & Prenzler, T. (1997), 'Officer Perspectives on Community Policing', *Current Issues in Criminal Justice*, vol. 9, no. 1, pp. 34–55.

Maher, L. & Dixon, D. (2001), 'The Cost of Crackdowns: Policing Cabramatta's Heroin Market', *Current Issues in Criminal Justice*, vol. 13, no. 1, pp. 5–22.

Manning, P. (1977), *Police Work*, Massachusetts Institute of Technology Press, Cambridge, MA.

Manning, P. & Redlinger, L. (1977), 'Invitational Edges of Corruption: Some Consequences of Narcotics Law Enforcement', in Rock, P. (ed.), *Drugs & Politics*, Transaction Books, London, pp. 279–310.

Manning, P. & Van Maanen, J. (eds)(1978), *Policing: A View From the Street*, Goodyear, Santa Monica.

Manning, P. (1977), *Police Work*, Massachusetts Institute of Technology Press, Cambridge, MA.

Marks, M. (2000), 'Transforming Police Culture From Within: Dissident Groups in South Africa', *British Journal of Criminology*, vol. 40, no. 4, pp. 557–73.

Marshall, G. (1965), *Police and Government: The Status and Accountability of the English Constable*, Methuen & Co Ltd., London.

Martin, C. (2000) 'Crime and Control in Australian Urban Space', *Current Issues in Criminal Justice* 12/1: 79–92.

Mason, G. & Tomsen, S. (eds) (1997), *Homophobic Violence*, Hawkins Press, Sydney.

Mathews, R. (1988), *Informal Justice?* Sage, London.

Matthews, M. (ed.) (1989), *Privatising Criminal Justice*, Sage, London.

Mawby, R. (2002), *Policing Images: Policing, Communication and Legitimacy*, Willan, Devon.

McBarnet, D. (1978), 'False Dichotomies in Criminal Justice Research', in J. Baldwin & K. Bottomley (eds), *Criminal Justice*, Martin Robertson, Oxford.

McBarnet, D. (1979), 'Arrest: The Legal Context of Policing', in S. Holdaway (ed.) *The British Police*, Edward Arnold, London.

McBarnet, D. (1981), *Conviction: Law, the State and the Construction of Justice*, Macmillan, London.

McConville, M. et al. (1991), *The Case for the Prosecution: Police Suspects and the Construction of Criminality*, Routledge, London.

McCulloch, J. (2001), *Blue Army: Paramilitary Policing in Australia*, Melbourne University Press, Melbourne.

McKillop, S. & Vernon, J. (eds) (1991), *The Police and the Community in the 1990s*, Australian Institute of Criminology, Canberra.

McLachlan, E. & Muri, K. (1997), 'The Future Lasts a Long Time: Public Police-Work and the Managerialist Paradox', in P. Francis et al. (eds), *Policing Futures: The Police, Law Enforcement and the Twenty First Century*, Macmillan, London, pp. 84–5.

McMannus, M. (1995), *From Fate to Choice: Private Bobbies, Public Beats*, Aldershot, Brookfield.

Messerschmidt, J. (1993), *Masculinities and Crime: Critique and Reconceptualisaton of Theory*, Rowman & Littlefield, Maryland.

Miller, S., Blackler, J. & Alexandra, A. (1997), *Police Ethics*, Allen & Unwin, Sydney.

Milte, K. & Webber, T. (1977), *Police in Australia: Development, Function and Procedures*, Butterworths, Sydney.

Moss, I. (1998), 'Using Complaints to Improve Policing', *Current Issues in Criminal Justice*, vol. 10, no. 2, pp. 207–13.

Moir, P. & Eijkman, H. (eds) (1992), *Policing Australia: Old Issues, New Perspectives*, Macmillan, Sydney.

Mugford, J. et al. (1993), *Australian Capital Territory Domestic Violence Research: Report to the Australian Capital Territory. Community Law Reform Committee*, Australian Institute of Criminology, Canberra.

Mukherjee, S. (1999), 'Ethnicity and Crime', *AIC Trends and Issues*, no. 117, Australian Institute of Criminology, Canberra.

Neal, D. (1991), *The Rule of Law in a Penal Colony: Law and Power in Early NSW*, Cambridge University Press, Melbourne.

Newburn, T. & Hayman, S. (2002), *Policing, Surveillance and Social Control: CCTV and Police Monitoring of Suspects*, Willan, Devon.

Neyroud, P. & Beckley, A. (2001), *Policing, Ethics and Human Rights*, Willan, Devon.

Noaks, L. (2000), 'Private Cops on the Block: A Review of the Role of Private Security in Residential Communities', *Policing & Society*, vol. 10, no. 2, pp. 143–62.

NSW Anti-Discrimination Board (1982), *A Study of Street Offences by Aboriginals*, Anti-Discrimination Board, Sydney.

NSW Law Reform Commission (1993), *People With Intellectual Disabilities and the Criminal Justice System: Policing Issues*, NSW Law Reform Commission, Sydney.

NSW Ombudsman (1999), *Policing Domestic Violence in NSW*, Office of the Ombudsman, Sydney.

NSW Office of the Ombudsman (2000), *Report on Policing Powers Introduced by the Crimes Legislation (Police and Public Safety) Act*, Office of the Ombudsman Sydney.

NSW Police Service (2000), *Domestic Violence Policy and Standing Operating Procedures*, NSW Police Service, Sydney.

O'Sullivan, J. (1979), *Mounted Police in NSW*, Rigby, Adelaide.

O'Toole, G. (1978), *The Private Sector—Private Spies, Renta Cops and the Police Industrial Complex*, Norton & Company, New York.

Palmer, D. & Cherney, A. (2001), ''Bending Granite?' Recent Attempts at Changing Police Organisational Structures in Australia: A Case of Victoria Police', *Current Issues in Criminal Justice*, vol. 13, no. 1, pp. 47–59.

Palmer, M. (1992), 'Controlling Corruption', in P. Moir & H. Eijkman (eds), *Policing Australia: Old Issues, New Perspectives*, Macmillan, Sydney, chapter 4.

Pasquino, P. (1991) 'Theatrum Politicum: The Genealogy of Capital', in G. Burchell, C. Gordon & P. Miller (eds) *Foucault Effect: Studies in Governmentality*, University of Chicago Press, Chicago.

Police Act (NSW) 1860.

Police Powers and Responsibilities Act (Qld) 2000.

Police Recruiting Act (NSW) 1853.

Police Regulation Act (NSW) 1850.

Police Regulation Act (NSW) 1899.

Polk, K. (1994), 'Criminal Justice Reform in Australia', in, D. Chappell & P. Wilson, (eds) (1994), *The Australian Criminal Justice System: the Mid 1990s*, Butterworths, Sydney, pp. 299–314.

Poynting, S. (2002), 'Bin Laden in the Suburbs: Attacks on Arab and Muslim Australians before and after 11 September', *Current Issues in Criminal Justice*, vol. 14, no. 1, pp. 43–64.

Prenzler, T. & Ransley, J. (eds) (2002), *Police Reform – Building Integrity*, Hawkins Press, Sydney.

Prenzler, T. (1995), 'Equal Opportunity and Policewomen in Australia', *Australian and New Zealand Journal of Criminology*, vol. 28, no. 3, pp. 258–77.

Prenzler, T. (2000), 'Civilian Oversight of Police: A Test of Captive Theory', *British Journal of Criminology*, vol. 40, no. 4, pp. 659–74.

Putnis, P. (1996), 'Police-Media Relations: Issues and Trends', in D. Chappell & P. Wilson (eds), *Australian Policing: Contemporary Issues*, 2nd edn, Butterworths, Sydney, chapter 11.

Queensland Criminal Justice Commission (1991), *Police Powers in Queensland: An Issues Paper*, Criminal Justice Commission, Brisbane.

Queensland Criminal Justice Commission (1993), 'Gender and Ethics in Policing', *Criminal Justice Commission Research Paper Series*, vol. 3, no. 3, pp. 1–8.

R v. Chief Constable of Devon and Cornwall, Ex parte Central Electricity Generating Board [1982] Q.B. 458.

Rafter, N. & Stanko, E. (eds) (1992), *Judge, Lawyer, Victim, Thief: Women, Gender Roles and Criminal Justice*, North Eastern University Press, Boston.

Reiner, R. (ed.) (1996), *Policing*, vols 1 & 2, Dartmouth, Brookfield.

Reiner, R. (1992), *Chief Constables: Bobbies, Bosses or Bureaucrats?* Oxford University Press, Oxford.

Reiner, R. (1992), 'Policing a Post Modern Society', *Modern Law Review*, vol. 56, no. 6, pp. 761–81.

Reiner, R. (1997), 'Policing and the Police', in M. Maguire et al. (eds), *The Oxford Handbook of Criminology*, Oxford University Press, Oxford, pp. 997–1049.

Reiner, R. (2000), *The Politics of Policing*, 3rd edn, Wheatsheaf, London.

Reiner, R. & Spencer, S. (1993), *Accountable Policing: Effectiveness, Empowerment and Equity*, Institute for Public Policy Research, London.

Reynolds, C. & Wilson, P. (1996), 'Private Policing: Creating New Options' in D. Chappell & P. Wilson (eds), *Australian Policing: Contemporary Issues*, Butterworths, Sydney, chapter 14.

Reynolds, H. (1981), *The Other Side of the Frontier: An Interpretation of the Aboriginal Response to the Invasion and Settlement of Australia*, James Cook University, Townsville.

Robinson, C. (1979), 'Ideology as History: A Look at the Way Some English Police Historians Look at the Police', *Police Studies*, vol. 2, pp. 35–49.

Sarre R. (1989) 'Towards the Notion of Policing by Consent and its implication for Police Accountability, in Chappell & Wilson, chapter 8.

Schlesinger, P. & Tumber, H. (1994) *Reporting Crime: The Media Politics of Criminal Justice*, Oxford University Press, New York.

School of Social Science and Policy (1997), *Report on Police Attitudes to Domestic Violence*, University of NSW, Sydney.

Sharpe, A. (2002), 'Policing the Transgender/Violence Relation', *Current Issues in Criminal Justice*, vol. 13, no. 3, pp. 269–85.

Shearing, C. (1981), *Organised Police Deviance*, Butterworths, Toronto.

Shearing, C. (1995), 'Transforming the Culture of Policing: Thoughts from South Africa', *Australian and New Zealand Journal of Criminology* (special issue), pp. 54–61.

Silver, A. (1967), 'The Demands of Order in a Civil Society: A Review of Some Themes in the History of Urban Crime, Police & Riot in Britain' in D. Bordua (ed.), *The Police: Six Sociological Essays*, Wiley & Sons, New York, pp. 1–24.

Silverman, E. (1995), 'Community Policing: The Implementation Gap', in Kratcoski, P. et al. (eds), *Issues in Community Policing*, Anderson, Cincinnati, chapter 3.

Skogan, W. & Harnett, S. (1997), *Community Policing Chicago Style*, Oxford University Press, New York.

Skolnick, J. (1966), *Justice Without Trial: Law Enforcement in a Democratic Society*, Wiley, New York.

Smith, J. (1992), 'Tabloid Television', *Polemic*, vol. 3, no. 2, pp. 120–3.

South, N. (1988), *Policing for Profit: The Private Security Sector*, Sage, London.

Sparks, R. (1992), *Television and the Drama of Crime*, Open University Press, Buckingham.

Sparks, R. (1996), 'Masculinity and Heroism in the Hollywood "Blockbuster"', *British Journal of Criminology*, vol. 36, no. 3, pp. 348–60.

Spitzer, S. & Scull, A. (1977), 'Privatisation and Capitalist Development: The Case of Private Police', *Social Problems*, vol. 25, no. 1, pp.18–29.

Squires, C. (1998), 'Cops and Customers: Consumerism and the Demand for Police Services', *Policing and Society*, vol. 8, no. 2, pp. 169–88.

Stanko, E. (1985), *Intimate Intrusions: Women's Experience of Male Violence*, Routledge & Kegan Paul, London.

Stanko, E. (1989), 'Policing Battering: Missing the Mark', in J. Hammer et al. (eds), *Women, Policing and Male Violence*, Routledge, London.

Stanko, E. (1995), 'Policing Domestic Violence: Dilemmas and Contradictions', *Australian and New Zealand Journal of Criminology* (special issue) pp. 31–44.

Strang, H. & Braithwaite, J. (2000) (eds), *Restorative Justice: Philosophy to Practice*, Ashgate, London.

Sturgess, G. (1996), 'Truth in Policing', *Current Issues in Criminal Justice*, vol. 7, no. 3, pp. 382–7.

Sturma, M. (1981), 'Police and Drunkards in Sydney', *Australian Journal of Politics and History*, vol. 27, no. 1, pp. 49–50.

Sturma, M. (1987), 'Policing the Criminal Frontier in Mid Nineteenth Century Australia, Britain and America', in M. Finane (ed.), *Policing in Australia: Historical Perspectives*, University of South Wales Press, Sydney, chapter 1.

Summers, A. (2002), *Damned Whores or God's Police*, 2nd edn, Penguin Books, Camberwell.

Swivel, M. (1991), 'Public convenience, Public nuisance: Criminological Perspectives on "The Beat"', *Current Issues in Criminal Justice*, vol. 3, no. 2, p. 237.

Tonry, M. & Norris, N. (1992), *Modern Policing*, University of Chicago Press, Chicago.

Travis G. (1983), 'Police Discretions in Law Enforcement: A Study of Section 5 of the NSW Offences in Public Places Act 1979', in M. Findlay, S. Egger, & J. Sutton (eds), *Issues in Criminal Justice Administration*, George Allen & Unwin, Sydney, chapter 14.

Travis, G. et al. (1995), 'The International Crime Surveys: Some Methodological Concerns', *Current Issues in Criminal Justice*, vol. 6, no. 3, pp. 346–61.

Van Maanen, J. (1978), 'Kinsmen in Repose: Occupational Perspectives of Patrolmen', in P. Manning & J. Van Maanen (eds), *Policing: A View From the Street*, Goodyear, Santa Monica.

Vold, G. & Bernard, T. (2001), *Theoretical Criminology*, Oxford University Press, New York.

Waddington, P. (1999), 'Swatting Police Paramilitarisation', *Policing and Society*, vol. 9, no. 2, pp. 125–40.

Walker, C. & Starmer, K. (eds) (1999), *Miscarriages of Justice: A Review of Justice in Error*, Blackstone Press, London.

Walklate, S. (1993), Policing by Women, with Women, for Women', *Policing*, vol. 9, pp. 101–15.

Weatherburn, D. & Lind, B. (2001), *Offender Prone Communities: An Epidemiological Approach*, Cambridge University Press, Cambridge.

White, R. (1994), 'Street Life, Police Practises and Youth Behaviour', in White, R. & Alder, C. (eds), *The Police and Young People in Australia*, Cambridge University Press, Melbourne, chapter 5.

White, R. & Alder, C. (eds) (1994), *The Police and Young People in Australia*, Cambridge University Press, Melbourne.

Wood, J. (1997), *Royal Commission into the NSW Police Service: Final Report*, vol. 2, NSW Government Printer, Sydney.

Wright, A. (2002), *Policing: An Introduction to Concepts and Practice*, Willan, Devon.

Xiaoming, Chen (2002), 'Community and Policing Strategies: A Chinese Approach to Crime Control' *Policing and Society*, vol. 12, no. 1, pp. 1–14.

Young, A. (1996), *Imagining Crime*, Sage, London.

Zdenkowski, G. et al. (eds) (1987), *The Criminal Injustice System*, vol. 2, Pluto Press, Sydney.

Index